Patti Smith

Also by Victor Bockris

The Philosophy of Muhammad Ali

Nothing Happens:
Photographs of Muhammad Ali and Andy Warhol

Making Tracks:
The Rise of Blondie (with Debbie Harry and Chris Stein)

Uptight:
The Velvet Underground Story (with Gerard Malanga)

Keith Richards:
The Biography

Lou Reed:
The Biography

The Punk Portfolio:
Photographs of Muhammad Ali, William Burroughs, Mick Jagger,
Andy Warhol and Friends

published by Fourth Estate

With William Burroughs

The Life and Death of Andy Warhol

Patti Smith

Victor Bockris

FOURTH ESTATE • *London*

First published in Great Britain in 1998 by
Fourth Estate Limited
6 Salem Road
London W2 4BU

1 3 5 7 9 10 8 6 4 2

A catalogue record for this book is available from the
British Library.

ISBN 1-85702-478-8

Typeset by Rowland Phototypesetting Limited,
Bury St Edmunds, Suffolk
Printed in Great Britain by Clays Ltd, St Ives plc

**To Terry Southern,
may he never be forgotten**

Contents

'Patti Smith is like Christmas on earth.'
Richard Hell

Introduction

The first time I saw Patti Smith perform was when she stepped into the spotlight as the opening act of a poetry reading at the prestigious St Mark's Church Poetry Project in February 1971. In the early seventies in New York a poet was one of the coolest things you could be. You can't imagine how many people who are successful people now started their lives as New York poets – something that is almost unimaginable today. In those days the St Mark's Poetry Project was on a par with Warhol's Factory, Mickey Ruskin's Max's Kansas City and the Gotham Book Mart as a bastion of the influential underground art movements that were the emotional engines of New York, just as the city was on the verge of becoming the cultural capital of the world.

Topping the bill that night was Gerard Malanga, who had been Andy Warhol's major domo between 1963 and 1969 and was one of the most striking poets of his day. His books *The Screen Test Diaries* and *Chic Death* (both illustrated by Warhol) are among the most accurate accounts of the time. The people sitting in the front-row seats had a more polished, confident uptown look than one normally associated with a St Mark's audience. Unknown to Gerard, Patti had called upon her contacts to bring their contacts, swelling the crowd to a virtual Who's Who of New York's smart set that season. Bobby Neuwirth had brought with him the rock contingent, which included the impresario Steve Paul with his two stars, the blues guitarists Edgar and Johnny Winter. The poet Jim Carroll was there with some fashion models

1

he knew, as were a number of more glittering literary figures than St Mark's poets usually faced at their weekly Wednesday-night readings. The influential rock journalist Lisa Robinson, an early Smith supporter, was there, as well as the ebullient talent scout Danny Fields. Andreas Brown, proprietor of the Gotham Book Mart, sat prominently in the first-row chair nearest the central walkway that led to the podium. Dressed in his standard outfit of fifties-ish tweeds, with a touch of the college boy still evident in his youthful features, he stood out as one of Patti's most powerful supporters and an evident tie-in to the uptown writing scene. To be supported by the owner of the Gotham Book Mart was to be taken seriously, without a doubt. His presence was perhaps the most unexpected and weighty, despite his low-key demeanour and appearance. There were also a scattering of Patti's friends from the Chelsea Hotel, and, above all, the artist and photographer Robert Mapplethorpe had gone out of his way to lean on some of his new high-society patrons. They had turned up in all their splendour, and lent as strong an authority to the evening as the rockers, the club set and the literati.

Malanga had also called upon his connections to attend the event and, despite recently having been dismissed from the Warhol Factory for the second time in two years, was still looked upon as, and looked like, a bona fide Warhol superstar, with the ends of his unbuttoned, elegant white shirtsleeves soaked in a musky Halston scent that gave him the aura of coming himself from some different world too. Various other Warhol people were scattered throughout the audience. Leading poets like Anne Waldman, Allen Ginsberg and John Giorno made up the full house.

Patti appeared promptly at 8 p.m., accompanied in the background by the lanky figure of Lenny Kaye. The audience gasped with astonishment. She was a figure of the future standing before them, looking like something many of them had never seen. The raw, rasping, heavily New Jersey accent with which she addressed the crowd gave Patti's reading its edge that night. The content of her work leant heavily towards the sexual, mixing up male and female without concern. She also revealed a sharp sense of timing by alternating the works she read on her own with the ones she read with Lenny's backing, and by keeping the set to a tight twenty minutes. Shorter sets were expected by opening acts, but poets so rarely got a chance to be heard that they often went on for as long as they could. Not Patti. She had the confidence and courage to machine-gun her poems at the sophisticated if slightly stunned crowd.

Patti 'took' St Mark's that night. Malanga, whose reading was a superb and passionate rendition of some of his best work, was still the centre of attention at Max's later on, but Lenny Kaye recognized that the changing of the guard started on that very evening. And within a year the rockers would have taken over Max's and other cultural outposts from the artists and poets.

I was with Andrew Wylie, a young poet who would later go on to great success as a literary agent. Andrew was twenty-four and I was twenty-three. Together we ran a small poetry press called Telegraph Books and had just accepted a book by Malanga. We were there that night to check out our latest acquisition.

Malanga later remembered:

> I thought Patti had something exciting about her. And there was such a spiritual commitment in her feelings about poetry. I felt that I had discovered in her a magic which I found very exciting. Patti was a breath of fresh air, there was something so liberating about her, in terms of her cocky attitude about life and poetry and who her heroes were. Her role models were Arthur Rimbaud and Frank O'Hara, and her idea was the fusion of rock and roll and poetry, which I think in her mind was the kind of thing Rimbaud would have been into had he lived in the twentieth century; she was identifying Rimbaud as a kind of punk poet, the first punk poet.

That September had a big spread of Patti's poetry in Detroit's *Creem* magazine. *Creem* was an irreverent rock magazine which would publish a lot of Patti's writing over the years and introduce such talented writers as Nick Tosches and Lester Bangs, lending credence to the notion that after the Beat Generation there was another literary movement in America: the rock writers. Malanga was shocked to read her comment in *Creem* about the St Mark's show: 'It was Gerard's night, and like at the Fillmore, I was supposed to be the dumb little group supporting the big star.' Patti was obviously not going to give anyone else credit or even acknowledgement for her success. Despite the comment, Malanga persuaded Telegraph to publish a book of her poetry. It was the only book we didn't even hesitate to agree on, it was so obviously right for its time. Patti took no small amount of persuading because for a short time in the spring and summer of 1971 she was high on the list of New York's 'Hot 100' who were going to Make It. She was turning down offers right, left and centre. So why did she give her first book to a small, unknown publisher which offered her no contract, no advance and no royalties? We had offered to print 1000 copies of her book in our uniform format and do our best to sell them at one dollar each, cheap even in 1971. What Patti seemed to like about Andrew and me was our drive and energy. We came on like the City Lights of the seventies, calling ourselves the Electric Generation and talking big. Like Patti we believed in poetry passionately and were dead serious about what we were doing. Patti responded to our intensity.

It was Andrew who clinched the deal. A short essay he published in the same month of the St Mark's reading may have convinced Patti that she had found someone on her intellectual wavelength.

In the untitled essay, which appeared in a tiny edition of a special Andrew Wylie issue of the Philadelphia magazine *Telegrams*, Wylie was direct and forceful in summing up where he stood on the poetry field at the beginning of the decade: he could no longer relate to long works like Ginsberg's *Howl* or Pound's *Cantos*. Living, he felt, in an extremely violent, fragile time, he was drawn to short, almost amputated works. The essay went on to express an intellectual's interpretations of the current vibrations he felt surrounded by, concluding that just to be alive in these times was an act of violence. The essay, which Patti received a copy of, most likely impressed her, as Wylie did, for its sense of urgency about making it now, about doing something *now*. This was a response to the very confused period that began the seventies, after the sixties had exploded in our faces at Altamont, in the eyes of Charles Manson, and with the increasingly dangerous drug culture that had changed from a peaceful, neighbourly social scene to part of a growing criminal culture so quickly that it had taken our breath away, leaving people confused and in many cases separated from each other all over the landscape.

What the culture clearly needed, as all cultures always do, was some kind of leader, or at least a voice it could call its own. Whether Patti Smith was aware of it or not, she had provided that voice for the first time at St Mark's Church on the now historic occasion of her first reading there. That was evident in the number of people who immediately approached her with ideas, directions, deals of their own, in which they wanted to mould her into something they could make money out of.

Since meeting Patti, we had done poetry readings together and even travelled together to London (Malanga, Wylie, Smith and I) to read our work and have photographs taken by Malanga. Patti's book *Seventh Heaven* was published in the spring of 1972. Designed, like all our books, in a uniform seven-by-five-inch paperback, it had a black-and-white photograph of the poet on the cover with the book's title above it and the author's name below it. We had accepted her manuscript as it was with no editing suggestions, down to the photograph she wanted to put on the cover. A dedication to Mickey Spillane and Anita Pallenberg was followed by a saying: 'and god created seventh heaven, saying let them/all in. and caused it to be watched over by the/ bitch and the aeroplane', and then a contents page, which flashed to the reader, like an advertisement, the names of Joan of Arc, Edie Sedgwick, Marianne Faithfull, Amelia Earhart and

Céline, as well as the words 'cocaine' and 'crystal', and titles like 'Death by Water', 'Girl Trouble' and 'A Fire of Unknown Origin', which almost rumbled with the promise of a short, sharp, fiery set of lyrics more than poems. Indeed, in flipping through its forty-eight pages, one noticed that most of the works were, if not always short, quick, since the lines were short: the whole book could have been read in twenty minutes, and was by those readers who snapped it up, eager to get to know more about this new figure who had suddenly arrived on our scene, but now for the first time with a package of something of hers they could take home and treasure. *Seventh Heaven* took Patti Smith's voice into a number of homes, even though its first edition only sold some 700 copies owing to poor distribution. It received more reviews than the majority of poetry books simply because, via a carefully orchestrated campaign of publishing record reviews and profiles in *Creem, Crawdaddy* and even *Rolling Stone*, Patti had been well on her way to becoming what she claimed she had always wanted to be, 'one of those rock writers'. The reviews were good, and *Seventh Heaven* stands today as Patti Smith's best book of poems. As a set they are tight, they work and you want them, and moreover, they are the child out of which one can see the single 'Piss Factory' and even the album *Horses* growing.

However, by the time the book was published Patti's attitude towards us had changed. I went to her loft on Twenty-Third Street to deliver forty copies of the book and found that the sweet, playful girl who had been so excited by our acceptance of her book, had changed to a wrathful harpy overflowing with anger. Before I could even walk across the room to unload my burden, she cut into me with a stream of invective. 'You guys are ripping me off!' she screamed. I was genuinely shocked and angry. In order to appease her I told her that a magazine in Philadelphia was dying to publish a big interview with her. She immediately calmed down and we set up an appointment for five o'clock the following day. No actual Philadelphia magazine existed, I was just thinking on my feet to cool Patti out, but the result was her first long interview, articulate and charming, which would later be published in a magazine founded mainly for that purpose. An excerpt follows:

> Well, see, what happened is I really didn't fall in love with writing as writing, I fell in love with writers' lifestyles, Rimbaud's lifestyle – I was in love with Rimbaud for being a mad angel and all that shit. Right before I met Telegraph Books two things happened that really liberated me. The major thing was reading Mickey Spillane. I started reading Mickey Spillane and Mike Hammer, his 'hammer language' like 'I ran. I ran fast down the alley. And back again.' I mean, he wrote like that. Three-word sentences and they're like a chill and they're real effective and I got real seduced by his speed and at the same time I started reading Céline. I've never been able to get through a whole book by Céline 'cause it's just too intellectual but the idea that he could freeze one word and put a period – he dared put one word 'yellow' and follow it by forty other words like forty movements, also like some kind of concerto or something. He's not as seducing to me as Mickey Spillane but I juggled the two. And then the third thing, I was reading Michaux. He's so funny.
>
> I think I'm a good writer. I'm a good writer in the same way Mickey Spillane or Raymond Chandler or James M. Cain is a good writer. There's a lot of American rhythms. I mean I can seduce people. I got good punchlines, I got all the stuff that Americans like. Some of it's dirty. There's a lot of good jokes. I mean, I write to entertain. I write to make people laugh. I write to give a double take. I write to seduce a chick. I wrote 'Girl Trouble' about Anita Pallenberg. Anita Pallenberg would read it and think twice and maybe she'd invite me over to the South of France and have a little nookie or something. Everything I write has a motive behind it. I write to have somebody. I write in the same way I perform. I mean, you only perform because you want people to fall in love with you. You want them to react to you.

I don't consider writing a quiet, closet act. I consider it a real physical act. When I'm home writing on a typewriter, I go crazy. I move like a monkey. I've wet myself, I've come in my pants writing . . . Instead of shooting smack, I masturbate – fourteen times in a row . . . I start seeing all these strange spaceships landing in the Aztec mountains . . . I see weird things. I see temples, underground temples, with the doors opening, sliding door after sliding door, Pharaoh revealed – this bound-up Pharaoh with ropes of gold. That's how I write a lot of my poetry.

Seventh Heaven, the first completed work written by Patti Smith on her own, would be recognized twenty-five years later by Deborah Frost in her essay on Smith in *Rock Women* as the first work in the trilogy, including 'Piss Factory' and *Horses*, that would form the base of her oeuvre and remain her finest, most complete achievement in the poetic field. It would also, by creating her public persona, pave the way for the work that would make her world famous as a rock-and-roll singer-songwriter.

Goat Girl
1946 – 64

Even as a child I always used to imagine that I was being secretly filmed. I'd pretend Bergman was shooting a movie. Or one of the saints, in shooting the whole earth, was doing a zoom on me.

Patti Smith

From an early age Patti Smith exhibited many of the characteristics that would be the hallmarks of her artistic persona: a wild and unpredictable imagination, a contentious relationship with religion, and a rebelliousness against conformity and traditional gender roles.

Patricia Lee Smith was born on 30 December 1946 in Chicago, the first child of Beverly and Grant Smith. The Second World War had been over for one and a half years. Her father, whom Patti later described as a one-time track star and former tap-dancer, was a factory worker. Her mother, whom Patti later described as a jazz singer with a 'cigarette tan', was a housewife, who would also work as a counter waitress in a drugstore. They lived on the South Side of Chicago.

In 1950 the Smiths moved to the East Coast city of Philadelphia, where they lived in what Patti described as GI housing in the largely black neighbourhood of North Philadelphia. Grant worked the night shift as a machinist for the Honeywell Corporation. Soon there were more children for Beverly to care for and for Patti to play with; her brother Todd and sister Linda were born shortly before and after the move.

'We lived in Philly till I was about eight years old,' Patti remembered. 'My grandparents lived in Upper Darby but I lived in North Philadelphia on Newhall Street. My mother used to take me to Leary's bookstore and would buy me a bag of books for a dollar, stuff like *Uncle Wiggly* and *The Wizard of Oz*, then we'd go to Bookbinder's or get steak hoagies at Pat's.'

When Patti was seven she came down with scarlet fever. The illness gave her severe, feverish hallucinations which provided fuel for her already vivid imagination. While the hallucinations would much later be valuable sources of creative juice, at the time they served only to make her feel 'different'. As a result of the scarlet fever, her hair started to fall out. 'I was a very sick little girl and skinny, they didn't even know if I would live,' Patti said later in a somewhat dramatic statement to a journalist. 'We had no money, and my brother and sister were in the hospital with malnutrition.' In Patti's description her family situation sounds more like life in a Third World country than fifties Philadelphia.

Patti's left eye always wandered, and her parents could not afford the operation to fix it. 'I had this cast eye that used to go up in my head. I had this creepy-looking eye patch, and I weighed about ten pounds and had duck feet and glasses. Kids used to be scared of me because they thought I had an evil eye.' Patti told herself from an early age that she was special, destined for better things, bigger things, and that kept her going.

When I was a little kid I always knew that I had some special kind of thing inside me. I mean I wasn't very attractive, I wasn't very verbal, I wasn't very smart in school. I wasn't anything that showed physically to the world that I was something special but I had this tremendous hope all the time,

I had this tremendous spirit that kept me going no matter how fucked up I was, I just had this light inside me that kept spurring me on. I was a happy child, because I had this feeling that I was going to go beyond my body physical, even when I was five in Philly – I just knew it.

Patti was introduced to music by her mother.

My mother sang, and first I was crazy about forties and fifties white jazz singers like Chris Connor and June Christy. When I was a child, I loved opera, loved Puccini. I loved Maria Callas. I'd sit there and cry. I didn't understand what it was about, I didn't understand Italian, obviously, but the sound, the concentration and perfection of that sound, would just take me soaring. I actually did opera when I was young. I played young tenor Gypsy boys in Verdi. As a matter of fact, had I lived at a different time and in a different place, had I lived in Italy, I'd probably have wanted to be in opera, but being an American in the fifties, trying to pursue opera in Philly, forget it. Nobody was gonna buy that.

One day, this boy who had an RCA victrola said, 'Wait till you hear this,' and he played 'The Girl Can't Help It' by Little Richard. My mouth just dropped – it was instant recognition, it really got me below the belt. Little Richard got my mind at six and I felt the desire to live.

The way Patti recounted her childhood, it was really just a waiting period till she hit the big time.

I had my whole life planned out since I was a little kid. I had an absolute swagger about the future. I wasn't born to be a spectator. The tragedy about the ugly duckling was that no one ever took him aside and said, 'Look. You're ugly now, but it's going to pay off later.' And that was my view of myself. I figured I'd just bide my time. I'm a real optimistic person. I was the kind of girl you would never find in *Mademoiselle*, but I used to tell my friends, 'I'm going to get into all those magazines when I grow up.'

Like many young girls growing up in the fifties, Patti rejected the overtly feminine images prescribed for girls by society. 'I was a relentless tomboy. I hated being a girl. I was always Flash Gordon, not his old lady. I never identified with any female at all. I hated the look of the 1950s . . . I would lurk about in limp taffeta and I stuck out like a boil on a bare back,' Patti wrote. 'At school dances I was a perpetual wallflower. I loved my family, but I felt estranged from everybody and as a child I felt like a visitor from an alien culture.'

Patti deified Grant, though he was distant and aloof. 'My father was very spiritual and intellectual but he was disinterested. Not in a bad way, but he worked hard at Honeywell and had his own intellectual pursuits. He worked all the time. My father was always into developing the country of his mind. He hungered to read about everything.'

When Mr Smith was not at work he would get lost in some epic Bible tale or wig out on one of the loony UFO books that flooded the market in the midst of the cold war. Bored with that, he might spend his energies searching for the perfect system to beat the ponies. Anything rather than dealing with his family. Patti's image of him as 'part God, part Hagar the Spaceman from Mega City' has a more satiric stab to it when you see that Hagar looks like a Viking on acid as drawn by R. Crumb. In fact, if you had to construct the Smith childhood in cartoon frames no one would be more suitable than Crumb: Patti marching along in nine-league boots and a footwide grin beneath a big bubble that bawls 'Keep On Truckin'. Never at a loss to praise her poor Dad, Patti insisted that he had planted in her a permanent hunger for reading, not realizing that it was probably just another attempt to gain his attention by emulating just what he did.

Patti's parents were polar opposites when it came to religion. Although he studied the Bible, Grant Smith was an atheist and taught his children not to be pawns in 'God's game'. 'He used to blaspheme and swear against God, putting him down,' Patti remembered. Beverly Smith fervently embraced religion (Patti would refer to her as a 'religious fanatic'), and taught her children the doctrines of the Jehovah's Witnesses. She even had them accompany her when she distributed copies of *Awake* to the neighbours, something that Patti found humiliating, especially when the neighbours yelled and threatened them. Not everything her mother taught her was so violent. 'My mother taught me to pray and when she explained to me that there was this higher order and we could talk to Him when we liked, I couldn't wait to get to bed.'

The Smiths escaped from their Philadelphia ghetto in 1955 when Patti was eight, relocating in the southern New Jersey suburb of Woodbury Gardens, where they moved into a standard single-storey ranch house: 'Mama called me her goat girl . . . little black sheep,' Patti wrote in the poem 'Autobiography'. 'I loved my brother and sister: Todd and Linda/We drank each others blood . . . we were double blood brothers/. . . we practiced telepathy/ no one could separate us . . . our minds were one.'

> I really loved that I was from south Jersey because it was a real spade area. I learned to dance real good . . . there was a lot of colloquial stuff I picked up, that's where I get my bad speech from. Even though my father was an intellectual, I wanted to be like the kids I went to school with so I intentionally never learned to speak good. I thought I couldn't use it on the dance floor so what good was it? And I never really liked white stuff. It embarrassed me.

She imagined the neighbours called them witches and also remembered a 'weird racial attitude' that she did not understand 'because I wasn't brought up with prejudices', but 'we didn't care,' she wrote. 'We were laughing and dancing and damned.' After four years in the city of Philadelphia, Patti had a hard time adjusting to country life. She spent most of her time at home with Todd and Linda. As the oldest she assumed the role of leader, and Beverly remembered her getting her brother and sister to clean by announcing, 'Okay, we're gonna play war and I'm the sergeant. Todd, you do the bathroom; Linda, you do this; and I'll go out. When you hear my footsteps, if you're not done you'll be court-martialled!' Alternately she would bark the order, 'Let's play mean father! You be the kids, and I'll beat you to death if you don't have the house clean.'

Patti always read. From traditional fairy tales, the Bible and comics, Robert Louis Stevenson's *A Child's Garden of Verses* she moved on to Louisa May Alcott's classic *Little Women*. The Smith family, like the March family in the novel, lived in an atmosphere of constant financial pressure, and like Jo March, Patti wanted to resolve the family's predicament by becoming a writer.

I really loved Jo, the unconventional one who struck out on her own. The writer. After I was seven when I read *Little Women* I wanted to be like Louisa May Alcott. I started to write. Jo was so great. I really related to her. She was a tomboy, yet guys liked her and she had a lot of boyfriends. I thought of myself as Jo in *Little Women*, raising a family. She was a real big influence on me, as much an influence as Bob Dylan was later. She was so strong and yet she was feminine. She loved guys, she wasn't a bull [dyke] or nothing. So I wanted to write. I had always been a daydreamer. I mean, I had a gang and stuff, I'd beat up Irish kids and things like that, but basically I was a daydreamer.

Patti's brother Todd later detailed his role in one of Patti's finest gang-related triumphs:

I became part of a gang at that time called the Buddy Gang Cool Cats. It was headed by our most capable warrior and leader, Patti, my sister. I was the last and youngest member, a loyal, never-say-die commando with little confidence that I would perform up to the leader's standards in our war against evil, Jackie Riley's gang. Remarkably there were no deaths associated with this warfare. Even the bloodshed was limited to an incredible piece of marksmanship by Patti in which she threw a small piece of slate stone at an advancing enemy. The slate whistled through the air with impending doom written all over it. The aim proved nothing less than perfection as it made contact, separating the enemy from his vaccination scab. We were now a true force to be reckoned with and now the enemy knew it.

Patti was very naive in her perceptions of herself as a female. 'I was so involved with boy-rhythms that I never came to grips with the fact that I was a girl. I was twelve years old when my mother took me inside and said, "You can't be wrestling outside without a T-shirt on." It was a trauma. In fact, I got so fucked up over it when my mother gave me the big word — that I was absolutely a girl and there was no changing it — that I walked out dazed on a highway with my dog Bambi and let her get hit by a fire engine.'

As Patti progressed her field of activities widened to include, for the first time, writing.

Jo's other activity, running a boys' school, inspired Patti with fantasies of having a school with lots of 'cool-looking rich boys' whom she would control. 'Jo in *Little Women* with all those fairy tales and plays introduced me to the writer as performer,' she pointed out. 'She would write those plays and perform them and get her sisters laughing even in the face of death so I wanted to be a chick like her, who wrote and performed what I wrote and so I used to write these dumb little plays and then I wrote these banal little short stories but I wasn't good. I showed no promise.'

In a pattern that was to repeat itself throughout her life, Patti's discovery of art — on the occasion her father took her to one of the many Philadelphia museums — superseded her commitment to writing, at least for the time being. 'I had never seen art up close before,' said Patti. 'I was totally taken by that expression of oneself. From then on, I wanted to be an artist.' Patti's interest further increased when an intelligent teacher showed her a mirror of her own features in the paintings of Modigliani and Soutine.

I was real self-conscious about being skinny, and I had one teacher who said I shouldn't be. She took me to the school library and she showed me art books and she said I looked like an El Greco or a Modigliani. That was the first time I could relate to something physical. I really was tormented because I was so skinny. When we got weighed in gym class I used to put locks in my pockets. With a lower-class upbringing, it was real desirable to have big tits and a big ass, and I wanted boys to like me. But they didn't – they liked me as a pal. Art totally freed me. I found Modigliani, I discovered Picasso's Blue Period, and I thought, Look at this, these are the great masters, and the women are all built like I am. I started ripping pictures out of the books and taking them home to pose in front of the mirror.

Patti stumbled into another conundrum when it dawned on her that the religious doctrines her mother obeyed strictly forbade any form of artistic expression. To actually practise art made damnation inevitable. 'By the time I was about twelve or thirteen I just figured, well, if that was the trip, and the only way you could get to God was through a religion, then I didn't want him any more.'

In 1959 when Patti was thirteen the Smiths had their fourth and final child. Patti's kid sister, Kimberly, would inspire at least one eponymous song. 'I was outside and there was this huge storm brewing. I was standing outside and I was sick . . . sick of being a Jehovah's Witness, because they said there was no place for art in Jesus' world. I said, "Well, what's going to happen with the museums, the Modiglianis, the Blue Period?" They said it would fall into the molten sea of hell. I certainly didn't want to go to heaven if there was no art in heaven.'

When I was twelve, our teacher gave us an assignment to choose a country that would be our country for the whole year. We had to report on it, and look for newspaper articles about it. I chose Tibet. But the teacher said, 'No, Patti Lee. Nobody has heard of Tibet. You won't find any articles, you won't find anything about it, you won't get a good grade.

You can't have Tibet. Pick a real country.' I stood firm. I said, 'I choose Tibet.'

Well, I was a fervent prayer in my youth. I prayed continuously that something would happen in Tibet so that it would be in the newspaper and it would become famous and I could do a great report. That was in January of 1959. In March of '59 Tibet was in the news, but not the way I had anticipated. Tibet was invaded by the communist Chinese, and the Dalai Lama's whereabouts were unknown. [In fact Tibet was annexed by China in 1951. But there was an uprising in 1959 and when this was suppressed by the Chinese army, the Dalai Lama fled.] This broke my young heart because, with childish conceit, I really thought it was my fault. I thought maybe I hadn't made my prayers clear.

We grew up at a time when nuclear war seemed imminent, with air-raid drills and lying on the floor under your school desk. To counterbalance that destruction was this civilization of monks living high in the Himalayas who were continuously praying for us, for the planet and for all of nature. That made me feel safe. When the Dalai Lama disappeared, I prayed for him constantly. I fell in love with Tibet because their essential mission was to keep a continual stream of prayer. To me they kept the world from spinning out of control just by that continuous state of prayer. I didn't quite understand the whole thing but I felt protected.

Patti's battle with religion would become the seedbed of her calling as an artist. Through writing, art and music, she would find her own spiritual resonance.

Religion is always to the exclusion of other people and that's why on my record, or in everything I do, I try not to exclude anybody. The imagery of religion is fantastic, but I can't get into the dogma ... the one thing cool about music, or the one thing cool about art, is that it's not to the exclusion of anybody. That's why I think art and music and all those things are the new answers for religion. People desperately want to believe in something, but because every time they try to believe in something they're given a bunch of rules, it doesn't happen.

Patti ran into another obstacle when she entered Deptford High School in 1960. The civil rights movement had recently gathered momentum and was regularly in the headlines. Deptford High was integrated but that only brought the conflict into the classroom. Patti's reaction was to date someone black. Her parents backed her up and their house became something of a sanctuary for like-minded students. This did not increase the Smiths' popularity but Patti insisted that she was not on a liberal crusade but was following her instincts. While the school's strait-laced white kids organized their lives around football games and cheerleading. Patti joined a jazz club where she could tune into the cool sounds of Miles Davis, John Coltrane, and Thelonious Monk. However things came to an ugly climax when the police called Patti's parents at 1 a.m. on a Friday asking them to come pick up their daughter, who was being held for breaking curfew. When Beverly arrived she found Patti's black boyfriend being held in a separate cell without being allowed to call his parents.

As her adolescence bloomed, so did Patti's sexual fantasies. The social repression of the fifties, lasting well into the early sixties, combined with the tight moral code of the Smith family, pitched Patti into a series of masochistic masturbatory fantasies that would help create the vivid images in her poems and songs. Just how integral masturbating was to her creativity was emphasized in the interviews she would give as a rock star:

I was horny, but I was innocent 'cause I was a real late bloomer and not particularly attractive. In fact, homely. See, nobody told me that girls got horny. It was tragic 'cause I had all these feelings inside me. I was like one of the boys in school who flap their legs frantically under the desk. I always had this weird feeling between my legs and I had no idea what it was. I didn't know girls masturbated. I never touched myself or anything . . . I did it all in my mind. I was so horny in school it felt like my body was filled with electricity. I felt like I had neon bones or something. All my report cards said, 'Patti Lee daydreams too much.' I didn't know what it was but I couldn't wait to get home each day. And when I got home I'd just lay down and let my mind spill out.

Remember when Anne Frank was real big and *Life* was doing all that stuff on Nazi atrocities? Well, I'd read that stuff and I'd get really crackin' down there. Anytime I'd read about a dog getting beaten or any weird thing, it would trigger me off, and the only way I could relieve myself was by lying in bed and putting a flashlight on inside of my brain. There'd be this flood of light and then these movies would start up in my mind. Nothing specifically dirty or anything, just a lot of abstract action. It was like being horny in a really vague way. My one regret in life is that I didn't know about masturbating. That's really sad. Think of all the fun I could've had!

Most girls, I guess nobody has to tell them, they just figure it out. I had to be told. Some girl actually had to show me with a hairbrush, demonstrate exactly what to do. I just never figured that stuff out naturally. When I was younger and couldn't come, I figured there was something wrong with me. I went to all these doctors, and I kept saying, 'There's something wrong with me.' Most broads don't come, but nobody told me that. I used to beg girls in the bathroom at school, 'Please tell me, is something wrong with me?' It was like, 'Would you look at my pussy and see if it's made right? I'll look at yours.' And all of a sudden they'd think I was a queer. The doctors would say, 'Oh-ho-ho. You're a normal young girl.' They'd say stuff like 'Tell your partner to engage in more petting.' Petting. Let me be your dog.

I never had any dates. I never really had any boyfriends. I was the girl who did the guys' homework. I was really crazy about guys but I was always like one of the boys. The guys I always fell in love with were completely inaccessible. I didn't want any middle-of-the-road creep. I always wanted the toughest guy in school, the guy from south Philly who wore tight black pants. Y'know, the guy who carried the umbrella and wore white shirts with real thin black ties. I was really nuts over this guy named Butchie Magic 'cause he let me carry his switchblade. But I couldn't make it with guys. I used to dream about getting fucked by the Holy Ghost when I was a kid.

I was always trying to pick guys up. I'd ask guys out and stuff like that. I had no pride. I was the biggest lurch at dances, waiting for the ladies' choice. I'd lunge at my prey like a baby wolf. I was really skinny, and guys would tell me I wasn't their type. But I was ready. I got along better with the niggers, but they didn't wanna fuck me either. They kept saying, 'You gotta stay a virgin 'cause if we find the right coloured guy he'll pay five hundred bucks for a virgin white girl.' I believed in love, so it never worked out.

Despite these various travails, Patti found a lot to enjoy during her junior and senior years. She hung out with a small group of socially aware students and among them found her first steady boyfriend. Although she rejected the role of 'a confused skirt tagging the hero', Patti recalled that she was definitely

searching for someone crossing the gender boundaries, someone both to be and to be with. I never wanted to be Wendy – I was more like Peter Pan. The only time I ever tried to cultivate being sexy was when I read *Peyton Place*. I was about sixteen and I read that this guy's watching this woman walk and he can tell she's a good fuck by the way she walks. It's a whole passage. He's telling Allison McKenzie, 'I know you're a virgin.' And she says, 'Well, how?' And he says, 'I can tell by the way you walk.' And I thought, Uh-oh, everybody knows! I was ashamed to be a virgin, so I tried to cultivate a fucked walk. I tried to figure out what it looked like. I figured I'd watch any hot woman I could. I mean, look at Jeanne Moreau. You watch her walk across the street on the screen and you know she's had at least a hundred men.

Music was an important consolation to Patti. 'My mother always got me great records when I was sick,' she remembered.

In 1963, I got Coltrane's *My Favorite Things*. I tried to hang at jazz clubs like the Showboat, just to see the musicians, but I was way too young, though I once made it into Pep's to see Coltrane for a few minutes before I got threw out. You had to be eighteen, so these people helped me get dressed up, trying to look older. I was basically a pigtails and sweatshirt kind of kid. So I got in for fifteen minutes and saw him and then they carded me and kicked me out. He did 'Nature Boy'. I was in such heaven seeing them, Elvin Jones and McCoy Tyner, that I wasn't even disturbed that I got thrown out.

Patti identified with jazz musicians so much she tried on the identity of a jazz poet. 'As a teenager I also imagined myself as a jazz poet – not a very good one. I'd just listen to Coltrane and then write poetry.' Her growing list of heroes now included John Lennon and Paul McCartney, Jean-Paul Sartre and Jean Genet, Jeanne Moreau and Joan of Arc.

Then I realized I was a lousy writer so I started to paint. I always had the desire to extend myself. I used to just telescope myself aesthetically right into perfection. I was a lower-class person with upper-class aesthetics. I was like a girl with no money living in a farm area reading *Vogue* magazine. Those were my two references. I got a lot of hope from *Vogue* magazine because there were all these skinny weird girls in it. But as far as having a pulse beat on my future, I just had a lot of desire. I was never discouraged. I was never discouraged by nothing.

Like many gifted but alienated students, Patti made a special connection with one teacher who empathized with her search for an identity in art and writing. Her teacher could see the creative soul behind Patti's clown mask, and his guidance helped ease the journey from high school to college, but he could not have guessed the secret dreams she later revealed to the writer Scott Cohen:

> When I was in high school, to me being a model was the heaviest. It was the logical extension of being an artist's mistress. Like in Modigliani's time, it was always the mistress that held the great artists together. Fuck art. It was obvious the chicks were where it was at. Besides wanting to be an artist's mistress, I wanted to be a movie star. Like Jeanne Moreau or Anouk Aimée in *La Dolce Vita*. I couldn't believe her in those dark glasses and that black dress and that sports car. I thought that was the heaviest thing I ever saw. Anouk Aimée with that black eye. It made me want to have a black eye for ever. It made me want to get a guy to knock me around. I'd always look great.

If Patti orginally felt like an alien and a wallflower, according to her high school yearbook by 1964 she had become something of a busybody – acting in the school play, singing in the school chorus, as well as being on the prom committee, the football committee and the bulletin board committee. And she took a nickname, Natasha, from a famous TV cartoon *Rocky and Bullwinkle*. From these entries we get our first glimpse of the mother hen who will ten years later pop up on the punk rock committee.

Piss Factory

1964 – 67

What does it mean to be called?
What does it feel like to be called?
What kind of life does one have
being called?

Patti Smith

Patti graduated in June 1964. She spent the summer between high school and college working in the Dennis Mitchel Toy Factory which produced equipment for children from prams to playthings. Her experience here would inspire what is arguably the first punk record – 'Piss Factory' – arising in part from the grim incident in which Patti had her head pushed into a toilet bowl full of piss by her fellow workers.

I used to get carsick when I did piecework at the factory in south Jersey. I'd have to inspect baby-buggy bumper beepers, and I'd wind up puking in the bathroom. I'd have to take little yellow pills. I inspected beepers, steel sheets. It depended, it changed every week. I cut leather straps for baby carriages, made big cardboard boxes for baby mattresses. Toys, strollers, all that stuff. The stuff those women did to me at that factory was horrible. They'd gang up on me and stick my head in a toilet full of piss.

One day, it was my lunch break. There was this genius sausage sandwich that the guy in the little cart would bring

23

and I really wanted one, but the thing is the guy only brings two a day and the two dykes who ruled the factory, named Stella Dragon and Dotty Hook, took these sausage sandwiches. There was nothing else I wanted. You get obsessed with certain tastes. My mouth was really dying for this hot sausage sandwich, so I was real depressed. So I went across the railroad tracks to this little bookstore so I was roaming around there and I was looking for something to read and I saw *Illuminations* by Rimbaud, you know, the cheap paperback of *Illuminations*. I mean, every kid has had it. Rimbaud looks so genius. There's that grainy picture of Rimbaud and I thought he was so neat-looking and I instantly snatched it up and I didn't even know what it was about, I just thought Rimbaud was a neat name. I probably called him Rimbald and I thought he was so cool. So I went back to the factory and I was reading it. It was in French on one side and English on the other, and this almost cost me my job, 'cause Dotty Hook saw that I was reading something that had foreign language and she said, 'What are you reading that foreign language stuff for?' and I said, 'It's not foreign,' and she said, 'It's foreign, it's communist, anything foreign is communist.' So then she said it so loud that everybody thought I was reading *The Communist Manifesto* or something, and they all ran up and, of course, complete chaos, and I just left the factory in a big huff and I went home. So I attached a lot of importance to that book before I had even read it, and I just really fell in love with it.

Arthur Rimbaud was born in the north of France near Belgium on 20 October 1854, and died of syphilis in Marseilles on 10 November 1891. Although he stopped writing at the age of nineteen, his poetry was so powerful and so revolutionary that it has continued to be a tremendous influence on writers over the last century. Rimbaud's extraordinary life and work took on the quality of a myth for many, including Patti, who would call him her 'brainiac amour'. 'When I discovered the poetry of Rimbaud

I actually stopped writing for a while because I felt that I'd found the ultimate language,' said Patti. 'Somehow I knew this was the perfect language. It looked like it glittered. I knew some day that I would decipher it.'

Rimbaud would emerge in her imagination as the first punk poet and there are extraordinary similarities between his thinking and rebel rockers from Brian Jones to Kurt Cobain. But what Patti would seize on was his dictum that to receive visions you must derange the senses, and his insight that women would soon come into their own as artists, unleashing powerful, magic abilities. Rimbaud was the perfect guide for the path Patti would explore.

One of Patti's strongest role models after Rimbaud was Bob Dylan.

My mother was a counter waitress in a drugstore where they had a bargain bin of used records. One day she brought this record home and said, 'I never heard of the fellow but he looks like somebody you'd like,' and it was *Another Side of Bob Dylan*. I loved him. I've always loved singing, but I never knew how to approach singing out of my poems. Dylan released that in me.

By the autumn of 1964 Patti had to decide whether to get a job or go to college. Her hellish experience at the factory made college seem attractive, but the Smiths were unable to afford the tuition for the private art schools of Philadelphia, so she accepted a place at Glassboro State Teachers' College under the pretence of wanting to become an art teacher.

For the adventurous Patti, Glassboro was a real let down. The students were so conformist and middle-class, so different from her expectations. As she searched for artistic inspiration, Patti wore a trenchcoat and dark glasses, slinking around the school corridors like a spy, making cryptic comments and trying to give the impression that she was a sophisticated, even decadent, libertine who had been to bed with lots of men. She presented such a strange and spacey persona (for the early sixties) that she believed the other students thought she was on drugs, some kind of commie pinko, or just a weird beatnik who didn't wash.

The two years spent there were disappointing and ultimately led to her disillusionment with college altogether. Patti's inability to adapt to Glassboro's standard teaching methods was clear the day she was assigned to a class of children at a nearby grammar school to oversee the making of paper-chain Christmas tree decorations. According to Dusty Roach's biography of Patti Smith, *Rock 'n' Roll Madonna*, Patti, left alone, took the project and ran with it, teaching the students something completely unrelated. Experimenting with the format that would make her famous in the seventies, Patti improvised a story of the kingdom of Alaria, where, among the foggy ice-capped Himalayan peaks, there lived a snow prince who would appear with clouds upon clouds of colourful balloons. The cold mountain winds would toss the balloons up and down, to and fro, and all about Alaria. Having laid down this groovy setting, Patti told the students to pretend that they were the wind by jumping up and down and then blowing with all their might. After the kids started gasping for air, she told them to sit down and immediately draw the wind. As Patti was bowling along, her horrified art instructor steamed over to the school library to look up the country of 'Alaria'. Discovering no such place, she panted back to the classroom to pop Patti's bubble. The upshot was that Miss Smith was henceforth forbidden to use her own teaching methods at the college.

Despite this flat rejection of Patti's creative teaching methods, she seized on her time there to learn as much as she could about all the magnificent artists and writers whose images kept exploding in her brain. 'I read a lot of Spanish poetry by Lorca and I wrote these long, stupid romances about men in love with their dead wives,' she remembered.

Very Spanish. Orange trees and glowing moons and incestuous brothers and sisters and fathers kneeling in the dirt trying to get their dead wives to show them some warmth.

Or killing their wives! It was always the same long story. Archaic language. Terrible, terrible stuff. My big line was 'Ach! You are as cold in death as you were in life!' I thought it was really great. I used to make up these long, dramatic poems about getting arrested by a beautiful blond Nazi guy and having pleasurable torture, but that didn't mean I wanted Hitler back or I was a racist. It's just . . . you're in the adolescent terrain, which is very violent.

Patti made a contact at Glassboro with at least one other student that would last for the rest of her life. Janet Hamill was one of a group of New Jersey writers with whom she aligned herself in the kind of communal working experience Patti felt most comfortable in. 'There was this little scene of New Jersey writers,' Patti reminisced.

I was secretly ashamed of my writing because all my best friends were great writers. I didn't have no confidence in myself. I was so romantic and I thought all you had to do is expel the romance. I had no idea the romance of language was a whole thing in itself. I had no idea of what to do with language. I mean, I used to record my dreams. I had no conception of style of words.

Just as Patti had made a connection with a teacher at Deptford, she encounted another sympathetic mentor among her professors at Glassboro, who 'really got it through to me that often criminals were failed artists, like Hitler wanting to be a painter. I learned all the stuff you have to do – like TB, eat hashish, sleep in gutters.'

One night home from college, Patti heard her father 'shouting from the TV room, "Jesus Christ! Jesus Christ!" I ran in panting,' she later wrote in an essay called 'The Rise of the Sacred Monsters' marking this milestone.

there was Pa glued to the TV screen cussing his brains out.
a rock 'n' roll band was doing it right on the Ed Sullivan

Show. pa was frothing like a dog. I never seen him so mad. but I lost contact with him quick. that band was as relentless as murder. I was trapped in a field of hot dots. the guitar player had pimples. the blond kneeling down had circles ringing his eyes. one had greasy hair. the other didn't care. and the singer was showing his second layer of skin and more than a little milk. I felt thru his pants with optic x-ray. this was some hard meat. this was a bitch. five white boys sexy as any spade. their nerves were wired and their third leg was **riging**. in six minutes five lusty images gave me my first glob of gooie in my virgin panties. my pussy dripped. my pants were wet and the Rolling Stones redeemed the white man forever. No wonder the Christian God barred the image.

That was my introduction to the Rolling Stones. they did time is on my side. my brain froze.

Philadelphia, a short distance from Woodbury Gardens in New Jersey, was a great city for rock and roll fans in the sixties. It attracted big acts and had its own Philly sound. Among the great DJs of the day none was as personable and exciting as Patti's favourite, Jerry Blavat, The Geater with the Heater. Patti's parents knew they could not ban rock and roll in the house, but Grant forbade the children to play it when he was there. Consequently as soon as he went to work Patti, Linda and Todd raced to the radio or record player. They sang the choruses together, pretending they were on stage. Patti's enthusiasm for the Rolling Stones was so extreme it became a more powerful influence on her poetry than the Bible. And for a while its frontline, Brian Jones, Mick Jagger and Keith Richards, took the place of the poets and painters as her number one heroes and role models.

1965 was the year Bob Dylan went electric and the Stones had their first American number one with 'Satisfaction'. It was the great pivotal year in which the leftover influences of the fifties were swept off stage and the mythical sixties began. It is notable that despite these heady influences Patti continued to see herself primarily as an artist and went on visiting Philadelphia museums, absorbing everything she could from the Renaissance to the twentieth century. In 1966 she even won a scholarship to the Philadelphia Museum of Arts' Saturday morning classes which gave her the opportunity to get some feedback about her work.

Fixated on modern celebrity, Patti became more interested in the artists' lives than their work. 'I got seduced by people's lifestyles, like Modigliani, Soutine, Rimbaud. At first, I had no interest in American artists at all. There just weren't any great biographies of genius American lifestyles, except the cowboys. And I'm a girl and I was interested in the feminineness of men. I was shrouded in the lives of my heroes.'

An inspiring example of American celebrity came to Philadelphie in the autumn of 1965 when Andy Warhol, then at the zenith of his career as a Pop painter, attended the opening of his first retrospective at the Institute of Contemporary Art on the University of Pennsylvania campus. He was accompanied by his stunning entourage of superstars, led by Edie Sedgwick. Their presence caused a riot of proportions previously associated only with rock stars. 'It was like seeing a black and white movie in person,' Patti recalled.

> Edie Sedgwick with the blonde hair and the dark eyebrows – she didn't mess around. Platinum hair and black brows. She was really something. I saw her and Andy Warhol in the Philadelphia Museum of Art. She really got me. It was something weird. Like I really think you know your future if you want to. There I was – I had really bad skin, I was really skinny and really fucked up – but I knew I was goin' to do work for *Vogue*, I didn't know how, but I just knew it.

Patti first saw the Rolling Stones in the flesh at Philadelphia's prime arena Convention Hall on the edge of the University of Philadelphia campus. A local boy drove her to the gig in his pick-up truck, entering the city via South Philly. The Stones were in their '19th Nervous Breakdown' phase, reaching the end of their first wind. Mitch Ryder and the Detroit Wheels opened for them and Ryder was much more blatantly sexual than Jagger, ripping off his shirt to expose a marvellous torso, but when the Stones came on to deliver their third twenty-five minute set of the day, having played two matinées in Chicago, they were simply magic. Patti remembered that night thirty years later in a conversation with Thurston Morre.

I was sitting in this auditorium, with mostly other white girls. And then the Rolling Stones came on and all of a sudden girls started screaming and ran towards the stage. I had a front-row seat. And I had no choice, they just pushed me into the edge of the stage. I had never seen anything like this ever. I was so embarrassed. They acted like such freaks, screaming. One girl broke her ankle. It was some kind of collective hysteria they had learned reading about people going to see the Beatles.

Mick Jagger looked very nervous. The funniest one was Keith because he was really young and nervous and his ears were big and he had pimples and his teeth were kind of bucked and cute. But I loved Brian Jones. He was sitting on the floor playing one of those Ventures electric sitars, and these girls kept pushing me and pushing me. They pushed me right on the stage and then I felt myself going under and I was gonna be trampled and out of total desperation I reached up and grabbed the first thing I saw; Brian Jones' ankle. I was grabbing him to save myself. And he looked at me. And I looked at him. And he smiled. He just smiled at me.

Sartorially Patti made a switch when she started Saturday morning art classes at the Philadelphia Museum of Art. Immensely impressed by the Jewish girls in art class, she returned to college in the fall, the spitting image of a hip Jewish art student in black tights and black turtlenecks. The costume gained her a reputation as a Vietnam war protestor, but Patti protested that nothing could have been further from the truth. Unaware that the US was even in a war she imagined herself being the mistress of Bob Dylan, Jackson Pollock or Houdini. This did her little good at Glassboro, where her academic record was even worse than it had been in her freshman year. 'I failed everything – I was so undisciplined.' She later boasted:

> Everyone in New Jersey thought I was weird. Sometimes in south Jersey I wouldn't get served in a restaurant because of the way I looked, and I never understood it – because I wasn't that conscious of Image. I would wear black turtlenecks because I liked it. I never tried to look any way for shock value or anything like that, but I always would affect people in a certain way. All I was was romantic.

In the summer between her sophomore and junior years in 1966, Patti fulfilled her image as a communist protestor by doing the worst thing imaginable among girls of her age. She became pregnant by some ne'er do well who conveniently disappeared, leaving her to face the problem to the soundtrack of *Revolver* and *Aftermath* with its signature song, 'Stupid Girl'. Given that abortion was both illegal and dangerous, Patti was lucky to be able to share this trauma with Grant and Beverly. She had made up her mind to carry the baby to term then immediately give it up for adoption, but would need their support to carry out such an emotionally and physically draining task. Her position was that she felt a calling to be an artist and knew that having the child would make that impossible. Luckily, although Beverly was ambivalent at first, her parents agreed to support her. Her mentor at Glassboro, Dr Flick, helped cover up the situation by arranging for her to take some phantom courses in New York, and found her a place to stay with a couple who would keep her out of sight. The period of isolation provided her with a useful time of introspection and study. If willpower is one of the major ingredients of success, Patti was beginning to reveal an ability to focus on and achieve her goals unusual in one so young and undisciplined. Her biggest problem was coming to terms with her all too evidently female body. 'Bloated, pregnant. I crawl thru the sand. like a / lame dog,' she later wrote in a withering description of the ordeal, 'like a crab. pull my fat baby belly to the / sea. pure edge. pull my hair out by the roots. / roll and drag and claw like a bitch. / like a bitch. like a bitch.'

In February 1967 the Rolling Stones released one of the biggest singles of the decade 'Ruby Tuesday/Let's Spend the Night Together', and Patti had a baby. The twin events helped propel her out of what might otherwise have become a quagmire of depression. 'Let's Spend the Night Together' was the big hit, she recalled. 'It's impossible to suffer guilt when you're moving to that song. I never considered the Stones drug music. They were the drug itself.' That month the Stones, now rivalling the Beatles, put out *Between the Buttons*, fourteen Jagger-Richards compositions that instantly became the coolest, hippest, hardest album of the year. On its cover Brian Jones looks as if his once angelic face had been put through a lemon squeezer. Patti zoomed in on his pain 'like some sick kodak'. Despite Patti's claim that she had a caesarian birth (and a big scar to back it up), she told at least one close friend that she had a regular vaginal birth, 'because she described to me what childbirth was like, how the force just came from her and there was nothing like the connection between souls and giving birth'. Regardless she stuck to her course, immediately giving the girl up for adoption with the only caveat that she not be raised a Catholic. Years later, she would give a simple explanation for giving up the child: 'I gave it up . . . because I wanted to be an artist. Simple as that. I wanted to create and recreate in my own way. I didn't want to create through another person – at that point in my life.' She would later fantasize about the daughter she gave up, imagining her playing the role of Patti Smith in the movie about her life. In 1979, she said, 'I have no desire to meet her, or to raise her, or to have some kind of emotional reunion with her.'

New York City

1967 – 69

**There's no place that seduces you
and perverts you and inspires you
like New York.**

Patti Smith

I n the spring of 1967, with sixteen dollars saved, Patti bought
some art supplies, got on a train and headed for New York,
the city of Big Dreams. According to Patti, her first two weeks
were spent sleeping on the subway or on building stoops, though
in reality she moved in with friends. 'New York was like a huge
cathedral,' said Patti. 'No one stared at me. I could hide. It's the
only place that really accepted me. New York and me get along
real good metabolically. It's a city of work.' Within days, Patti
found a job uptown at Brentano's bookstore on Fifth Avenue,
smack in the centre of Manhattan.

When I came to New York people immediately accepted me
in the sense that I was anonymous. I was a very naive person.
Even with getting 'in trouble', I was sort of virginal, and
there were so many weird things in New York. A lot of sexual
stuff – not just happening to me, just happening – that I
had to realize was a part of life. I had lived such a sheltered
childhood, so family-oriented, and all of a sudden I was on
my own. And that's when I learned that anything is possible.
People don't realize we have these built-in seven-league

boots. The body can go anywhere. It is physically capable of sustaining almost any kind of abuse, or any dream.

With a job and a place to live, Patti was free to pursue her mission. 'I came to New York not to be an artist but an artist's mistress,' she told the writer Scott Cohen. 'I have a completely French view of art. I used to read biographies of great people like Piaf, who really dug their men and worked for them.' First, she had to find an artist. There were many places she might have looked for one in the New York of 1967. Andy Warhol's Factory was in full swing, and anybody could walk right in, presuming they had the confidence, and meet any number of artists. Cooper Union, the tuition-free art school on the Lower East Side, or the blooming St Mark's Poetry Project, then at the height of its fame under the wing of the poet Anne Waldman, were both enclaves for artists. Perhaps the most obvious place she could have looked was Max's Kansas City, the downtown watering hole that catered to artists, the underground elite and slumming celebrities. However, Patti ventured into none of these places, choosing instead to investigate the Pratt Institute of Art in Brooklyn, where she fantasized she would discover the man of her dreams.

On venturing out to the environs of Pratt, she came upon the man who would for ever change her life, becoming Peter Pan to her Wendy. Looking for a friend, she stumbled into the wrong apartment and came upon the sleeping form of an elfin sprite, not unlike herself in appearance, a nineteen-year-old art student named Robert Mapplethorpe.

Patti always had a knack for joining forces at just the right moment with the person who could best help her catalyse her vision of herself, thereby facilitating her development as an artist. In Robert she recognized her twin who would nurture and inspire her. The recognition was immediate and mutual. Patti needed Robert. Robert needed Patti. Coincidentally Robert was also employed by Brentano's, in their Greenwich Village store.

Shortly after their meeting, Patti moved into the apartment that Robert was sharing with Pat and Margaret Kennedy.

Margaret Kennedy immediately pinned Patti as manipulative and controlling, according to Patricia Morrisroe in her biography of Mapplethorpe. Though she could be sweet, Patti could also be cruel, and seemed to hate other women, especially attractive ones. She would criticize Margaret's cooking and do everything she could to intimidate her. For example, when Margaret's in-laws visited from Wisconsin, a completely nude Patti walked casually into the living room and said hello, shocking the conservative Midwesterners. It became obvious that this foursome would not work.

Robert was so enamoured of Patti that instead of staying in his Waverly Avenue apartment with the Kennedys, he elected to move and find another place with Patti. Soon they were living together in a floor-through brownstone on Hall Street in Brooklyn. Here their relationship really took off. 'I was nineteen years old, really shattered,' said Patti. 'I'd been through a lot of hard times. I had all this powerful energy, and I did not know how to direct it. Robert really disciplined me to direct all my mania – all my telepathic energy – into art. Concentrating on the God within, or at least a creative demon. I was really emotionally fucked up.'

'The streets around Pratt,' she wrote, 'were run by painters and poets. Everybody had a vision. Everybody was broke. Nobody had a TV.' Instead of watching TV, they watched each other. Robert recognized how equally disturbed and creative Patti was, and knew if she could just be grounded long enough she would make something of her demons. Patti felt confident that Robert might be somehow able to complete her and under his direction she slowly began to bloom. Theirs was a bleak little apartment that Robert brightened with Indian cloths, religious objects and his own work, while Patti went about creating a writer's workshop: hanging the famous photograph of Rimbaud from the cover of the New Directions edition of *Illuminations* over her desk, laying down an appropriately hip soundtrack, alternating tracks by French beat chanteuse Juliette Greco with cool jazz or the Rolling Stones. Robert spent his energies creating his own art nest, replete with sketchpads and objects to add to his sculptures. Unlike Patti's eclectic musical tastes, Robert's soundtrack would often consist of a lone Vanilla Fudge album, played over and over relentlessly for up to twelve hours at a stretch.

At their new apartment on Hall Street their creativity really began to flourish. Patti and Robert had left Brentano's to work at F. A. O. Schwartz, the famous toy store, Patti as a cashier and Robert as a window trimmer. Then Patti took a job at Scribner's bookstore. When Robert complained that his job as a window dresser was really cutting into his time to 'make art', Patti jumped in with an offer to support him. She could afford this because she was skimming the till at Scribner's. Gerard Malanga remembered her technique:

> Patti was working at Scribner's and she told me to come by, I could get any book. She implied she'd be giving me any book I chose for free – at least I thought I was going up there to get a free book. I picked out a book I wanted, it was David Bailey's book of photographs, *Good-bye Baby and Amen*, a big coffee-table book which cost forty dollars, which was pretty expensive at the time. We went to the wrapping table and she personally wrapped up the book for me, tied it up with string, then looked at me and said, 'Why don't you give me twenty bucks?' I realized it was not going to be a freebie. I gave her the money and she put it in her pocket, escorted me to the door and handed me the package. I said, 'Thanks a lot.' I was happy. I'd spent less than I would've spent, but I realized she had a scam going. She wasn't giving money to the store, she was putting the money in her pocket! She was giving the book away for free, but making money on it! She had a whole thing going. And obviously I wasn't the only one.

While Patti toiled away at Scribner's, Robert stayed home and decorated their apartment with tapestries and beaded curtains, and pursued his art. At night with rock and roll blaring from the hi-fi, he would smoke pot, take speed or drop acid, while

Patti, who eschewed drugs at the time, made a simple dinner, then joined him with her sketchbook. They saw each other as the brother and sister in Jean Cocteau's *Enfants Terribles*. 'They were both totally enraptured by the idea of being artists and living outside of society,' said Patti's friend from Glassboro, Janet Hamill, who frequently visited Patti in Brooklyn. 'But they wanted to be rich and famous, too. Fame was particularly important to Patti, because, after losing the baby, she needed a way to reaffirm herself. Robert and Patti were always telling each other, "We're going to make it, and we'll do it together!" '

'We were twenty years old, we lived in Brooklyn, totally isolated,' Patti recalled years later. 'I worked in a bookstore, I came to the apartment, and we spent most of our time drawing, looking at books, and spending all of our time together, hardly ever seeing other people. And I flourished.'

Patti moved from drawing to painting, and then to writing. Through writing, Patti could turn herself into a composite of her cultural heroes.

> I felt the people I could learn from were the rock-and-roll stars. In the sixties it was Jim Morrison, Smokey Robinson, Bob Dylan, the Rolling Stones. I can still get excited about Humphrey Bogart. I like people who're bigger than me I'm not interested in meeting a bunch of writers who I don't think are bigger than life. I'm a hero worshipper.

As Patti started to feel more confident, she began to explore the wonderland of New York, taking the subway out to Coney Island with Robert, or running and dancing through the streets of Manhattan by herself, dreaming of the heroes who had lived and worked there, from Billie Holiday and Frank O'Hara to Jackson Pollock, whom Patti described in her writing as 'the great dancing abstract expressionist', whose 'jazzy dance steps burst into some of the most exciting paint splashes in history'. In a piece she wrote describing her early days in New York, entitled 'The King Curtis Death Kit', she paid homage to Pollock and Franz Kline, the Ladies Home of Detention on Greenwich and

Seventh Avenues, Marcel Duchamp, Dylan Thomas, Cassius Clay and Houdini, George Raft, Janis Joplin and Jim Morrison. Then she skipped and skidded from Second Avenue and Tenth Street, up past Madison Square Gardens to 42nd Street, where she played pinball in Playland, and cut west to Twelfth Avenue, where the helicopter yard was empty and forbidding. The piece ended as Patti gazed raptuously at the Empire State Building, seeing in its immensity and style the imagination of the city. Patti had sometimes had a hard time finding herself in the swirling confusion of the late sixties, but she had a lot of fun, and continued to believe fervently that fate had in store for her great adventures, adventures in poetry, adventures in love.

A problem came up though when Robert did not seem as adventurous as Patti sexually. When she became involved with another artist and decided to move in with him, Robert collapsed, crying out that if Patti left him, he would become gay! 'It was more than a fight,' Robert recalled. 'We split up for a little while.'

After she left, Mapplethorpe flew out to San Francisco, capital of the gay world, to fully explore his sexuality. 'The first fight I had with Patti, I went to California,' Robert remembered. 'I left school and just went out there for about four weeks. I flew out not knowing anyone and met some boy on the plane who was sort of a hippie, and he was going to stay in a commune so I just went with him. It was amazing. Everybody took all kinds of drugs.'

Robert returned to Brooklyn and, having come to terms with his homosexuality in San Francisco, soon fell in love with a young man with whom he began having an affair. Patti stopped by one day to collect some of her things and found Robert surrounded by photographs of naked men and various accoutrements of his new gay lifestyle. It just didn't make any sense. If Robert was gay, it negated everything they had shared. According to several friends, Patti went berserk.

Her hysteria had a domino effect and apparently so unnerved the man she was living with that they broke up, and Patti fled to the sanctuary of Janet Hamill's apartment on West Twelfth

Street in Greenwich Village. For a time Janet felt Patti was really suicidal.

To distract herself from these events, in May 1969 Patti took leave of absence from Scribner's and flew to Paris with her sister Linda to search for Rimbaud's ghost. 'We stayed at the Hotel of Strangers, in the attic room where Charles Cros and Rimbaud lived together,' Patti claimed.

In fact, I'm sure I slept in the same bed because the proprietor said nobody rented this room because it's the attic room. It was like in the movies when they go into the haunted house and they hit everything and there's tons of dust and spiders and the bed is shaped like bodies. It was a tiny bed on a metal ramp. You could see the outline of bodies where the people had slept. It was so dirty. I said, 'I will pay anything, just let me stay up there.'

Patti and Linda stayed in Paris for nearly three months. They joined a group of street performers, working with the musicians and fire-eaters. Patti's instrument was a toy piano and she also became an expert pickpocket.

I used to work the cafés between the Dom and the Coupole on weekends with this fire-eater, Adrillias, and a little street-circus. I had a little black dress on and looked like Piaf. In Paris, everyone's a poseur. The French are the best actors in the world. They're not deceitful, but everyone's conscious of his image: they're very involved in delineating their images. When I left the States I was still very much into image. I wore my black suit and my dark glasses . . . feeling cool . . . everybody's into that. Paris to me is completely a city of images. I always felt that I was in a black and white 16mm film.

In Paris, she continued her metamorphosis from painter to writer.

I wanted to be an artist, I worked to be an artist for maybe six years and as soon as I became a good artist all of a sudden I couldn't draw because in 1969 it began that I put my piece of paper and my canvas in front of me and I could see the finished product before I even touched the paper and it was frightening to me. I'm not interested in the finished product, I'm interested in creating the moment. I mean, the finished product is for the people who buy the stuff, you know. And I'm not interested in doing stuff so other people can get their rocks off. I was still painting but my paintings were becoming more and more like cartoons, and the words were standing out more than the images. I had gone to Paris to find myself as an artist, but I came back to New York filled with words and rhythms. After putting seven years into it, I gave up art just like that in one day.

Writing allowed Patti to celebrate the people she admired most. In a significant switch, however, although she wrote poems about Bob Dylan and Brian Jones, the majority of her new subjects were female. This was a vital step in her development because, although the subjects certainly qualified as heroines, as she would later admit, the poems were in fact all about Patti. In writing, she both started to remake herself from a combination of different parts of all her heroines and took her first step towards becoming a songwriter and singer, whose work was all autobiographical. 'I didn't know hardly any of the girls I wrote about,' Patti pointed out. 'I could only write about my best friend Judy when she was away from me for a year. Then all of a sudden she became a muse. I met Edie Sedgwick a few times but she had nothing to say to me. Who was I? But I thought she was swell, she was one of my first heroines. I don't like women who are attainable.'

Patti did not leave Paris so much as she fled it, spooked by weird hallucinations about her father and, separately, the Rolling Stones, especially Brian Jones. She sent Linda back home to find out how Grant was doing and went straight to Robert's. He took her in and kicked his boyfriend out. It turned out that her father had had a heart attack but would be okay. Robert, on the other hand, having long neglected his dental hygiene, had ulcerated sores on his gums and a serious infection. Patti moved him to Manhattan's artists' haven, the Chelsea Hotel on West Twenty-Third Street. Stanley Bard, who ran the legendary hotel, had long been in the custom of taking in poverty-stricken artists whom he believed in, often taking their art as collateral for or sometimes in payment of their rent. Despite his never having heard of Patti Smith or Robert Mapplethorpe, Patti soon talked him into giving them the key to the smallest room in the hotel on the tenth floor. Flashing him one of her more charming grins, Patti dashed out into the lobby to drag the sick and shivering Robert into the elevator. And so they ascended into what would become the true launching pad for both of their careers.

The same month Patti moved into the Chelsea, Brian Jones of the Rolling Stones died by drowning in his swimming pool. Patti's sorrow over his untimely death had a profound impact on her. 'I was with her the night that Brian Jones died,' recalled a friend. 'She was just crying hysterically. I was upset too, but she just kept talking about "Baby Brian Jones" and "Baby Brian Jones's bones." ' Patti began writing a 'Black rock and roll mass, based on numerology and spells – like in medieval language, but with rock and roll rhythms'.

'At this time I was writing my Brian Jones poems,' said Patti.

Of course they were rock-and-roll oriented because they were about Brian, and I would write them in rhythm of the Stones' music. I wasn't trying to be 'innovative' – I was just doing what I thought was right, and being true to Brian. William Burroughs was there [in the Chelsea], and Gregory Corso, and the Jefferson Airplane and Janis Joplin and Matthew Reich [a musician tipped for stardom in the sixties who would marry the actress Genevieve Waite and then have a breakdown from which he would never fully recover] – who was also an early influence on me – and it was really a good time. It was time for us to strike out on our own . . . Robert as an artist, and I had been writing some of my poetry.

'That night stretched like a cloud,' she wrote of the night Jones died.

Brian was still holding on. I wanted to speak to him but I got caught up in the lace border of his cuff. I traced the delicate embroidery until it stretched across my field of vision like Queen Anne's Lace. it was morning. it was dazzling. it was July 3rd. by night fall the whole world knew that Brian Jones was dead. the Stones were moving toward a mortal mergence of the unspoken moment and that hot dance of life.

The next step in Patti's ascent was a series of visits to New York's hippest locale, Max's Kansas City, on Seventeenth Street and Park Avenue South, a short walk from the Chelsea. One night on the way to Max's, Patti and Robert came across an abandoned pair of shoes. 'We had no money to get anything to eat, no money for art supplies – we were considerably down,' said Patti.

Then, in the streetlight, there was a perfect pair of pointy-toed alligator-skin shoes, really high-end and expensive, just sitting there. They had to be worth three or four hundred dollars. I looked at those shoes and said, 'Clothes or art?' Robert replied, 'Both.' He took off his huraches, put on the shoes with no socks, and stuffed in newspaper to make them fit. All of a sudden he was a new man. He couldn't buy anything to eat but he had new shoes. Later he came home and put them into an installation. Now those shoes are part of his work, probably in somebody's collection. That was what I liked. Everything was always Life or Art. It was magical when something could cross over and be both.

Max's was the only club that catered to the denizens of the underground art world. Andy Warhol and his entourage had made it their nightly hangout in the sixties but by the seventies

Max's had begun to be taken over by the rock-and-roll crowd. The club was divided into two main areas. The front room was the domain of painters and artists who were friends of the owner Mickey Ruskin, while the back room was the province of the elite of the downtown *demi-monde*, and entry had to be earned.

When they first started coming to Max's, Patti and Robert couldn't get in at all. 'I couldn't understand why they couldn't get in,' said Leee Black Childers, a photographer and downtown *bon vivant* who haunted the back room with the drag queen Jackie Curtis. 'I thought Robert was quite cute. Patti'd be in ugly, dirty, ripped clothes. I guess Mickey Ruskin thought they didn't have the right look. The doorman was the one who was saying no. Patti and Robert would sit on the kerb out in front of Max's and talk to everyone as they came and went. Everyone would take them glasses of wine and things and so it didn't take long until they were getting in.'

Still they weren't really 'in'. They would sit alone at a table, nursing a Coke and maybe splitting a salad, waiting for someone to talk to them. 'We hung out at Max's every single night until like three in the morning trying to get a big break,' Patti remembered. 'I don't even know what we were trying to get a break for. We hung out there every night for about six months and nobody even said hello to us.'

A breakthrough occurred when Danny Fields invited them to join his table. Fields was a popular figure at Max's who had managed Iggy Pop and Detroit's MC5, among others, and being invited to his table conferred on them considerable status. 'She and Robert used to come to Max's every night, stand in the doorway, and stare at all the chic people and wish that they would be invited to sit down or hang out with them . . . Finally I said, "Well, come sit down, you two, who are you?"' For Patti and Robert this was the big payoff for all their endless hours of hanging out. No one knew quite what to make of them at first. Were they lovers, siblings or best friends? Straight, bisexual or gay? Artists, writers or groupies? Luckily, no one cared. Max's housed a scene where such ambiguity was itself a form of cachet.

'1969 to 1972 was my peak period, when I made the transition from psychotic to serious art student,' said Patti. 'I like to work. I like that anguish you go through when you're writing something. I like to battle with language.' Patti would spend the first three years of the seventies turning herself into a successful poet. Though the possibility of being in a band or doing rock and roll was hinted at in conversations with her friend Penny Arcade, she put distance between herself and the concept for the time being. Patti was eerily prescient about what the times required. The early seventies would be a confused transitional period for the rock musicians who had thrived in the sixties. A plethora of ambitious and talented artists would destroy themselves in their attempts to make themselves the stars of the early seventies. Patti had always been ambitious, but now she watched and waited for the perfect moment she knew would come.

The Outrageous Lie
1969 – 70

Everyone began to think of themselves in mythological proportions.

Leee Black Childers

Patti Smith made her first appearance in front of an audience in 1969 in the Theater of the Ridiculous play *Femme Fatale*. The cast included the Warhol stars Mary Woronov, Jackie Curtis, Penny Arcade and Jayne (then Wayne) County. *Femme Fatale* was written by Jackie Curtis, the star of Warhol's post-assassination-attempt film *Women in Revolt*, alongside Candy Darling. Unlike Candy, who was drop-dead gorgeous in drag, Jackie was clearly a man in a dress, and played it that way, with frizzy hair and glitter make-up over unshaved stubble. The play was based on Jackie's experiences with the underground actress Penny Arcade and John Christian, who had starred in a John Vaccaro play based on his own life called *Cockstrong*. By the time the play went into production, Christian was suffering from drug-induced agoraphobia and refused to leave his apartment. Jackie decided that John's part would be played by a woman, and cast Patti Smith. A star is born.

Patti had become involved with the Warhol set hanging out at Max's Kansas City with Robert Mapplethorpe. From day one Jackie Curtis mistrusted Smith, telling Penny Arcade that she thought Patti was a 'social climber'. Leee Black Childers concurred. 'Jackie never liked her. She didn't want to be around her at all.' But Patti had a look that was completely her own and something to be valued. 'Some people thought Patti was this ugly girl,' said Penny Arcade, 'you know, when ugly was a sin. But she wasn't ugly, it was just that nobody looked like that then. She was really skinny and weird, a precursor of the whole punk thing.'

Around this time the Warhol drag-queen crowd developed a concept called the Outrageous Lie. According to Leee Childers, the concept was first invented by Jackie Curtis, who became its biggest proponent. The idea was that if you simply lied you would surely be caught, but if you created an absolutely Outrageous Lie, it would be believed. So Cyrinda Foxe (the Warhol star of *Bad*, who would later marry David Johansen of the New York Dolls and Aerosmith's Steven Tyler) began telling people that she was shot off the back of a motorcycle in Texas by Hell's Angels and had the scars to prove it. Wayne County had a fabulous brown silk jacket and told everyone that it was given to her by Joan Crawford – never mind that she had found it at a flea market. According to Childers, who was Jackie Curtis's friend and room-mate at the time:

> Like all things that happen, it had a purpose. It was the right time for the Outrageous Lie. Everyone began to think of themselves in mythological proportions.
>
> At the rehearsals for *Femme Fatale*, Patti confessed to us that she had become pregnant at nineteen and as the baby grew, it became impatient and it kicked until wham! this leg came right through her stomach wall and was hangin' out! Now we were all kids, including Patti, and we all went, 'Ooohh, ooohh, my God, it kicked its way straight out of your stomach?' Now I don't think that could ever happen, but we all believed it at the time. I think she believed it because that's the other thing about Outrageous Lies, you gotta believe it or they don't work.
>
> Jackie studied what'd gone before, in the way of who got away with what. Jackie's particular case was hopeless because she was a man in a dress, who would never ever look like a

woman. Still she studied it and she worked it and she passed it on, and what she passed on, among many things, was the concept of the Outrageous Lie. If the lie is so outrageous, not only can you get away with it but it creates a centre of glamour around you. And that was Patti's Outrageous Lie and it existed for years and years and years with me, until finally I told it to someone one day at a party, and the person said, 'A baby can't kick a leg through someone's stomach and both of them live,' and then I went, 'Oh!' And so it was the era of the Outrageous Lie. And the relevance of that was, we lived it. Each of us told our individual one or two or three or four, depending on our energy and the amount of speed we took, we told our Outrageous Lie. But we also basically lived the Outrageous Lie, we lived the completely Outrageous Lie – Jackie Curtis, Candy Darling, Holly Woodlawn, Jayne County and Patti Smith. There was no possible reason that that girl should have been a great star, on the face of it. If you analysed what she had going for her – nothing. Don't ever analyse! Because she had everything going for her, which was in her brain. And she used the Outrageous Lie like we all did, to bridge the gap; to get into Max's Kansas City, to get into St Mark's Church, and once she was there, there was no doubt in anybody's mind that there was some amazing something happening, and she didn't need the Lie any longer. Don't get me wrong about the Outrageous Lie, I think it's a nice, healthy thing, I wish people would do it more.

The play's director Tony Ingrassia basically hired Patti for the way she looked, since nobody had seen her act. But Patti surprised everyone. 'She had great instincts as an actress. She could have been a great actress, she was fabulous, the audience loved her, you could feel it,' said Leee Childers.

Patti played every scene so perfectly. The Theater of the Ridiculous is based on improvisation and so even if you're given the lines you've got to be able to do something [with them] because the lines generally don't mean much. And Patti astounded everyone with her stage presence and with her confidence. Audiences adored her. She could have gone on to become a great actress. She still may do that. She has the magic that audiences immediately see. Jackie was way over the top and Penny is very much of a burlesque woman, but Patti played it very still, very stiff, very intense, very mean, very threatening and it worked like crazy. Patti always got raving applause at the end of the show.

After her success in *Femme Fatale*, Patti went on to appear in Ingrassia's production of *Island* with Wayne County and Penny Arcade. Ingrassia rewrote and restructured the play especially for her. According to Childers, Ingrassia loved working with Patti. She was easy to work with and took direction well. 'You told her what to do and she did it. She didn't try to do it, she just did it.' 'I think she was very serious about her acting, and very proud of it too,' concluded Bebe Buell, someone who would soon become another friend.

Though these improvisational plays were as off-Broadway as you could get, within a certain group of people they were important and got Patti noticed. Andy Warhol came to almost every performance, according to Childers. 'He was there so much it was embarrassing because we had to keep it up. The first time it's a thrill, but the eighth time? Oh, my God, Andy is still here! He was coming all the time, he was entranced with it. He was entranced with Cherry [Vanilla] and Wayne and the whole production, but very much part of the entrancement was Patti.' The play was set on the deck of a Fire Island beach house and Patti would be on the 'beach', closest to the audience. 'She was two feet from the audience,' said Childers. 'Very much a focal point, almost like the fool in Shakespeare, commenting on all the fools . . . the real fools up there on the deck. She was on stage most of the play talking about the idiots on stage!'

After being on the fringe looking in at the party, Patti had made her grand entrance. Her persistence had paid off.

The Outrageous Lie: 1969–70

While keeping their room at the Chelsea, Patti and Robert now also rented a loft together just down the block at 206 West Twenty-Third Steet. (Ironically, given Mapplethorpe's later subject matter, 206 West Twenty-Third would in the nineties be the site of an S & M theme restaurant called La Nouvelle Justine where patrons eat out of dog bowls and are served by drag queens dressed as dominatrixes.) Robert spent most of his time working in the loft on his art projects and this left Patti free to network. She was looking to stretch out, take her new taste of success in the Ingrassia plays and find some action. Not having found the support she needed among the drag queens, she soon hooked up with the eminently heterosexual Bobby Neuwirth, who had been one of Edie Sedgwick's lovers. Neuwirth was supposedly the coolest of the cool, a musician who had appeared in the documentary *Don't Look Back* with his good friend Bob Dylan. Gerard Malanga remembers the Neuwirth of that time as someone with 'a really nasty attitude'. 'He just had no manners, he was a very crude person, just an unbearable person to be with in the seventies,' said Malanga. 'I could never see what Bob Dylan saw in Bobby Neuwirth.' Maybe it was his ability to stroke the egos of people he liked. He looked at one of Patti's books and, Patti said, 'immediately recognized something in me that I didn't even recognize in myself'. Neuwirth was the first person to take Patti seriously as a poet and encourage her. 'He really loved my poetry. He built up my confidence and kept inspiring me to keep the music in my poetry. He said we needed a poet.'

Neuwirth introduced Patti to the rock-and-roll crowd – Kris Kristofferson, Janis Joplin, who occasionally cut Patti's hair, the Winter brothers, Johnny Cash. 'I was acting real unimpressed then because I thought I was gonna make it in the art world,' Patti remembered. However, it was writing, not art, that was coming to dominate her existence. Slowly Patti began to get articles and record reviews published in the rock magazines. 'I wanted so much to be a rock writer,' Patti would say, 'I used to devour those magazines.'

The Chelsea Hotel was a heady place to be in the late sixties and early seventies. The British writer Miles, who was in New York working on a William Blake record with Allen Ginsberg, remembered that 'there was a whole gang of people then, a sort of moving party at the Chelsea, of which Patti was a part. Almost any night you could call down to Josie on the switchboard and say, "Where's the party?" and she'd say, "It's in Dr Johnson's apartment" – Dr Johnson, the black professor, she often had parties – or else it would be in Harry Smith's room.' Harry Smith was a filmmaker and collector of records, artefacts and books who influenced many sixties artists, including Bob Dylan and Allen Ginsberg. He also influenced Patti. 'Harry really encouraged me,' she said. 'I used to sit in his room at the Chelsea and sing for him.' (When Harry Smith died in 1991, his collection was donated to the Anthology Film Archives in New York, where Patti Smith now heads the fund-raising committee.) The Canadian poet and singer-songwriter Leonard Cohen lived at the Chelsea, as well as the writers Arthur C. Clarke and Arthur Miller. 'I remember one meal where both Patti and Allen Ginsberg were present,' recalled Miles.

> At the El Quixote. We never ate anywhere else, 'cause there's a connecting door between the Quixote and the Chelsea bar. Everyone would gather at the bar, it would get late and you'd get hungry, and it was just so easy to go next door to get a table. Quite often Leonard Cohen would have to pay, because Harry Smith would say something subtle like 'You're the only rich dude here, why don't you pay?' That sort of thing. Even when Patti moved next door [to the loft] she still seemed part of the Chelsea scene, everybody knew her and she was there every day.

William Burroughs visited the Chelsea at this time and he was another influence. 'Burroughs showed me a whole series of new tunnels to fall through,' said Patti. 'He was so neat, he would walk around in this big black cashmere overcoat and this old hat. So of course Patti gets an old black hat and coat, and we would walk around the Chelsea looking like that. Of course he was never too crazy about women, but I guess he liked me 'cause I looked like a boy.'

Patti also met the poet Jim Carroll at the Chelsea. Carroll would later fuse music with his poetry but at this time he was mainly a nineteen-year-old heroin addict, although one with a literary reputation, having had part of his novel *The Basketball Diaries* published in the *Paris Review* at the age of sixteen. His book *Living at the Movies,* poems about life at the Chelsea, was later nominated for a Pulitzer Prize. Patti courted Carroll, supplying him with money and food. Patti was 'one of the few women I knew who actively encouraged my addiction,' said Carroll. 'I think she would have been disappointed if I had stopped!' Before long Carroll had moved into the Twenty-Third Street loft with Patti and Robert. Like Neuwirth, Carroll encouraged Patti to write. 'She seemed to fully accept my advice to concentrate on writing, putting aside her drawings,' wrote Carroll in his book *Forced Entries.* 'Patti possessed something which caused me great envy, it being a quality I was in short supply of – ambition. The best and healthiest kind of ambition. An ambition totally integral to her vision, and the work which was a manifestation of that vision.' Patti encouraged Carroll to put the lyrics he was writing to music, to sing, even to front a band, but the thought of facing an audience horrified him. 'I do believe that a poet would possess a stronger intuitive sense of phrasing with a rock song,' he wrote. 'That there is a way to tap into the emotions of an audience simply by the cross of a certain phrase, even a single word, against a certain chord. There's no doubt in my mind. But I respect the craft. I believe in technique . . . and my singing abilities are so serious a handicap that it would take a whole new scale to make the entire thing less ludicrous.' Carroll would overcome his horror of performing and go on to some critical acclaim as a recording artist in the eighties, but his self-confessed lack of ambition would prevent him from achieving any lasting success in rock and roll.

In the autumn of 1970 Patti met the next man who would play a role in her artistic growth. Sam Shepard, an underground playwright who had already notched up six Obie awards from the *Village Voice* for his twenty plays, was only twenty-six and, like Jim Carroll, something of a sensation. He played drums with a rock band called Holy Modal Rounders and possessed the charisma of a rock star. Fitting the mould of her previous romantic partners, he was slim, rangy and tall, with deep blue eyes and a winning smile. Though he was married at the time to a beautiful woman named Olan and had a young son, he and Patti nevertheless began a passionate love affair.

As in the past, Patti's sexual relationship turned into fuel for her art. 'I learned from Sam,' said Patti.

> Because Sam is one of the most magic people I have ever met. Sam is really the most true American man I've ever met in as far as he's also hero-oriented. He has a completely western romance mind. He loves gangsters, he loves cowboys. He's totally physical. He loves bigness. You know Americans love bigness. In his plays there's always a huge Cadillac or a huge breast or a huge monster. His whole life moves on rhythms. He's a drummer. I mean, everything about Sam is so beautiful and has to do with rhythm. That's why Sam and I so successfully collaborated. Intuitively he worked with rhythm in his blood. I do it intellectually. He does it from his heart. We were able to establish a deep communion.

For the first time Patti was having an affair with somone that her soulmate, Robert Mapplethorpe, felt threatened by. But Patti was deeply in love and nothing could dissuade her. In an act that had greater significance for Patti than Sam they each had a tattoo engraved by the Italian beatnik artist Vali, who lived in the Chelsea and had been a heroine of Patti's since she was a teenager. She gave Patti a prophetic lightning bolt. Sam got an appropriate hawk moon. 'Patti said Sam was beautiful and special and talented and that he was going to go somewhere,' said Bebe Buell, who met Patti after the affair with Shepard was over.

'He was an important force in my life,' said Patti.

We wrote the play and took it right to the stage. We wrote *Cowboy Mouth* on the same typewriter – like a battle. And we were having this affair. He was a married man, and it was a passionate kind of thing. We were talking about two people – two big dreamers – that came together but were destined for a sad end. It was the true story of Sam and me. We knew we couldn't stay together. He was going back to his wife, and I was going on my way. But even though it was an unhappy love affair, it was a very happy union. He inspired me to be stronger and make my move.

Patti's last time on a stage acting was on 29 April 1971, playing Cavale to Shepard's Slim in *Cowboy Mouth*, the play they had written together. The title was taken from Dylan's song 'Sad-Eyed Lady of the Lowlands' by Patti, who dominated the writing of the play, later published in one of Shepard's collections of works.

In the most telling part of the play, Patti (Cavale) spoke about rock and roll as the new religion which would replace the High Church in pomp, ceremony and revelations:

CAVALE: I mean I can't be the saint people dream of now. People want a street angel. They want a saint but with a cowboy mouth. Somebody to get off on when they can't get off on themselves. I think that's what Mick Jagger is trying to do ... what Bob Dylan seemed to be for awhile. A sort of god in our image, you know? Mick Jagger came close but he got too conscious. For awhile he gave me hope ... I want it to be perfect, 'cause it's the only religion I got ... in the old days people had Jesus and those guys to embrace ... they created a god with all their belief energies ... and when they didn't dig themselves, they could lose themselves in the Lord. But it's too hard now. We're earthy people, and the old saints just don't make it, and God is just too far away. He don't represent our pain no more. His words don't shake through us no more. Any great motherfucker rock and roll song can raise me higher than all of Revelations. We created rock and roll from our own image, it's our child . . .

Terry Ork, a downtown entrepreneur who would later manage Television, brought the renowned director of *Rebel Without a Cause*, Nicholas Ray, to see a rehearsal and there was talk of filming a performance, but it was not to be. After one performance of the play, Sam got cold feet and left town. He couldn't face enacting his adulterous relationship in public. It was like having a love affair on stage. He left for Vermont, leaving Patti waiting at the theatre to go on, and later took his wife and son to London, turning his back on the wildness of New York.

Patti had never been so humiliated as she was by Shepard's change of heart and abrupt departure, and she would express her own pain for everyone to see. On more than one occasion she was carried out of Max's by friends, crying and drunkenly screaming Sam's name. Patti was beginning to live out her legend on the public stage. But the success of her February reading at St Mark's Church was still resonating, and Patti was nothing if not a survivor. There were poems to write, identities to forge and new lovers to discover. Patti Smith was on the move.

Seventh Heaven
1971 – 72

**and god created seventh heaven.
saying let them all in. and caused
it to be watched over by the bitch
and the aeroplane.**

Patti Smith

Since the St Mark's poetry reading in February, Patti had been swamped with offers and advice about what direction her 'career' should take, for it was indeed beginning to look like a career despite any protestations. The former club owner Steve Paul, who managed the careers of Edgar and Johnny Winter, thought Patti had enormous potential as a rock-and-roll singer and suggested she put aside her writing for music. He had an act in mind pairing Patti with the guitarist Rick Derringer, whom he also managed. Things went so far as to have photos of the duo taken. 'They were gonna be Ricky and Patti, or Ricky D and Patti Lee, something like that,' Bebe Buell recalled. There was some talk of Patti becoming the singer for Allen's band, Blue Oyster Cult, but nothing came of that either. 'Steve Paul thought perhaps she could be the Barbra Streisand of the seventies,' said Lisa Robinson. 'But Patti knew she didn't want to be a pop leather queen.' Patti didn't want to do music unless she could do 'exactly what I want to do', and nobody was offering to let her do that. Yet.

Buoyed up by the encouragement from Bobby Neuwirth, Jim Carroll and Sam Shepard, Patti concentrated on her writing. Rather than dwell on her loss and write a lachrymose book about Sam, she penned a series of celebrations of her heroes and heroines from whose composite characteristics she now set out to construct the new Patti Smith, the one who would no longer place herself under a man's thumb but would shine as her own individual star.

Over the summer she had a brief affair with the multi-instrumentalist Todd Rundgren, who would later produce her fourth record, *Wave*. Rundgren had started with a band called the Nazz and become a producer and engineer who also had several hit singles of his own in the seventies. According to Bebe Buell, who would be Todd's next girlfriend, Patti had strong feelings about Rundgren. 'She really loved him with all her heart,' said Buell. 'She told me how she felt about him, she told me how the "Room of Burning Fire" was about him, a song or a poem. It was about a bad visit with Todd and after she went home and started a fire with a pile of paper . . . They were very dear connected souls.' Bebe began to visit Patti for advice about her relationship with Todd. 'What we'd do is put on records and sing along to them, using hairbrushes for microphones, and stand in front of the mirror and sing,' said Buell.

In September *Creem* magazine ran a selection of Patti's rock-and-roll poetry. Patti was again living with Robert Mapplethorpe, who proved his true friendship for Patti by taking her back and devoting himself to her care after the dramatic break-up with Sam Shepard. Robert was the only man in Patti's life who did not at any point feel threatened by her. Even Sam had destroyed some of Patti's drawings during an argument, an act friends thought was a result of his jealousy of Patti's own prodigious talent. Mapplethorpe, more than any of her other lovers, was able to support her totally at times when she might otherwise have lost her mind. His care was selfless and in the true spirit of artistic collaboration and support.

Around this time, Patti began to hang out at the Gotham Book

Mart, whose owner, Andreas Brown, was a kind of equivalent to the Chelsea's Stanley Bard, recognizing and helping to support young artists who showed promise. 'Patti always looked bizarre and emaciated,' he recalled. 'I felt sorry for her.' (Gotham would later publish Patti's third book of poetry, *Witt*.) Returning to the loft every night, Patti would 'sit at the typewriter and type until I felt sexy,' she confided, 'then I'd go and masturbate to get high, and then I'd come back in that higher place and write some more.' From this vantage point as she fought to extricate herself from the influence of the St Mark's, New York school poets, Patti rapidly penned the poems to her heroes which would become *Seventh Heaven*.

The writing methods Patti applied to the book were described in detail in an interview she gave in 1972:

Most of my poems I write two ways. I write them from first writing a letter to someone who will never receive the letter or I write recording a dream like 'Skunk Dog' was a complete dream. Judy was a girl I was in love with in the brain. I'm in love with her because we have similar brain energy. We can travel through time, we have this fantastic way of communicating. But she doesn't let me touch her. She's one girl that maybe I would like to have done something to, I was really obsessed with her and she wouldn't let me. Then she went away to Nepal and right before she left she grabbed me and kissed me and I was so shocked I pushed her away and she said, 'You blew it', just 'cause I was too chickenshit. As soon as she reached out for me I got scared. I'm a phony. So anyway, Judy was away and I loved her so much I couldn't stand it. I started dreaming of her. So I was trying to write her a letter, but when you really love someone it's almost impossible to write them, you know. It's people you love the most who you can't communicate with verbally. I had such a strong mental contact with this girl that I couldn't talk to her. So I was at the typewriter and for me writing is a very physical process. I write with the same fervour as Jackson Pollock used to paint. I started writing down a line, just words but you know words that were perfect, words like kodak, radiant, jellybitch, and I just tried writing these words. I was trying to write her a letter but I had no idea where she was so obviously it was a piece of narcissism. I was trying to project, with words and language, a photograph of Judy.

Her first book presents her most cut-and-dried self portrait in the mirror images of her male and female heroes. Having straddled the gender barrier all her life, she comes down on both sides of it. Her female models, Marianne Faithfull, Anita Pallenberg, Joan of Arc, Amelia Earhart and Edie Sedgwick, have in common that they gambled with their lives to achieve distinction and for the most part lost. The same can be said of their male counterparts: Brian Jones, Jimi Hendrix, Jim Morrison, Keith Richards and Bob Dylan. In both galleries however there are one or two who fall but rise again like Marianne Faithfull and Bob Dylan. And it is these characters whom Patti praises or wants above all to be. 'Most women writers don't interest me because they're hung up with being a woman, they're hung up with being Jewish, they're hung up with being somebody or other,' Patti said. 'I mean, to me Erica Jong ain't a woman, she's just some spoiled Jewish girl who'd rather whine than go out of her brain.' But on another occasion she said:

When I was writing my *Seventh Heaven* book, I was in my early twenties and going through this crisis that I had to learn to become a girl. I started buying dresses and gold bracelets and trying to walk in high heels, buying silk stockings, garter belts, sitting around completely self-conscious with all this stuff, trying to figure out what all this girl stuff meant. I still don't know how to put on make-up. I still don't know how to walk in shoes higher than sneakers.

'Patti was still so girlie,' recalled Bebe Buell. 'She liked to put on a dress. She liked to make dinner and do laundry . . . she could be downright subservient to a man. It wasn't a contradiction to her. She felt you could embody all the things that men embody but you could still be a woman.'

Adopting yet another mask, Patti now cast herself as Stella Kowalski from the Tennessee Williams play *A Streetcar Named Desire*, and pontificated about the pleasures of being punched around by a lover. 'It was the first time I considered that a woman's true position was on her back. The first time I assumed a completely passive role . . . I'm different now, I don't mind getting knocked around a little.'

'The French poet, Rimbaud, predicted that the next great crop of writers would be women,' Patti reminded Nick Tosches.

> He was the first guy who ever made a big women's liberation statement, saying that when women release themselves from the long servitude of men they're really gonna gush. New rhythms, new poetries, new horrors, new beauties. And I believe in that completely. Everytime I say the word pussy at a poetry reading, some idiot broad rises and has a fit. 'What's your definition of pussy, sister?' I dunno, it's a slang term. If I wanna say pussy, I'll say pussy. But all these tight-assed movements are fucking up our slang, and that eats it.

In the autumn of 1971, Patti retreated into a relationship with yet another new lover, Allen Lanier, the keyboardist in a successful heavy-metal band, Blue Oyster Cult. Patti commented:

> Everybody was asking me to do stuff. So I went into hiding. I'd been through so many shattering experiences, especially with men . . . Bobby [Neuwirth] broke my heart, he really did, and I was dispersing myself all over New York. So it was the right time for me to just sit down and find out what was going on inside of me – I had been working on the surface for so long. I was never phony, it's just that I was moving more on an image basis than on a heart or soul basis.

Choosing Lanier was a good example of Patti's survivor instinct. He was quite different from her other lovers but perfect for what

Patti needed now. She needed a place to hide out, slow down, cool out and take stock. She had been frantically busy for three years, writing, performing and bouncing from one passionate affair to another. She had spread herself too thin, let her heart get broken too often. She needed to reconnect with that part of herself that required letting the subconscious take over. Another reason she recognized that Allen Lanier was right for her now was that she wanted to get in touch with her feminine side and stop being the aggressive outgoing tomboy. In retrospect she viewed this relationship as highly successful. She felt that the next time she went out she was going to have to really make it. This was a pit stop to check out and repair her inner workings. Part of it had to do with getting in touch with the woman inside. For a while she tried to lead the life of a housewife – for artistic reasons!

Lanier proved to be as successful as Mapplethorpe at focusing Patti's energy. As the least flamboyant of Patti's extraordinary gallery of lovers, Allen Lanier might seem at first an unlikely candidate for a prime collaborator as she metamorphosed from a poet to a rock and roll singer. However, Allen had a lot to offer. Unlike Shepard, Carroll, Neuwirth and Mapplethorpe, Lanier was not a tortured artist but rather a stable, dependable man who treated rock and roll as more of a job than a calling. Through him Patti was able to learn a lot about the nuts and bolts of the music business. Withdrawing from the limelight for a time, she absorbed everything around her like a sponge. This was clearly the period in which she put together the pieces of the puzzle that would together form the act that would take her right to the rock and roll stage.

Before the end of 1971, Allen moved into the Twenty-Third Street loft with Patti and Robert. Mapplethorpe was not at all threatened by Allen, and he fitted easily into the daily life of their little art factory. But Patti eventually wanted more privacy to nurture her relationship with Allen and besides, she no longer found it amusing to witness the constant parade of Robert's downtown tricks and uptown patrons flowing through the loft at all hours. Allen and Patti began looking for an affordable apartment in Greenwich Village, and Robert's patron Sam Wagstaff would soon buy him a loft downtown.

Although Patti had always longed to write for rock magazines, now that she had the gig she realized it was not going to work.

> I stopped doing rock writing because I started interviewing people like Rod Stewart who I admire but because of my ego and my faith in my own work I don't like meeting people on unequal terms. So I figured I'd stop doing that and would wait until they discovered me and we can meet on equal grounds. I couldn't wait to meet Rod Stewart and then when I met him I didn't want to ask him about his work; I wanted to show him mine.

This dilemma was even more pronounced in an interview she did with Eric Clapton. After asking him what his favourite colour was, she turned off the tape recorder and ran away, leaving a bemused Clapton stroking his beard.

Instead, Patti concentrated on becoming a poet. In January 1972 she made a two-day trip to London to give a poetry reading with Gerard Malanga, Andrew Wylie and Victor Bockris. It was a tentative step on to the international stage and she made a considerable impact on the small though influential London poetry scene. One hundred and twenty-five people showed up, an unusually high number for a poetry reading which normally attracted an average of fifteen people. This was due in part to Malanga's reputation combined with Lou Reed's. Reed was in town recording his first solo LP. A summit meeting between the Velvet Underground's great interpretational dancer and the composer of 'Heroin' made the weekly music papers. Malanga gave an outstanding reading, holding the attention of the entire audience. Patti was unknown in London, although a nude still of her from Sandy Daley's film *Robert Having His Nipple Pierced* had appeared on the cover of the weekly listings magazine *Time Out*, but she wowed the crowd. Telling them she had forgotten to bring along what she had planned to read, Patti, wearing a baggy white T-shirt, seduced the crowd by recounting one of her adventures. Some of the awed poets who stayed afterwards told Bockris and Wylie they had changed the London poetry scene overnight. The reading also gave Patti the chance to visit Sam Shepard. The always accommodating Gerard Malanga, who had done more than anyone to encourage Patti as a poet, gave the couple the key to his room in the chic Portobello Hotel, where they spent an afternoon. Shepard came to Malanga's photo session outside Ezra Pound's house the following morning, though his meeting with Patti was supposed to be a secret.

Patti made a second pilgrimage to Paris in the summer of 1972, accompanied again by her sister Linda. This time, rather than searching for Rimbaud, her visit focused on Doors singer Jim Morrison, who had died there one year earlier and was buried in Père Lachaise, the famous cemetery. She would later write about a vision at Morrison's grave in a 'final' essay for *Creem* magazine, 'Jukebox Crucifix':

I went to Paris to exorcise some demons, some kind of dread I harbored of moving forward. I went with this poetic conceit that we would meet in some melody hovering over his grave. but there was nothing. it was pouring rain and I sat there trying to conjure up some kind of grief or madness.

I sat there for a couple of hours. I was covered with mud and afraid to move. then it was all over. it just didn't matter anymore. racing thru my skull were new plans new dreams voyages symphonies colors. I just wanted to get the hell outa there and go home and do my own work. to focus my floodlight on the rhythm within. I straightened my skirt and said good-bye to him.

I went to Rimbaud's grave afterwards, and stood there and felt totally cold. And then I just said, 'Fuck it. I'm going home and doing my own work. I'm not standing over the graves of these people.'

Back in New York in July 1972 she saw the Rolling Stones at Madison Square Garden on the final night of their US tour. It gave her hope for the future of poetry.

> Jagger had done two concerts and was on the brink of collapse – but the kind of collapse that transcends into magic. He was so tired he could hardly sing. What was foremost was not the music but the naked performance. It was his presence and his power to hold the audience in his palm. He could've spoken some of his best lyrics and had the audience just as magnetized. I saw the complete future of poetry. I got so excited I could hardly stand being in my skin and that gave me faith to keep on going.

In September 1972, Telegraph Books published *Seventh Heaven*. Patti carried it around with her for weeks: 'I liked to carry it on buses and hope people would recognize it was me on the cover. I'll stand behind that book, I think it's a damn good book.'

In her first in-depth interview given to publicize the book, she talked about her self-image and her ambitions, giving a more revealing account of herself than she would ever give again into a tape recorder.

> I'm not a fame fucker, but I am a hero worshipper. I've always been in love with heroes. That's what seduced me into art. But poets have become simps, there's this new thing the poet is a simp, the sensitive young man always away in the attic, but it wasn't always like that. It used to be that the poet was a performer and I think the energy of Frank O'Hara started to re-inspire that. I mean, in the sixties there was all that happening stuff. Then Frank O'Hara died and it sort of petered out and then Dylan and Allen Ginsberg revitalized it, but then it got all fucked up again because instead of people learning from Dylan and Allen Ginsberg and realizing that a poet was a performer they thought a poet was a social protester. So it got fucked up.

I ain't into social protesting. I've found it has more to do with the physical presence. Physical presentation in performing is more important than what you're saying, quality comes through of course, but if your quality of intellect is high and your love of the audience is evident and you have a strong physical presence you can get away with anything. Billy Graham is a great performer even though he is a hunk of shit. Adolf Hitler was a fantastic performer. He was a black magician. And I learned from that. You can seduce people into mass consciousness.

The book caused more of a stir than most poetry books by new authors and Patti started thinking of herself as a successful writer. It definitely furthered her reputation in the ranks of the underground and the avant garde, where being published by anyone other than yourself was considered a success. To capitalize on the attention which the book's publication received she returned to the stage and gave as many readings as possible. 'I sell 'cause I got a good personality and people really like me,' she blathered excitedly. The book only sold 700 copies. 'When people buy my book they're really buying a piece of Patti Smith. That book is autobiographical. It sheds the light of my heroes on it.'

Asked if she was bisexual, Patti claimed that she was

completely heterosexual. I tried to make it with a chick once and I thought it was a drag. She was too soft. I like hardness. I like bone. I like muscle. I don't like all that soft breast. Most of my poems are written to women because women are most inspiring. Who are most artists? Men. Who do they get inspired by? Women. The masculinity in me gets inspired by female. I get, you know, I fall in love with men so they can't take me over. I ain't no women's lib chick. So I can't write about a man because I'm under his thumb.

'Patti loved the power that being a woman brought her but she wanted to be a boy too,' said Bebe.

She told me one time, 'I'm not Todd's type, I'm not beauti-ful and blonde, and I look like a boy,' and I said, 'For a boy you have the biggest breasts I've ever seen!' A lot of people didn't know how big her boobs were because of the way she wore them. She would wear a nice baggy T-shirt or a man's shirt with a good flattening bra or no bra which brought them down even flatter. She was very endowed. My god, I almost fainted when she showed them to me!

Patti felt her function as a poet was to:

number one entertain. Another thing I do is give people breathing room. In other words . . . I don't mean any of the stuff I say. When I say that bad stuff about God or Christ I don't mean that stuff. I don't know what I mean. It's just it gives somebody a new view, a new way to look at something. I like to look at things from ten or fifteen different angles. So it gives people a chance to be blasphemous through me. The other thing is that through performance I reach such stages in which my brain feels so open, so full of light, it feels huge it feels as big as the Empire State Building, and if I can develop a communication with an audience, a bunch of people, when my brain is that big and very receptive imagine the energy and the intelligence and all the things I can steal from them.

She named her three favourite living American poets as Jim Carroll, Bernadette Mayer and Muhammad Ali:

Because they're all good performers. Ali's got great rhythms. He's a good writer in a certain frame of reference. He's entertaining. Bernadette Mayer because I like what she does conceptually. She's real speed-driven.

I get a kick out of myself. I act like a bitch, a motherfucker. It's like when I'm doing this interview I act real tough and then my boyfriend comes in and I apologize to him and say, 'I'll be finished quick, baby.' I'm like a chameleon. I can fall into the rhythm of almost any situation as it calls for me to. I'll be a sexpot, I'll be a waif. I'm flexible. I can marry the moment.

Before the end of the year Middle Earth Books in Philadelphia published Patti's second volume of poetry, a slim pamphlet entitled *Kodak*.

Learning to Stand Naked
1973 – 75

I always thought of myself as a writer and a poet. I am now honestly starting to think of myself as a singer.

Patti Smith

In early 1973, Patti acquired a manager, Jane Friedman. Friedman ran the Wartoke Concern, a publicity firm, and had a good head for business. Her original and creative approach to her work had garnered her clients like Stevie Wonder, and her guidance would allow Patti to focus on her music and grow as an artist. However, Jane was not eager to manage Patti Smith, who looked like she lived on five dollars a day. Not one to give up easily, Patti, whose ability to find people's Achilles' heels got her over a number of hurdles, pretended she had terminal tuberculosis and Jane agreed to see her. Instantly charmed by Patti's happy ugly duckling routine, she agreed to take her into the Wartoke family. Patti had what Muhammad Ali calls 'the Art of Personality'. She was able to get people to do whatever she wanted by using the right key for the right hole. Jane was a natural manager. She liked to take care of people and used her imaginative ideas to produce the results they wanted in their careers.

The coolest place on the downtown scene that season was the

Mercer Arts Center, a three-storey building that housed a video room, various workshops and a club called the Oscar Wilde Room. New York's premier group the New York Dolls were the house band. The New York Dolls were very influential as far as the downtown (and later the world) music scene was concerned. They were the first New York City rock-and-roll band to really make a splash. In the sixties, there were Long Island groups like the Vagrants and the Rascals, and after that was the Greenwich Village folk-rock scene with bands like the Magicians and the Lovin' Spoonful, and no one could ever forget the Velvet Underground. But in 1973, the Dolls ruled downtown New York. They wore sequinned pants with off-the-shoulder tops, ladies' pumps or platform boots, and hair sprayed and teased out to there, though the original music they played was based as much on American rhythm and blues as rock. By their very existence, the Dolls gave a certain inspiration and focus to the New York rock scene, which spawned groups like the Forty-Second Street Harlots, the Miamis and Teenage Lust. In the up-for-grabs atmosphere of the fast-changing New York underground, 1973 was a good year for poetry. Jane, who regularly furnished acts for the Mercer, dreamed up a slot for Patti to do ten minutes of material opening for the Dolls. It quickly became a regular gig.

The relationship between Patti Smith and Jane Friedman is the stuff of showbiz legend. When they met, Patti was in the midst of putting together a poetry act, soon to be dubbed Rock n Rimbaud. Using props like a megaphone and a toy piano, borrowing a little courage from Lenny Bruce, she dived on stage only to find herself facing a tidal wave of vicious catcalls and jarring japes. Rather than caving in and running off crying, 'They don't like me!' Patti shot back better than she got, putting away the yobbos with tougher, funnier lines. The word Jane used to describe her at the time perfectly sums up the soul of Patti Smith circa 1973 – Valiant. Until she joined forces with Friedman, Patti had not known how to capitalize on the momentum her work and her appearances generated. Friedman began to book Patti on a regular basis so she could hone her performance skills.

She performed regularly at the Mercer Arts Center that spring, reading her poetry and learning to deal with feisty audiences. Patti turned her defensiveness into her shtick, modelling herself as much on the talk-show host Johnny Carson as on Rimbaud. The result was a surreal combination of literary and pop-culture references, delivered in a bebop style.

Patti was beginning to feel a sense of urgency – now she was in a hurry to make it. In May she played Kenny's Castaways, opening for the singer Cathy Chamberlain's Rag and Roll Revue. Again, the bill was an incongruous pairing, but the audience was charmed. There was a critic for the *Village Voice* there that night who wrote that Patti was 'in the vanguard of cultural mutation; a cryptic androgynous Keith Richards look-alike poetess-appliqué'.

'When I wrote that poem "Rape", I thought there were great jokes in it, like "I'm a wolf in a lamb skin trojan",' Patti responded.

> I think of myself not as male or female or rapist but as a comedian. When I'm writing, I'm just like a novelist. Novelists have to slip into the skins of all kinds of people and so do I. I'd like to taste everything in life and I probably won't get a chance to rape or murder anybody, so sometimes I just psyche myself up to feel like a rapist or a murderer. To write that rape poem, I read all these articles about Richard Speck. [A notorious mass murderer who killed seven student nurses in the sixties.] He was a really disgusting guy – he wore ski sweaters and had short hair. And I just lurked about the room for a while, letting the saliva come out of my mouth, till I felt like Speck.

Patti was still spending time hanging out at the Gotham Book Mart, receiving support and encouragement from Andreas Brown. One hot summer afternoon the *Interview* magazine writer Glenn O'Brien ran into her there. After chatting for a while, they left the store and headed down Fifth Avenue together. As they approached the New York Public Library they were surrounded by a group of Hare Krishnas who were chanting, 'Hare

hare Rama Rama hare Krishna hare Krishna.' Patti yelled at them, 'I BELIEVE IN KALI!' (the Hindu goddess of destruction). Going even paler than usual, the whole group turned on their heels screaming and ran away as fast as they could, grabbing their flowing robes around themselves so as not to fall over and get hit by a truck. Laughing hysterically, Glenn and Patti made their way downtown, where everybody believed in Kali.

In September the Gotham Book Mart published Patti's next book of poems, *Witt*, aligning her with established poets such as W.H. Auden and Edith Sitwell. This was heady stuff for a guttersnipe from New Jersey but somehow oddly fitting. Patti was that rare bird who is able to relate equally to the salons of the establishment and the dungeons of the underground. Gotham's Andy Brown also gave Patti a show of her drawings in the gallery above the shop, bringing her another giant step towards being an established New York artist. In the first intelligent assessment of Patti's poetry, Kate Bullen published a piece in the *Oxford Literary Review* called 'Sexual Bruising'. 'Patti Smith first received her telepathic wisdom rhythms in the petrol scented plains of America's "Garden State", New Jersey,' it began.

> She soon jumped her small town compass, slipping into her sexy black pants, balanced out by her schoolboy jacket. In the early seventies Patti Smith was a member of Warhol's androgynous beauties living under the fluorescent lights of New York City's Chelsea Hotel . . . Her performances were sexual bruisings with the spasms of Jagger and the off-key of Dylan. Her musical poems often came from her poetical fantasies of Rimbaud.

'By the time Gotham Book Mart published *Witt* in 1973, Patti had become a legend on the New York poetry circuit,' wrote Nick Tosches.

> She was feared, revered, and her public readings elicited the sort of gut response that had been alien to poetry for

more than a few decades. Word spread, and people who avoided poetry as the stuff of four-eyed pedants found themselves oohing and howling at what came out of Patti's mouth. Established poets feared for their credence. Many well known poets refused to go on after Patti at a reading, she was that awesome.

'There's a lot of New Jersey in my stuff,' she told Tosches.

South Jersey. It's all railroad tracks, hanging out by the tracks. I guess it all goes back to that. Most of the cool people I knew in south Jersey are dead now, or in jail, or disappeared. A couple are pimps in Philly. I haven't seen them in about twelve years, but a week doesn't go by that I don't think of 'em. The coolest things I have, the coolest rhythms, all come from my life in south Jersey and Philly. All my dance steps, all my sensibilities. I think about all that old stuff a lot when I'm on stage. Those people, they haunt me in a real sweet way.

Back in 1971, when she was a cashier at Scribner's, Patti had met the musician Lenny Kaye. Lenny was a cashier at Village Oldies on Bleecker Street at the time. 'We spoke secret cashier talk, and were both from New Jersey,' said Patti.

But we connected, really connected with our feet, when we put on 'The Bristol Stomp' [a fifties hit by the Dovells] one day. There were no customers, and I walked in this record store and I was talkin' about there's no place to dance in New York. He says, 'Whaddya mean? There's a dance floor right here, my dear.' And we danced. Meanwhile, I'd read this great piece on a cappella music. By Lenny Kaye. But I didn't know this cashier's name, I didn't realize the cashier was the same guy that writ the story. I called him and said, 'You don't know me, but . . .' And he said 'Oh, I've seen you around.' I was pretty infamous at that time; there wasn't anybody hotter looking than me in New York in 1971, you ask anybody. It was the Keith Richards look.

Anyway, Sam Shepard the playwright decided it was time for me to go out into the world – got me a reading. I wanted to make a real assault, so I called up the boy who writ the piece, 'cause he told me he played guitar, and he came over, and it was the same guy as the record store. We started laughin' cause we were way ahead of the game. We'd danced together, broken through a lot of veils, we were in a certain rhythm.

Ed Friedman, who worked at the St Mark's Poetry Project, witnessed an outstanding performance by Patti that summer: 'It was amazing. It was the biggest audience that we had. There could've been easily fifty, sixty, seventy people on this rooftop of a big industrial loft.'

The same month Allen Ginsberg told a journalist in Philadelphia, 'What Patti Smith seems to be doing may be a composite – a hybrid – of the Russian style of Declaimed Poetry which is memorized, and the American development of Oral Poetry that was from coffee houses now raised to pop-spotlight circumstances and so declaimed from memory again with all the artform – or artsong – glamour that goes along with Liddy Lane . . . maybe. Then there's an element that goes along with borrowing from the pop stars and that spotlight too and that glitter. But it would be interesting if that did develop into a national style. If the national style could organically integrate that sort of arty personality – the arty Rimbaud – in its spotlight with make-up and T-shirt.'

Lenny Kaye, who was friendly with Jane Friedman, was also at the rooftop reading and said hello to Patti. He had just returned from Europe, and their reunion was filled with excitement as they exchanged remembrances of Paris.

Patti resumed her alliance with Lenny Kaye in November 1973.

She started coming in and hanging out in the store again. We'd shoot the breeze. It was around then that she was going to do another reading, at Les Jardins, which was on top of the Hotel Diplomat on Forty-Third Street. She asked if I'd do my songs, so I think we changed, instead of 'Mack the Knife', we did 'Annie Had a Baby' [an oldie by Hank Ballard and the Midnighters], and we did [the originals] 'Jesse James' and 'Ballad of Bad Boy'.

Patti and Lenny's desire to revitalize rock and roll was a direct response to the boring and predictable music of the day. 'Much of the sixties era relied on older ways of thinking,' explained Lenny.

Like the emphasis on hit singles to make or break a group, for instance, or the submergence of instrumental displays to the needs of the song at hand . . . but much clearly pointed forward: a fascination with feedback electronics, caged references to the drug experience along with more 'worldly' concerns, and a sense that, somehow, things were going to be a lot different from this point on.

Jane Friedman tried to book Patti at one venue or another at least once a month. She and Lenny were now appearing regularly as a duo. According to Lenny,

We decided to start doing a real act versus an art project. The scene that nurtured us was the CBGB's poetry and art scene. Our first gigs were at Max's. I would take my little Princeton amp and my guitar up and sit around, and she would sing a few songs with a piano player, then she'd read her poems and then she'd call me up and I'd do my three songs, and then I'd sit down, and she'd finish up. That was the way it was.

'When she first started calling attention to herself, Miss Smith was a particularly evocative, pop-oriented instance of a whole movement in Lower Manhattan avant-gardism,' John Rockwell would later write in the *New York Times*.

She was a performance artist before that became fashionable, a chanting poet who lifted her words beyond language with the power of music. From the first she used the idiom of rock, but she wasn't so much a rocker as a poet-shaman who used rock to make a statement. The art was raw, bizarrely theatrical, populist. But it was art, nonetheless.

Patti and Lenny were not thinking of themselves as a rock band just yet, but rather as an act: a poet who used rock-and-roll imagery and rhythms accented by an electric guitar. Chris Stein, then playing with the Stilettoes, one member of which was the pre-Blondie Debbie Harry, recalled one of the duo's early shows:

The first time I saw Patti she was speaking at some Notre Dame show. She did a poetry reading and then brought Lenny out to play with her. He was playing real lousy, just bashing these chords out and drowning her out and she'd abuse him. It was almost a comedy routine that they did. She was just poking fun at the whole rock-and-roll syndrome.

That December, between Christmas and New Year, Patti did a four-night stand opening up for the folk protest singer Phil Ochs at Max's. For the first time Lenny Kaye stayed on stage the whole time. Patti was moving closer to music and further from plain spoken poetry with each show.

Early in 1974, Patti appeared at trendy downtown cabaret, Reno Sweeney. Lisa Robinson, the doyenne of the New York rock press and Patti's first champion, reviewed the show:

What Patti was doing right was very interesting and important as well. Although she was tired, she looked fabulous in a black satin pantsuit and white satin blouse. She moved comfortably through a variety of musical changes; seemed at ease with herself, even in a black feather boa, and not at all self-conscious. Mixed in with some of her poems were 'Speak Low', the tribute to Ava Gardner, and 'One Touch of Venus' that went with it; Cole Porter's 'I Get a Kick Out of You', dedicated to Frank Sinatra, whom Patti described as the 'Picasso of America'.

Andy Warhol, whose *Interview* magazine had featured Patti in 1973, attended one performance. Joey Ramone, whose band would soon explode in the vanguard of punk, attended another.

Nobody could pin down just what Patti Smith was doing, but they wanted to find out. 'We knew we were having an effect on the audience. That's what gave us the strength to keep going,' said Lenny.

> Patti was always possessed with a great deal of charisma, she always could reach out and grab an audience, and was always riveting. I never got tired of watching her. She'd be funny and then she'd read these poems and it wasn't like you had to think about what they meant, the images were really strong, they were totally street.

More and more people were turning up for Patti's shows, but as far as she and Lenny knew, they were the only ones in New York with a mission to wake up a complacent scene. Patti was friendly with the poet and bass player Richard Hell, but neither she nor Lenny had ever seen his band. Often credited with being the man who invented punk, Hell had formed a band with Tom Verlaine called the Neon Boys, which evolved into Television, and they began playing regularly at a club on the Bowery called CBGB's. Formerly a biker bar, CB's emerged as one of the only places in New York where a band could play original music. Tom Verlaine and Richard Lloyd of Television had stumbled by one day and asked the owner Hilly Kristal if their band could play on Sunday nights and for some reason Kristal agreed, and a new era of music inauspiciously began.

Word spread fast in the small downtown rock scene. After attending the première of the film *Ladies and Gentleman, the Rolling Stones* (a documentary of their 1972 tour) Patti and Lenny stopped by CBGB for the first time to check out the new group. It was 14 April 1974.

Patti had not experienced the kind of thrill she got that night for a long time, and then it had come from seeing bands like the Stones or Dylan, never a band of her generation. Television were indeed a sight to behold, with the frontline of Tom Verlaine, Richard Lloyd and Richard Hell, three magnificent, ethereal, pop-eyed, raw electric stimulants.

Around this time Richard Hell wrote a prescient essay for *Hit Parader* where he stated:

> Rock & roll has continued on this track of self-consciousness, witness Bowie, Ferry, Smith and Springsteen. Their works are filled with allusions to other rock and roll, their stage acts are studied, they have carefully designed the image of themselves that they mean to project. They all probably perceived themselves as stars before musician or vocalist or writer and that their greatest talent is for attracting media attention. I think this is great. The art-form of the future is celebrityhood ... the occupation of rock and roll is so appealing now – it's an outlet for passions and ideas too radical for any other form.

(Hell went on to found *People* magazine.)

Patti Smith shared with Richard Hell and his partner Tom Verlaine a poetry background and they also embraced the sixties British Invasion bands and the garage rock of the Velvet Underground. Patti soon fell in love with Tom Verlaine. Though she was still living with Allen Lanier, Patti had a modern attitude towards monogamy, and didn't feel guilty. Besides, Allen was having his own affairs on the road. She told Television's manager Terry Ork, 'I want Tom Verlaine. He has such a Egon Schiele look. You gotta get that boy for me.' To Ork it was a cut and dried affair: 'Tom was enamoured of Patti as a poet and scenemaker. He believed that she was gonna make it. Plus, I guess he liked her physically, they had the same kind of body structure.' Patti saw Tom as a creature of opposites. 'The way he comes on like a dirt farmer and a prince. A languid boy with the confused grace of a child in paradise. A guy worth losing your virginity to,' is how she described him in a piece in *Rock Scene*. 'Everybody knew that Patti was nuts for Tom,' said Television's rhythm guitarist, Richard Lloyd. 'But I think Tom was ambivalent. He did not want to get swallowed up by anybody.'

Hell wasn't upset when Patti started going out with Tom, apart from being nervous that the affair would boost Tom's dicey ego even further. 'I think both Patti and Tom played this dialectic, this "us versus them" thing. They could use it to their advantage or they could drift into the mainstream themselves. They would talk to each other about their career and what this whole thing was about,' observed Terry Ork.

The painter Duncan Hannah, a neighbour of Patti's, would run into her at the laundromat. When he asked what she was doing, Patti replied that she was just 'washing my old man's clothes', meaning Allen Lanier. Patti told Hannah about the triangle between Allen, Tom and herself, the relationship she wrote about in 'We Three'. She told Bebe Buell that Tom was 'the most beautiful guy in the world'. Debbie Harry once accidentally came upon Tom and Patti kissing behind CBGB's. 'Tom blushed and Patti went, "Fuck off!" Patti didn't really ever talk to me much,' said Debbie.

Her earlier steps on to the stage had been tentative, but this time Patti was ready for the challenge of being a star. At the beginning of 1974, Patti and Lenny decided to add a piano player to their act. Danny Fields was having an affair with a beautiful young guy named Richard Sohl, so when Patti and Lenny said they wanted a keyboard player, Danny introduced them to Sohl. 'We advertised for a piano player,' Patti remembered.

> And all these guys came in saying, 'Hey, wanna boogie?' Me and Lenny were stoned, trying to talk all this cosmic bullshit to them, like, 'Well, what we want to do is go over the edge.' Finally Richard Sohl came in wearing a sailor suit, totally stoned and pompous. We said, 'This guy's fucked up.' Lenny gave him the big cosmic spiel and Sohl said, 'Look, buddy, just play.' We felt like we were the ones getting auditioned! So Sohl said 'Whadaya want? Ya want some classical?' He played a bunch of Mozart. 'Ya want some blues?' He played a bunch of blues. I mean, the fuckin' guy could play anything! So we started talkin' and it turned out that he'd been raised as a Jehovah's Witness, which I had been, too. We'd

both rebelled against the same shit, and that helped. So we just brought him in.

Patti and Lenny christened Sohl DNV, which stood for Death in Venice, because of his resemblance to the character of Tadzio in the Thomas Mann novella.

'He had this one element, which was totally important for us, he could space out,' Lenny emphasized.

He could get a space and just go, and not worry that the song ended, and he had the technique. I mean, as a guitarist I was pretty rock 'n' roll, I was very rhythmic, I didn't have a lot of solo strings. I certainly was untrained, but he was classically trained, so he could move everything harmonically, and he was so atmospheric in his playing that where ever we went he could go, and we went any place.

Jane Friedman's company had an office behind a billboard on Times Square where the band rehearsed. The band rehearsed for hours at a time, and Patti developed a close friendship with Richard Sohl. Soon, Patti depended on Richard as much as she did on Lenny. In a lot of ways the group was at its purest when it was a trio, a perfect balance of communication and trust.

In June 1974, Robert Mapplethorpe, who was beginning to have some success with his photography thanks to the influence of his powerful patron Sam Wagstaff, gave Patti some money to make a record. She recorded two songs at Electric Ladyland Studios, 'Piss Factory' and 'Hey Joe', the B-side. Tom Verlaine played lead guitar on 'Hey Joe'. 'We recorded at Electric Lady, in studio B, which is a lot different than studio B is now, it was about the size of a table at the time,' Lenny recalled. 'We did two takes of "Piss Factory", we did "Hey Joe" first, and then Tom Verlaine overdubbed his guitar part and I overdubbed a little bass drum going boom, boom-boom, and that was it.'

'Piss Factory' recounted Patti's experiences working in the factory in Pitman, New Jersey. To her it was the most truthful thing she ever wrote, direct autobiography. 'In fact,' she said later, 'the truth was stronger than the poem.' The song ends with her vow to leave that squalid life behind: 'And I'm gonna go, I'm gonna get out of here, I'm gonna get on that train and go to New York City, and I'm gonna be somebody . . . I'm gonna be a big star.'

'Hey Joe', written by Dino Valenti, was originally a hit for a Los Angeles band called the Leaves. The song was frequently covered in the sixties, notably by Jimi Hendrix, in whose studio Patti was now recording. Patti brought the song up to date and made it her own by delivering a hard, scrappy account, opening with a rap about Patty Hearst, kidnapped scion of the wealthy Hearst family, asking if she had been 'gettin it every night from a black revolutionary'.

Patti latched on to the Patty Hearst case, realizing the astonishing free publicity it gave her. As she told a friend, every time she heard Patty's name on the radio or TV she wasn't sure if they were talking about Patty Hearst or her, Patti Smith. It was a little bit like what was happening with the Watergate tapes for Andy Warhol, who had been promoting the idea of taping everything all the time for ten years, and suddenly found the same idea in the headlines every day. Patti instantly grasped the significance of the photograph of Patty Hearst wearing army fatigues and a beret, grasping a machine gun, in front of a Symbionese Liberation Army flag. She recognized that its guerrilla-girl message fitted perfectly her aura as a revolutionary rock-and-roller. In fact, she was only one step away from posing in a very similar manner herself. Robert Mapplethorpe would shortly make his own self-portrait grasping a machine gun, wearing a black leather coat. The image contained the basic allure of rock and roll, whose mostly male practitioners' slogan was essentially, We've come to your town to steal your daughters, rape them, and they'll like it. There's no doubt the Patty Hearst case gave Patti Smith a big push in the media.

Some say 1,000 copies of the record were pressed, others say 1,500. In some accounts it cost $1,500 to produce and in others $1,000 or $2,000. Some accounts credit Lenny Kaye and Robert Mapplethorpe with paying for the effort, others just Robert. One report claimed 'the record label Mer was an ur-Altaic root meaning "to dare" and a Tibetan word meaning "flood".' Another insisted *mer* was both an Indo-Germanic root meaning 'to die' and an old English word for the sea. No serious attempts were made to distribute the record in any organized way. You could order it by mail or buy it in record shops around the city such as Village Oldies and Greenwich Village Disc, but also in bookstores such as the Gotham Book Mart and the East Side Bookstore. Most of the copies were signed by Patti. The single was later, in 1977, recognized as a classic and picked up by Sire Records for international distribution. It was then written about as 'perhaps the most important record she ever made' and 'the first punk record'.

Patti's first record is a perfect example of her technique. She would take a poem, chanting over a one- or two-chord backing, and segue from that into a classic rock song. By repeating this method she scrambled the ingredients until she constructed a song of her own. 'All our things started out initially as improvisations,' she explained. 'Lenny and I work out tunes as they go along. I have words and know how I think they should go, so we just pull it out and pull it out further until we get somewhere.'

The 'first edition' of 'Piss Factory' soon became a collector's item. Meanwhile Patti continued using the stage as a rehearsal room. It was there that her great rendition of 'Gloria' was born. There she stretched the list of heroes she invoked to include CBGB's mascot, Jonathan, a dog whose turds, distributed liberally around the club, helped create the unique aroma of CBGB. As she reached the first climax of her performing career Patti became her songs, dissolving into the brilliant shower of words called 'Land'.

One Philadelphia critic wrote:

As a performer, Smith owed much to the incantatory chants of Allen Ginsberg and the jazz recitations of Jack Kerouac, but her real antecedent was the ancient tradition of the shaman – the tribal sorcerer who acted as a medium for extrasensory worlds. With her hypnotic torrent of images, Smith could truly transport an audience outside itself. While Jim Morrison might have defined the other side, it was Smith who actually broke on through.

At the end of that New York summer, Patti Smith and Television had become the key bands in the rock-music revolution that would become punk. The two bands performed together at Max's Kansas City from 28 August to 2 September 1974, cementing their place in the hierarchy and sharpening their skills. The 'Piss Factory'/'Hey Joe' single had just been released, and everyone was feeling the momentum beginning to build. Patti revelled in the enthusiasm of the Max's audience. Though many of them were there to see Television, they certainly stayed to see Patti, many for the first time. For anyone who saw these shows there was no doubt that something, something brand new, was happening. Television were careening through 'Hard On Love', 'Fuck Rock and Roll' and 'Love Comes in Spurts', and Patti was making her surreal combinations of Brian Jones, Patty Hearst and the Velvet Underground. Playing at a rock club with a rock band and having the musical backing of Lenny and DNV, Patti had begun to change her whole approach. She was doing a lot more singing rather than her usual scatting Kerouac bebop.

'At that Max's job it was like a bird flew out of my mouth or something,' she said.

'That night I noticed for the first time that she could sing,' recalled Bebe Buell. 'And I saw the difference. Her voice went from her throat to her chest. Patti actually had power and control. And she got real good.' She was a smart performer, noted two reporters from the *New York Times* who were working on a profile of her. 'Using techniques similar to those recommended by Antonin Artaud, who created the "Theater of Cruelty", she sets up a powerful dramatic tension by alternating scaring and eliciting protective feelings from an audience. She aims for the groin and the spine, and as soon as people realize she wants them to like her, they usually do, and things start to cook.'

'I don't think we really started taking it seriously as anything until we played Max's,' recalled Lenny Kaye. The Max's performances were the first of a series of climaxes. Patti and Lenny began to see that they might be in the vanguard of a rock renaissance. Bearing this in mind and with a generosity rarely seen among rock musicians, Patti wrote a remarkable piece about Television called 'Learning to Stand Naked' which would be published in the October issue of *Rock Scene*.

> It's the rule of rock & roll somewhere somebody must stand naked [a reference to a Bob Dylan lyric].
>
> In the sixties we had the Stones, Yardbirds, Love and Velvet Underground. They didn't hide behind an image. THEY WERE THE IMAGE.
>
> Already a new group has begun an attack. Starting from the bottom with completely naked necks. A group called TELEVISION who refuse to be a latent image but the machine itself! The picture they transmit is shockingly honest. And the lead singer Tom Verlaine (initials TV) has the most beautiful neck in rock & roll. Real swan like – fragile yet strong. He plays lead guitar with angular inverted passion like a thousand bluebirds screaming. You know like high treble. And like Todd Rundgren he is blessed with long veined hands reminiscent of the great poet strangler jack the ripper.

At the Max's shows, Patti attracted the attention of the man who would become her most influential supporter after Lisa Robinson, the *New York Times* pop-music critic John Rockwell. He compared her to the poet-rocker Lou Reed for her 'absorption with demonic, romantic excess'.

As two of her most ardent fans, Stephen Holden and John Rockwell propelled her commercial fortune. Holden, then working in A & R, tried to sign her in 1974, and actually went so far as to record a demo with the band, but his taste was just ahead of the times and his efforts failed. However, word of Patti Smith was rapidly spreading beyond the confines of downtown New

York. In September, Britain's *Melody Maker* reported that Patti Smith 'finally and deservedly made the top billing' at Max's. 'Patti is sharp one minute and innocent the next,' wrote their US correspondent Chris Charlesworth.

> She's a bitch straining at the leash in most of her songs, all of which are prefaced by some kind of unusual story. Her ability to hold the audience's attention is her main selling point: drift away and you'll miss something you wish you hadn't. Her version of 'Hey Joe', recorded by a minor record company, is becoming an underground hit in the city even though the radio stations don't play it because of the suggestive remarks about Patty Hearst in the intro.

Among Patti's hardcore fans, her move from poetry towards rock and roll was cause for celebration but also concern. The poetry community had come to appreciate the attention she had helped bring to it with her increasingly popular readings. Patti was at the top of her form after three years of performances, and many believed (and this debate continues today) that she was at her best and purest as a poet backed by Lenny. However, there was a small but growing group of people, punk rockers, who hung out at CBGB's, and they welcomed Patti's presence in this new, fresh musical movement. There is a long tradition of poets singing their poems, and many people were excited by Patti's emergence and keen to see where she would go next.

In November, Patti went to California to play in a tiny bookstore in Berkeley, and then scored an audition night at Bill Graham's Fillmore West in San Francisco. In California she encountered her most fervent fans. One of them was Damita Richter, a twenty-year-old junkie and prostitute who wore a Catholic schoolgirl uniform and knee socks with cowboy boots and a black leather jacket. She met the band in a record shop. 'Patti came over all flirtatious and asked me who I was. I said, "I am Damita." So then she introduced me to Lenny Kaye. I hung out with them for a week but I would not let Lenny fuck me. I told him I had cancer of the uterus.' Lenny was bowled over by Damita's approach and thought she was one of the great spirits of the punk era.

The group then went on to LA to play the Whiskey A Go Go. At the Whiskey they were greeted by a tiny audience, but the band were excited by their West Coast shows because they sensed that out there they were beginning to connect with a burgeoning national punk-rock underground.

'Kids are more maniac in Berkeley than anywhere else in America,' said Patti,

even more than CBGB's. It's just so incredible. They'll scream and do interpretive dancing. They don't give a shit about being cool. The East Coast is much more hip, no question about it, but on the West Coast the people have more abandon. 'Ask the Angels' [a song written about San Francisco] is a celebration. See, I think this time around rock and roll is going to get a shot in the arm from New York the way it did from San Francisco in the 1960s. I think all the New York groups will be signed whether they're good or not. I think it will be a big phenomena. But the thing is, that song, which is about what's happening in New York, is really dedicated to the kids in California. In New York, the audience always tries to be cooler than the performer, whereas in California they give up that right to the performer.

The California trip convinced Patti and Lenny that the need for someone to fill out the sound was a pressing concern. According to Lenny,

We had fifty guitar players come down. And it was the first time we actually had to think: What are we doing and who do we need to do it with? Do we want this great blues guitar player? We were working in such weird formats that we needed someone who fitted us rather than would take us some more traditional place. We resisted the idea of having a rock-and-roll band for a long time . . . We enjoyed staying outside of tradition. We always felt it was important to keep a sense of surprise in the music.

'We had days and days of guitar players, all sort of maniac baby geniuses from Long Island, kids with $900 guitars who couldn't play anything. Mother had sent them – in a cab!' said Patti.

We'd make them do forty minutes of 'Gloria'. I'd go off on this long poem about a blue T-Bird smashing into a wall of sound or some shit like that and Lenny would keep the same three chords going, louder and louder. If the guy auditioning dropped out first, that meant he wasn't any good. These kids couldn't believe it, they thought we were nuts. Finally Ivan Kral came in. This little Czechoslovakian would-be rock star. He said, 'I am here to be in your band.' He was so cute. And we said, 'Oh, yeah?' So we did 'Land of a Thousand Dances' and it went on so long I thought I was gonna puke. But Ivan was so nervous he wouldn't stop, and we figured that was really cool. He ain't no genius, but he's got a lotta heart, Ivan does.

Ivan Kral had actually been playing at the time of the audition with Debbie Harry's band, now called Blondie. Patti and Lenny were familiar with his guitarwork from seeing him at CBGB's. It was an unspoken law that bands didn't raid each other's players, but Patti was re-writing the rules. Although in this case there was an added incentive that Patti had made it clear to Debbie on one of the rare occasions she spoke to her that there wasn't room for both of them in this scene, and since Blondie didn't stand a chance Debbie should quit now, and split.

It wasn't the last time the two divas would clash. Debbie remembered Patti showing up when Blondie were auditioning drummers.

I had Clem Burke there and she said [to Clem], 'Hey, you're pretty good, what's your name?' I said, 'Patti, I'm working with this guy.' She just went 'Oh.' You know, instead of 'Oh, pardon me,' like she hadn't done anything. Basically [Patti] told me that there wasn't room for two women in the CBGB scene and that I should leave the business 'cause I didn't stand a chance against her! She was gonna be the star, and I wasn't.

At the time Blondie were considered the band least likely to succeed. The rivalry between Patti and Debbie was of long standing. 'If there was one person in New York who could get Patti going, it was Debbie,' said Bebe Buell. 'I always noticed tension [between them], and I don't feel she took Debbie seriously. Debbie was a great talent, a great presence and a powerful beauty. Patti just sort of dismissed it. I'm not sure what the thing was with her and Debbie. I noticed that she was always uncomfortable around Debbie Harry type girls.'

Debbie had all the physical attributes that Patti adored in women. Patti's place in history as being the pop-poet will be remembered, but without Debbie Harry there would be no Courtney Love, there would be no Madonna.

On 1 January 1975 Patti read at the St Mark's Poetry Project's New Year's Day Extravaganza with Yoko Ono, Allen Ginsberg, Jackie Curtis, Robert Wilson, John Giorno and some fifty other poets. The event was reported in the *Voice* as a turning point in the seventies' culture. Patti was the most outstanding performer of the night. This success and a few scattered gigs round New York by the new four-piece Patti Smith Group aroused interest among several record labels, but the rough-edged punk sound jarred on music-business ears and in any case the band were not ready. What they needed was a regular gig to hone their skills and work on the presentation of their new songs.

This was achieved over a two-month period in the spring, when the Patti Smith Group were given a weekend residency at CBGB's, sharing the bill with Television. Patti had never played CBGB's before, but it turned out to be the making of her and of the club, which was sold out every night of the combined Television and Patti Smith package. Still, to put it into perspective, the price to get in was only two or three dollars and there was a long guest list, so the take at the door was still only in the low hundreds. But if the cash take was low, the buzz was definitely through the roof.

From Talking Heads to the Dictators, from the Ramones to Blondie (who had just lost yet another band member, the bass player Fred Smith, who replaced Richard Hell in Television), a truly diverse group of rising bands found their core audiences at CBGB's, which became the ultimate cool club of mid-seventies New York. It attracted not only the budding punk-rock fans but also the arty people who were initially drawn there to see Patti Smith. Patti remembered walking to the club during these exhilarating days: 'It was never dark, always twilight, and you'd have these old guys warming their hands over trash bins. The place was always so packed, and the feeling so intense. It was like a revival meeting.'

CBGB's was only a block away from Robert Mapplethorpe's Bond Street loft, so he frequently dropped by to hear Patti perform on his way to the leather bars. Blondie lived across the street, the Ramones were one and a half blocks away, Richard Hell could walk to the club in less than ten minutes. The audience found themselves not just watching Patti play but, on any given night, watching Patti play along with the leading members of the cutting-edge bands of the New York underground. And as word spread people like Lou Reed started dropping by too.

The British audience got their first detailed reports of Patti Smith from one of her first champions in the rock press, Charles Shaar Murray, who described a CBGB's show in the *New Musical Express*:

She can generate more intensity with a single movement of one hand than most rock performers can produce in an entire set. She's an odd little waif figure in a grubby black suit and black satin shirt, so skinny that her clothes hang baggily all over her, with chopped-off black hair and a face like Keith Richards' kid sister would have if she'd gotten as wasted by age seventeen as Keith is now. She stands there machine-gunning out her lines, singing a bit and talking a bit, in total control, riding it and steering it with a twist of a shoulder here, a flick of the wrist there – scaled-down bird-like movements that carry an almost unbelievable degree of power, an instinctive grasp of the principles of mime that teach that the quality and timing of a gesture are infinitely more important than its size. Her closing tour de force, an inspired juxtaposition of 'Land of 1,000 Dances' with a rock-poem about a kid getting beaten up in a locker room, was undoubtedly the most gripping performance that I've seen by a white act since the last time I saw the Who.

Patti was not unmoved by the experience of playing in such a supportive and welcoming environment. 'I would almost burst into tears 'cause of all the stuff that was happening,' she told Nick Tosches.

I'd look out at that long line of neon beer signs over the bar and that dog running around shitting while I'm in the middle of a beautiful ballad. There'd be a bunch of niggers beating the shit out of each other over by the pool table [this must have been one of Patti's hallucinations since no one who spent time at CBGB's ever witnessed any racial violence] and all these drunks throwing back shots [a possible reference to Legs McNeil]. It was the greatest atmosphere to perform in, it was conspiratorial. It was real physical, and that's what rock 'n' roll's all about: sexual tension and being drunk and disorderly!

I think all the groups had one similarity in that we wanted to elevate the idea of rock while still trying to keep it simple. It was a real reaction against disco music and the glitter-rock thing. Our lyrics were much more sophisticated, and we weren't into artifice at all. The whole punk phenomenon in England was much more reactionary and more 'high style'. We didn't comb our hair, not because we were making a political statement, but because we just didn't comb our hair. We were never really a punk band. We were predecessors of that; trying to create a space for people to express anti-corporate feelings. Rail against the big arena acts and the glitter bands. Bring it back to the streets, the garage. The people who came after were THAT genre. We were the grandparents, the first one to be signed out of CBGB's.

'We helped put CBGB's on the map,' said Lenny.

All of a sudden, the place would be packed out on Friday and Saturday, and it was a pretty good crowd on Thursday and Sunday. And after that, things started rolling on the Bowery. But it helped us too, because playing seven weeks, four nights a week at CBGB's, all these things that we were working on crystallized. We had Ivan, and Jay Dee Daugherty started playing with us occasionally on drums. By the time we finished CBGB's, we were, much to our surprise, like a band.

Like Ivan Kral, Jay Dee Daugherty was already in a band, Lance Loud's Mumps, when he got the call from Patti. The period 1974–75 was a time of musical chairs in the various New York punk bands, with players moving from one to another. Jay Dee Daugherty was gradually worked into the group during the two-month period. Once more, Patti had pinched a musician from another band whose profile was mostly provided by its lead singer. Lance Loud had starred in the groundbreaking *American Family* soap-opera documentary on channel 13. Hard feelings abounded as, with success approaching increasingly fast, the demon of competition entered a field which had so far been predominantly mutually supportive and friendly. In fact, apart from Television, Patti was never friendly towards or supportive of any of the other punk bands in New York.

Jay Dee's entrance into the Patti Smith Group was something

he had actively sought. After he had been invited by Jane Friedman to sit in for a couple of nights, Jay Dee started calling the manager daily, persistently forcing his way into the group. Even though the Mumps' Christian Hoffman would write him a thirty-page letter listing the reasons why he should feel bad for what he had done to the Mumps, reducing Daugherty to tears, Jay Dee was thrilled to be engaged in as well-defined a group as Patti's. As much as he recognized the potential of Patti over Lance, he also recognized that although there was a collaborative approach towards the music they made, Patti and Lenny ran the show and they were all working towards forwarding Patti's career. Lenny Kaye acted, when necessary, as a bridge between Patti and the rest of the band, interpreting her moods, marshalling their energies.

Just how precise Jay Dee's initial perceptions were would become apparent down the line. But Patti said Ivan had been the one who wanted a drummer, and when Jay Dee joined, 'we had to give him a crash course in everything. We'd tell him about the Arabs and sixteenth-century Japan and flying saucers. The poor kid had to carry all these books and records home every night.'

The members of the Patti Smith Group were defined by several different parameters, apart from how they worked. Patti, Lenny and Richard Sohl were all big potheads, who smoked grass ritualistically every day, whereas Ivan and Jay Dee were more inclined to bolt down some beers and hoover up a few lines of coke. Above all, Patti defined each member of the band as she saw him and, despite reality, pinned them by her way of thinking. Consequently, to some extent each member of the band was forced to acquiesce in Patti's image of him. She brought out in each of them aspects of their personalities of which they had not been aware, but at the same time constricted them by not accepting who they really were.

'There are many spectacular moments in rock and roll, but few magic ones when you witness the birth of a great, great artist,' recounted Leee Black Childers. 'Lisa Robinson is one of the toughest critics you could possibly face, but she and I would sit on these rickety chairs in this club that stank and was in a dangerous neighbourhood openmouthed because Patti was doing astounding things with cadence and rhythm and image. She was telling us rock and roll in a different way, and we were astonished that all of New York wasn't already clamouring at her feet.'

Patti's shows at CBGB's in March to April 1975 could not have been better timed. Dylan was launching *Rolling Thunder,* Springsteen was breaking out and the Stones were touring that summer. Record executives swarmed down to the club in a feeding frenzy. One relatively quiet midweek night the godfather of punk, Lou Reed, escorted Arista president Clive Davis to a show, and coached him through it.

Davis was impressed by the music and Patti. He recognized behind the act a shrewd, ambitous woman who wanted to be a star and knew 29 was late to start. 'I have to be in a rush,' she told him, 'I don't have the strength to take too long becoming a star.' Davis was struck by how strong a sense of herself Patti had.

Patti felt comfortable with Clive Davis. He had an outstanding record for discovering artists like Janis Joplin and Arista was young and growing. She believed he would nurture her, not just look for hit singles. In April he signed her at $750,000 for seven albums.

'At this point, with the success, everyone changed a little bit,' said Terry Ork. 'A lot of the Dionysian element evaporated with the pressure of Clive Davis coming down and all that. They [the bands] had to make it and they weren't making it, they hadn't signed big deals. New wave was dying and it did die, disco won out. People felt they had sold out because it was the only option. There was kind of a death throe.'

Patti's monetary ambitions were relatively modest (she would spend most of the advance on new equipment for the band), but she demanded from her contract an assurance of creative autonomy that a new artist rarely gets. It meant, for instance, that Patti created and approved her own ad campaigns. It was Patti who came up with the line, 'three-chord rock merged with the power of the word'. It also meant she exercised a producer's control over her records, no matter whom she called in to advise her. 'My record contract was one of the most unusual contracts of its time,' she told William Burroughs later, 'because although I got a lot of money and a lot of faith put into me, I also got full artistic control of what I did. I mean, I don't think even Bob Dylan had that at the time of his first contract!'

On 26 June 1975, while the Rolling Stones played Madison Square Garden, Patti appeared at a small downtown club called the Other End. Amy Gross, writing a profile of Smith for *Mademoiselle* magazine, described the show: 'She walks in during the first act, greeting friends, touching hands – there's something of the young Frank Sinatra in her now, his con-man cool, his wiry grace. Underneath the black silk shirt is a Keith Richards T-shirt, in honour of the Stones' visit to New York. Also in New York is Bob Dylan, who is perched unobtrusively at the bar. She is exuberant, clowning.' 'Somebody told us he was there,' Patti told a friend. 'My heart was pounding. I made a couple of references, a couple of oblique things to show I knew he was there.'

Afterwards, Dylan went backstage to introduce himself to Patti. He looked healthy and relaxed. Though physically unimposing, Dylan can never be separated from his myth and it was the mythical Dylan – the brooding, volatile poet-star of *Don't Look Back* – that had everyone in the room excited.

Those present noticed a distinct sexual tension in the room and found Dylan to be an intense and compelling sexual provocateur. He had everyone in his thrall just making small talk, even Patti, though when the photographers' flashbulbs began popping, she laughingly pushed him aside, saying, 'Fuck you, take my picture, boys!' Dylan smiled, made a gesture of prayer towards Patti, and disappeared into the night.

Patti clearly recalled the meeting and noted not only Dylan's effect on her but also hers on him:

He came back to see me and there was the same kind of sensation that I used to have in high school, like when you meet a guy in the hallway . . . it was just like that – teenage. We were like two pit bulls circling. I was a snotnose. I had a very high concentration of adrenaline. He said to me, 'Any poets around here?' And I said, 'I don't like poetry any more. Poetry sucks!' I really acted like a jerk. I thought, that guy will never talk to me again.

He had been in hiding for so long, and he wanted to come out, and in the club he kinda saw in me someone who was potentially as strong as him, who has a lot of energy – the kind that makes you totally uncomfortable with the world – and he recognized that. On stage I was into improvising, linguistically, and I was especially inspired that night because he was there. But of course I learned that from him, and yet it was almost like it was a new thing to him. I said, 'You have to remember where that came from!' He started getting really turned on by the idea of the band – my guys following me or pushing me and not faltering or wondering about what musical changes to go into because I've just spread the song out like a hand. He saw somebody doing something that he didn't think was possible, and he said, 'I wish I would have stayed with just one group – if I'd had the same group all this time, how well we would have known the ins and outs of each other.'

And the day after there was this picture on the cover of the *Village Voice*. The photographer had Dylan put his arm around me. It was a really cool picture. It was a dream come true, but it reminded me of how I had acted like a jerk. And then a few days later I was walking down Fourth Street by the Bottom Line and I saw him coming. He put his hand in his jacket – he was still wearing the same clothes he had on in the picture, which I liked – and he takes out the

Village Voice picture and says, 'Who are these two people? You know who these people are?' Then he smiled at me and I knew it was alright.

'I'm moving hard now because I know I can do it,' Patti told Lisa Robinson at the end of 1975.

Horses

1975

I came into Rock and Roll for political reasons, to be like Paul Revere. I knew we weren't great at the beginning, but we felt like human alarm clocks — Wake up! Wake up!

Patti Smith

At the beginning of the summer of 1975 Patti and her band went into seclusion to rehearse their material for the upcoming recording dates. After a lot of deliberation, Patti chose John Cale to produce the record. She joked that she was attracted by his face on the cover of his *Fear* album, but Cale's association with the Velvet Underground, the sound of his own solo albums, and his production work with Nico and Iggy Pop were the real reasons she made this choice. The band decided to record in the studio Jimi Hendrix had built in Greenwich Village shortly before he died, and where Patti had recorded 'Piss Factory'. Electric Ladyland on Eighth Street, New York's downtown rialto, had been modernized but still carried a lot of mystique.

The recording of the first album, *Horses*, over August and into September, became a battle of wills between John Cale and Patti.

After the CBGB's experience, Patti felt her songs were ready to be recorded, but Cale disagreed. He made the band rethink all their material from scratch. But first he had them replace all their equipment, which was beaten to hell by having been played on the road for years. Then, as Lenny said, 'he went right to the songs'. This resulted in many days of heated debate in the studio. 'Everything wound up pretty much the way it had started,' said Lenny, 'but we all understood it a bit more.' Lenny felt that Cale's main contribution was to set the 'psychological aura' in the studio. Cale recognized that his main task would be transforming a poet into a singer.

'It was not clear what persona this record was going to have until I had her improvise against herself,' said John Cale.

At that point something clicked. There was a track she did where she read poetry. I had her read poetry against her poetry and there were two lines going on and I had her mix it. When Clive Davis heard that, he said, 'Hey, you've got a collaborator.' And that's exactly the thing that made that record different. She was really a poet and you had to respect the fact that she was not a musician but out of sheer bravado and desire was making herself into a rock-and-roll singer and basically wanted to be Keith Richards. But I was awed that she had gotten all that input from Bob Dylan and Lou Reed to some extent. She had a Welsh Methodist idea of improvisation, in that it was like declamation. Lou was kind of psychological, but a lot of Patti's impulses came from preaching.

For Patti, *Horses* was

the culmination of all my most heartfelt adolescent desires. All I was looking for in a producer was a technical person. Instead, I got a real maniac artist. I went out to pick out an expensive watercolour painting, and instead I got a mirror. It was really like a season in hell for both of us. But inspiration doesn't always have to be someone sending me half a dozen American Beauty roses. There's a lot of inspiration going on between the murderer and the victim. I had to solidify everything I believed in. We came into the studio really half-assed and glib, then I had to pound my fists into John's skull day and night.

Cale imposed his discipline on the band and the result was that the songs became tighter and the band more confident, allowing them to experiment more. 'Birdland' and 'Land' were transformed. 'We went through all kinds of voyages,' said Patti. 'Usually [on "Land"] there's Mexican boys and space guys, weird Burroughs stuff like Arab guys and Christian angels fucking in the sand, pulling out each other's entrails.'

In 1975 recording studios came replete with every stimulant known to mankind, from cocaine and marijuana to amphetamines, opiates and alcohol. The combination of any variety of these with a minimum of six raging egos was bound to make the recording of *Horses* impossible to describe accurately. Furthermore, any description that attempted to be accurate would have to be a contradiction. In 1976, for example, Patti said, 'production-wise John wanted to put strings on the record and get new musicians. If you're into some Velvet Underground fantasy forget it. John is into the Beach Boys – totally. He wanted to just get rid of the band and take me into the studio with an orchestra.' Twenty-three years later she said, 'Sometimes we'd get all excited in the studio. John and I would have a really happy moment together, hugging, then at other times we'd have tears streaming down our faces. It was like two crazy poets dealing with showers of words. But we didn't have any motivation other than to do something really great.'

Everybody in the band related to John Cale in a different way. Jay Dee loved Cale's solo albums, and had met him briefly in California in 1969 at the Beverly Hills Hotel, where Cale had a suite while producing the Stooges. He thought he was great to work with, a great catalyst, and appreciated his eccentric sense of humour. Jay Dee also felt that though Cale could be difficult in the studio, he nurtured the integrity that existed in the band and in addition he brought his expertise and musical and technical inspiration to the project.

Lenny was also a fan of Cale's solo work, and was confident that he would understand the band's artistic ethos. He was not at all aware of Cale's love for the music of the Beach Boys and his tendency to monopolize any relationship he had, which meant in this case turning the Patti Smith Group into the Beach Boys. By the time they had finished the album, Lenny had a pretty clear understanding of how the collaboration had worked: because he had produced records himself, Lenny sympathized with John's approach, yet since it led almost immediately to a direct confrontation between John and Patti, coming at least once to blows, he was torn between his total allegiance to Smith and his understanding of Cale's dilemma. Basically, Cale forced the band to fight for its music, which ended up having a positive influence on the album. The essence of the conflict lay in Patti's desire to create spontaneously and Cale's to build layer upon layer of sound like Brian Wilson on a Beach Boys album.

During the making of the album, the continuing triangular relationship between Patti, Tom Verlaine and Allen Lanier caused friction, yet spurred creativity. On one occasion both Tom and Allen were in the studio at the same time. With Cale there too, there were moments when masculine anger flashed towards the edge of violence. Some onlookers got the definite impression that Patti enjoyed the tension created in the rivalry for her attention. Others thought it caused her distress. According to Cale, the most interesting sessions were the ones in which Allen Lanier felt obliged to flex his muscles. Given her history of playing her men off against each other, it seems likely that Cale's presence was primarily positive even if she did at one point launch herself at him like a torpedo.

Even before *Horses* was released, Patti was expressing her ambivalent feelings about Cale's role as producer. She spoke to Chris Charlesworth of the *Melody Maker*, intimating that she had produced the record.

What John did for us was to make us aware of each other. He said that we were really nebulous, and weren't that close, and I thought we were, you know? But after that recording . . . Well, we really broke past everything, got to know each other's fragile stuff. We're like brothers and sisters. I wasn't made to feel guilty or nervous about any of the subject matter. John kept pushing me to improvise and extend.

Months later, on a tour of England, she was even more dismissive about Cale's role on the record. When the writer Steven Lake criticized the sound of *Horses*, she told him, 'Forget about Cale. He had nothing to do with anything. I mixed the record myself, blame me for the way it sounds. The album was spewed from my womb. We ignored all Cale's suggestions.'

All the songs on *Horses* were written by Patti and a member of her band, Tom Verlaine or Allen Lanier. What made them commendable was the application of Burroughs's cut-up technique to the sound and sometimes partial content of classic fifties and sixties rock and pop lyrics. It was, as John Rockwell wrote, this elaboration of rock standards 'that provides the most striking songs in her repertory,'

'All the cuts are long,' she said, 'except "Elegy" for Jimi Hendrix which is two and a half minutes. We recorded it on September 18th, the anniversary of Hendrix's death.' Another song was about her little sister, Kimberly, and she re-wrote Van Morrison's 'Gloria' and interpolated 'Land of a Thousand Dances' by improvising about the 'sea of possibilities'.

Patti received her ideas equally from reading and dreaming. She wrote 'Birdland' for example, after reading the *Book of Dreams* by Peter Reich (son of psychiatrist Wilhelm). 'Break It Up' came from a dream about Jim Morrison lying naked on a marble slab with stone wings. Patti plays the part of a small boy repeatedly yelling 'break it up' until the wings break and Morrison is free to rise up, like Jesus, and escape. Again it was the combination of twentieth-century classic imagery with bubble-gum rock that blew the listener into that free space of unlimited possibilities that rock at its best offers.

Near the end of the recording Patti was down to 93 pounds (42 kilos), having lost 11 pounds working in the studio. She gave an interview to the writer Tony Glover, telling him:

> The thing is, art always wins. Art will survive, and I'm gonna die – so I'm not gonna give art all the best moments of my life. If you live in the moment, nothing comes first – but the energy I have left after my art I save for love. What you have to do is try to capture meaningful moments – and we got some incredible truly frightening moments on this record. 'Land' still frightens me.

Lenny added, 'Just as Patti projects personas and refuses to be defined as a woman or rock-and-roll singer, she just goes with whatever is happening to the boundary of art – we want to shatter that boundary and get out there.'

According to Patti's contract with Arista, she had total control of the album's design. There was no question but that Mapplethorpe would take the picture. The question was who would choose the image and what it would say. Despite mammoth conversations covering every possible angle, when it came to the shoot it was a matter of five minutes in the making. Robert had chosen a white wall in Sam Wagstaff's apartment on which the sun cast the perfect light at a certain time. Patti dressed in a white boy's shirt and threw her black boy's jacket over her shoulder, refused to comb her hair and turned an arrogant, impudent face to the camera. The image Robert captured in the first few frames resonated with as powerful a force as the Rolling Stones' first cover, Dylan's first electric cover or the Velvet Underground's famous banana cover by Andy Warhol. Within its first year *Horses* sold some two hundred thousand copies, but it instantly freed millions of women all over the world by saying they could do anything they wanted to, that men no longer dominated the field.

Many people actually bought the record for its cover. It became an instant icon. All those years of treating clothes as objects of art had paid off. As Tony Hiss and David McClelland pointed out in their profile of Patti, 'Her costume is replete with metonymic significance. Every article of clothing evokes a name and every name evokes a state of mind. For someone who looks rather like the 101st Neediest Case, Patti pays a great deal of attention to the way she dresses.' Patti expanded on her look: 'A black boy's suit jacket from Saks Fifth Avenue. Once, I went to Saks and watched a thirteen-year-old Catholic boy and his mother choose a suit, then I bought the same one. It's my Baudelaire dress suit. Sometimes a black schoolboy's tie or a black ribbon satin tie. Then white shoes, a tribute to the Rolling Stones' *High Tide and Green Glass* greatest hits album. Brian Jones always wore white shoes.'

'Patti's great to photograph,' Robert told this writer not long after the session for *Horses*. 'I know that I'm going to have something great out of each session that I do. I guess a lot has to do with our relationship. I think you can get too involved with [someone]. It seems to be better after you're not sexually involved.'

It's difficult now to comprehend how strange the image of Patti on the cover of *Horses* was in 1975. Women rock singers were supposed to be glamorous and sexy in the traditional way, with make-up and carefully styled hair. Arista Records' president Clive Davis hated the photo and fought to have it changed or at least airbrushed (to remove Patti's 'moustache'), but Patti had been given artistic control and she stood her ground. The cover of *Horses* completely captured the essence of Patti and the moment. It offered a new image of a rock-and-roll woman, ambiguous, androgynous but strong and in control. In 1991 the cover was voted one of the 100 best album covers of the rock era by *Rolling Stone* magazine.

As the band prepared for the album's November release and rehearsed for a US tour, Patti continued seeing Dylan, with whom she was rumoured to have had a brief affair. He wanted her to join his Rolling Thunder tour that fall. Patti told her friend Miles, whom she'd known since her days at the Chelsea Hotel:

Dylan told me to come to this party. Actually I thought he was inviting me for a drink – he asked me to come to some bar at Gerde's Folk City, where he first started in New York. So I went, and there's a million people there – well-known people, and I thought he was asking me for a drink, he couldn't have asked all these people – is this a coincidence? But it was a party for a birthday and they were also going to announce Rolling Thunder.

First, him and Joan Baez got up and sang 'One Too Many Mornings', which was one of my favourite Dylan songs. I'd seen him a lot in between all this time. Anyway, different people got up: Bobby Neuwirth, Jack Elliott got up, Jim McGuinn got up and sang his horse song; Bette Midler got up and sang this song – she didn't do such a hot job . . . she did this weird thing – she came over and threw this glass of beer in my face! Just walked up! I never met her before. It was like a John Wayne movie! I was real shocked. And then Dylan made me go up there. I had no band, no song prepared, but I understood that why I had to go up there was to save face. Since I couldn't hit her I had to do something to maintain my dignity, so I got up there with Eric Andersen, and I said, 'Just play a droning E chord behind me.' So I just made up this thing. I looked at Bob, and made up this thing about a brother and sister. But while I'm doing it I start thinking about Sam Shepard – he was in my consciousness – and so I told this story, really got into it, made this brother and sister be parted by the greed and corruption of the system – I did a good job and lots of people liked it. I was real proud.

There was a lot of tension. Phil Ochs was there, and Phil Ochs could always bring out that *Don't Look Back* side of Dylan. Bob wouldn't talk to Phil Ochs. The two of them . . . it was like there was a noose in the middle of the room and they were circling around, trying to get each other to hang themselves. [Phil Ochs would commit suicide by hanging on 9 April 1976.]

Anyway I'd got everything I need from him, I guessed it was time to turn the beat around. So I said, 'I'll give you one tip. Use your fists.' And he says, 'Aw, I can't hit the air with my fists or nothing. People will think I'm copying you!' I said, 'Well I've imitated you for twelve years, you can spare a little imitation.' So he just laughed. Seeing him laugh is great, 'cos he has a lot of pain. He's like the Duke of Windsor. But he's also got a streak in him that won't give up being a contender. And that streak is what gives him so much life – that streak makes him keep creating, keep putting himself out there. Dylan's such a fucking maniac. He's intense and that intensity has only been successfully revealed through abstract expressionism in rock and roll.'

Despite trying to focus on the release of her own record, Patti attended some of the Rolling Thunder rehearsals:

At those rehearsals . . . I just told him what I always tell him . . . that I think we could do something great together because he's such a great improviser. I suppose that creation is improvisation, but I'd like to see him do it on stage. I told him there was no space for me on that tour. And he knew it but at that point it was so early in my career and he felt that I should be exposed to the public. I thought it was real sweet of him, but he's so restless – at this point we're not chemically suited to be around each other – both of us have so much electrical energy we need some kind of calming factor. It's like if you have an electric chair you need somebody to electrocute, you don't bring in another electric chair.

Horses' release on 10 November 1975 was cause for celebration. Patti had fulfilled her desire to wake people up to a new form of rock and give the fans an album that would make them feel the way she had when purchasing a Dylan or Stones album in the sixties. It was a kind of manifesto and Patti was suddenly thrust into the spotlight as a rock politician. The album received the kind of reviews artists dream of and attracted the more literate critics from *Rolling Stone* to the *New York Times*. It was the first record to emerge from CBGB. A stream of debut albums from Blondie to the Dead Boys would soon follow, but by getting there first and doing such a magnificent job Patti had snatched the crown. Clive Davis and his staff at Arista could not have been happier. How often does a new contender break in the music press and the mainstream press on a first album?

Patti's longtime fan, the critic John Rockwell, wrote a review of *Horses* for *Rolling Stone*:

> Her first record, *Horses*, is wonderful in large measure because it recognizes the overwhelming importance of words in her work. John Cale, the producer, has demonstrated the perfect empathy he might have been expected to have for Smith, and he has done so mostly by not distorting her in any way. The range of concerns in *Horses* is huge, far beyond what most rock records even dream of . . . All eight songs betray a loving fascination with the oldies of rock. The homage is always implicit – the music just sounds like something you might have heard before, at least in part – and sometimes explicit.
>
> Smith is a genuine original, as original an original as they come. *Horses* is a great record not only because Patti Smith stands alone, but because her uniqueness is lent resonance by the past.

Patti certainly could not have expected a better response to a first album. *Horses* was trumpeted in the American press as a bona fide musical event. The *New York Times* described it as an 'extraordinary disc, every minute of which is worth repeated hearings. *Horses* may be an eccentricity, but in a way that anything strikingly new is eccentric. It will annoy some people and be dismissed by others. But if you are responsive to the mystical energy, it will shake you and move you as little else can.'

The British music press was split. Steve Lake in the *Melody*

Maker was vicious: 'Precisely what's wrong with rock and roll right now is that there's too many academics pretending to be cretins, and too many cretins pretending to be academics,' he wrote. 'And it's time we started shooting them down in flames. Let Patti Smith and John Cale be the first heads to tumble. There's no way that the completely contrived and affected "amateurism" of *Horses* constitutes good rock and roll. That old "so bad it's good" aesthetic has been played to death. *Horses* is just bad. Period.'

At the *New Musical Express*, Charles Shaar Murray took a polar opposite position:

> *Horses* is some kind of definitive essay on the American night as a state of mind, an emergence from the dark under-current of American rock that spewed up Jim Morrison, Lou Reed and Dylan's best work, out of Gasoline Alley, to Desolation Row, a thrashing exorcism of public and private demons. *Horses* is an album in a thousand. God knows, it's an important album in terms of what rock can encompass without losing its identity as a musical form, in that it intro-duces an artist of greater vision than has been seen in rock for far too long.

While paying homage to rock's great romantics from Keith Richards to Lou Reed, *Horses* marked the acceptance of the white female voice as a powerful instrument in rock. Patti was singing in an instantly recognizable, literate but hard voice that would in time spawn a new generation of female rockers. 'She shocked me the first time I saw her,' wrote Amy Gross. 'Real old-fashioned shock . . . This 27-year-old skinny punk who hammered out dirty poetry and sang surreal folk songs. Who never smiled. Who was tough, sullen, bad, didn't give a damn . . . I felt both ravaged and exhilarated.'

Another witness, Cleveland-based blues singer Adele Bertei, dropped everything and moved to New York the first time she heard Patti sing:

At the time music was about divas or rock goddesses. It was nothing to do with boyish little tykes like myself who could sing blues. I didn't think there'd ever be a place for me. Then Patti Smith came out with an album that rocked my universe. She was androgynous, outspoken, obviously well-educated and well-read. She became like a mentor to me. If she dropped references to Brancusi [the Romanian sculptor], I'd go out and find art books. If it was Rimbaud, I'd read him and learn about the French decadents. Because I didn't have much of an education, Smith in a sense was my first teacher.

In France, *Horses* won the prestigious Grand Prix de Disque presented by the Académie Charles Cros. The album's cover photo was published everywhere, giving Mapplethorpe's work wide attention. 'We had always dreamed about becoming successful together,' Patti said. 'It was all part of our grand scheme.'
Patti's fellow *Creem* magazine alumnus Lester Bangs eloquently summed up the qualities of the album:

This is not a spoken-word album, and if you couldn't understand a word of English, you couldn't miss the emotional force of Patti's music. *Horses* is a commanding album, as opposed to demanding: you don't have to work to understand or like it, but you can't ignore it either. It refuses to be background music, it stops the action in a room when it is on, and leaves its effects when it's over whether you like it or not.

In the British music paper *Sounds*, John Ingham concurred: 'Ladies and gentlemen, I give you the record of the year. Quite simply this is one of the most stunning, commanding, engrossing platters to come down the turnpike since John Lennon's Plastic Ono Band, and for the same reasons.' In the *Village Voice*, New York's most influential rock critic Robert Christgau dubbed her 'the first credible rock shaman'.
While *Horses* climbed the charts, reaching number 46 on *Bill-*

board's Hot Hundred, astonishing for something so completely out of the mainstream, Patti and her band took to the road for a creative three-month tour. Her opening act was a solo John Cale. Every place they played was sold out. Cale came out every night at the end of her set and played 'My Generation' with the band, culminating with Lenny launching himself into John's arms and Cale carrying him off stage.

Patti's first national tour was the most exciting journey she had ever taken. Her ecstasy was infectious as she jumped up and down, clapping her hands and rapping away in between songs with feverish intensity. It was *A Hard Day's Night* crossed with *Don't Look Back*, filmed by Godard with Patti as Anna Karina and Lenny as an improbable but willing Jean-Pierre Léaud. As they played into 1976, America's bicentennial, it was also brand new and red, white and blue. Backstage after each gig or in the hotel Patti got to exercise her love of language in a series of mythmaking interviews that stand as little works of art in themselves:

> I think masturbating is a really important function in art. People say I go too far, but there's no too far to go. I can come up to twelve times a day. I can have a lot of brain travel through masturbation. That's where I get a lot of my mental images. Besides, when I'm on the road it means I'm away from somebody I love. It might mean I'm not going to be making love for a month, so I have to get that shot on stage. To me fucking and masturbation and art are all the same because they all require total concentration.
>
> I want people to applaud too, just like Lenny Bruce. Do you think Lenny Bruce didn't want to be loved by everybody? My goals on stage are no different to Edith Piaf's or Mick Jagger's. I want everybody to love me.

Patti's achievements in 1975 were crowned by a *New York Times Magazine* profile, 'Gonna Be So Big, Gonna Be a Star, Watch Me Now!' by Tony Hiss and David McClelland, which was published on 21 December. 'Patti Smith is having a wonderful time these days,' it began. 'I have a lot to learn about records and mixing and things like that,' she told them, 'but nobody can tell me about the magic. The magic is completely under control.'

The Field Marshall of Rock and Roll

1976

**She was such a physical wreck.
I liked her for that.**

Johnny Rotten

The official public designation of punk rock as a movement came with the publication of the first issue of *Punk* magazine in January 1976. According to *Punk*'s creator and editor, John Holmstrom:

> It was pretty obvious that the word was getting popular. *Creem* used it to describe this early seventies music; *Bomp* would use it to describe the garage bands of the sixties; a magazine like *Aquarian* would use it to describe what was going on at CBGB's. The word was being used to describe Springsteen, Patti Smith and the Bay City Rollers. So when Legs McNeil came up with it we figured we'd take the name before anyone else claimed it. We wanted to get rid of the bullshit, strip it down to rock and roll. We wanted the fun and liveliness back.

'Something was going to happen,' added *Punk*'s resident punk, Legs McNeil. 'No one in New York had any money. The city was nearly bankrupt – that's when President Ford said to the city: "Drop dead!"'

Patti spent the first four months of 1976 on the road in the US performing at an increasingly frenetic pace and receiving great reviews. The Bottom Line in the heart of downtown New York was the greatest showcase for rock and roll in the city. From its stage Lou Reed recorded his live album *Take No Prisoners*. Now it was Patti's turn to take the room, which she did with all the panache of a seasoned entertainer. Her three weekend nights were sold out, with two shows on Saturday, one going out live on WXPN, and they added a second show on Sunday. Each concert began with the happy Lou Reed chestnut, 'We're Gonna Have a Real Good Time Together'. Reed, the actor Richard Dreyfuss, Peter Wolf of the J. Geils Band with his wife Faye Duna-way were among the many others in the audience. It was like Patti could walk on water, like she had melded with each liquid moment as she stunned the crowd with in-between-song patter like Lenny Bruce's kid sister. 'I am . . . the first . . . Patti Smith,' she intoned, 'Or maybe the second Anna Magnani! I've been reading all these articles about me, [the *New York Times* had just come out with their Sunday magazine profile] and I'm checking myself out . . . And I think what it is . . . I got a lot of . . . post-humous appeal!!!!!' 'AAAAAAAAHHHH HA HA HA HAHA HA,' the crowd went, screaming, pounding the tables.

'It's possible to accuse Patti of taking herself too seriously,' wrote Robert Christgau in the *Village Voice*, 'but you can't say she doesn't have a sense of humour about it. She knows that her audience – "my kids", she calls them, more maternal than you'd figure – has the earmarks of a cult. And she knows that her band can be described as a critics' band.'

Patti was feeling her power. At the end of her version of 'My Generation' (recorded for a live release) in Cleveland on 26 January, she ad-libbed 'I'm so young / I'm so young I'm so goddamn young / I'm so young / I'm so goddamn young / I'm so young / I'm so goddamn young . . . we created it: let's take it over.' Other cover versions included the Velvet Underground's 'Pale Blue Eyes' and 'Louie, Louie'. 'We were happy,' said Patti. 'We had really great camaraderie. We had a mission.'

The Field Marshall of Rock and Roll: 1976

'We're past the midpoint of a decade now,' she told her friend Nick Tosches, 'and I think a lot of people are ready to take a leap. I think we've had enough mediocrity. There is no way that singers like Elton John or Helen Reddy can ever transport people the way that Jim Morrison or Jimi Hendrix did. I don't feel that people will allow this shit to go on much longer. The heart of rock 'n' roll is integrity.'

'The whole point of Patti Smith was beyond gender, beyond politics, beyond, beyond,' Lenny Kaye explained.

> Any time you were defined, you were caught. I used to use that quote from Mayo and the Red Crayola, one of my favourite sixties albums, where they say 'Definitions define limit.' That was our philosophy. We wanted to have freedom to have a hit single, or to have twenty minutes of abstract noise. And what do you call that? Is Albert Ayler punk? I don't know. On the other hand, we liked the attitude of punk. So, it was kind of a toss-up. I mean, we were feeling like missionaries, carrying the word out there and trying to stir trouble up wherever we went.

Also in January *Creem*, the magazine that had featured her poetry back in 1971, ran a cover story on her by Tony Glover titled 'Patti Smith: Sweet Howling Fire'. Nick Tosches interviewed her for *Penthouse*, a definitive sign that she had broken out from the rock and local New York City press. Asked if she had many encounters with groupies, Patti complained:

> Yeah, but they're almost always girls. They're usually pretty young, too. They try to act heavy and come on like leather. I always act as if they're real cool. I never go anyplace with them. They bring me drugs and poetry and black leather gloves and stuff like that. I don't really know what they want. I mean, I think they're actually straight girls. The guys that I get, they're always such great losers. Really pimply-faced fuck-ups with thick glasses, but a lot of heart, y'know? My heart really goes out for those kids 'cause I can still taste

what it feels like to be sixteen and totally fucked up. I remember everything. And I figure if I came out of it okay, then these kids are going to be okay, too. They just need to be told that they're going to be okay, that's all.

On 20 February, she was quoted in the *New Musical Express* saying, 'I'd rather be remembered as a great rock-and-roll star than a great poet. To reach the highest point of something our generation created.' On 13 March, Arista released the live version of 'Gloria'/'My Generation' (with John Cale on bass) recorded in Cleveland in January.

Patti introduced a new motif into her daily babels from the stage of New York's prestigious Avery Fisher Hall the same month, protesting that 'the people own the airwaves'. Patti had already been banned from WBCN, the key FM radio station in the Boston area, an important market for new wave at the time, and one of the few stations open to playing the new music. Patti had let loose with a string of 'fuck's and 'shit's during an interview, knowing that it was live with no delay. American radio has strict guidelines on which words are illegal to say over the airwaves, and radio stations that do not comply, for whatever reason, are heavily fined. However, in her battle against censorship, Patti was apparently not concerned with who suffered the consequences of her actions.

The single most important event of 1976 for Patti was meeting Fred Sonic Smith, who had been in Detroit's proto-punk band the MC5. It is somehow fitting that Lenny played Cupid on this occasion, introducing Patti to Fred on 9 March 1976 during a party given by Arista at a tiny hot dog joint, Lafayette Coney Island, in downtown Detroit. Fred was standing in front of a white wall in a navy blue coat. The meeting inspired two songs, 'Godspeed' (in which the coat gets a mention) and '25th Floor' about the hotel room they partied in later that night. The connection was immediate and for the next four years Patti was more attached to Fred than any other single person. Since Fred was

married and Patti was still with Allen it would be two years before
they went public.

Fred Smith was in his late twenties and at this time led a group
called the Sonic Rendezvous Band who played mostly in the
Detroit area. Patti was immediately drawn to the tall, quiet guitar
player. There was something slightly remote and inaccessible
about him, but those were the very qualities that attracted her.

John Sinclair, formerly leader of Detroit's white panthers and
manager of Fred's first band the MC5, penned a good description
of Patti's show at the Ford auditorium: 'Not so much a singer as
an electronic female shaman who chants, moans, shakes and
screams her visions into being, Ms Smith presented the most
powerful compelling stage performance seen in these parts since
the demise of Iggy and the Stooges. She did have the good taste
to call Motor City mainstay Fred Smith to the stage for the band's
encore on "My Generation".'

'The first night we met,' Patti said, 'he appeared on stage with
us, and I could tell by the way he played what kind of person he
was – better than me, stronger than me.' After the show they
went to Patti's hotel together. She wrote '25th Floor' about that
night, which later appeared on *Easter*. The song refers to her
'fender duo sonic' and also mentions the Detroit River, which
runs behind the hotel where she and Fred first got to know each
other.

'He was just Patti's type – a tall, brooding blond – the strong,
silent type,' said Jay Dee. 'It was love at first sight for Patti. It was
personal chemistry. The MC5 thing was icing on the cake. She
loves tall guys with crooked teeth.'

When the band hit San Francisco Lenny hooked up with Damita again, but Damita discovered a different Patti: 'When I got
there Patti was really mean to me. I thought, what's going on?
During a soundcheck she jumped off the stage and started poking me in the chest saying, "I know you slept with you know
who." She had found out that I had been dicking around with
her boyfriend Allen Lanier. I spent the whole week in tears.
When they left Patti said, "Well, I forgive you." I was like, "Oh,

fuck you!'' I hated her because I had come all the way from Hawaii to be with them and I felt it was unnecessary for her to be cruel.'

Back in New York, Patti was still dividing her time between Allen Lanier, living with him in their Greenwich Village apartment across from the Kettle of Fish, and Tom Verlaine, in whose building she kept an apartment. The two men had satisfied the poles of Patti's personality. From Lanier she had learned everything she could about how to be in a successful rock band, how it was like being in the army, with preparations for tours being boot camp. 'Allen brought out something in her that gave her the confidence to execute her music, the strength to be a singer,' said Bebe Buell. 'He was also open and receptive to her poetry and envisioned music with it, the same as Lenny. That was their bond. He certainly wasn't her physical type.' He was a small, wiry man, about Patti's size, with the long hair and standard garb of the heavy-metal rocker (jeans and a leather jacket), but he did not possess big hands, crooked teeth, a beautiful neck, etc. His looks were not striking, neither did he have the charisma of a rock star. However, what he did not have physically he more than made up for mentally and personally. Everybody liked him. You never heard a bad word about Allen Lanier. Patti's overnight success in 1975 had put her ahead of Allen in the rock-star stakes, adding an element of strain to the relationship. But Allen had always been the least dramatic of her boyfriends, the kind of guy who could spend hours just lying around the house or playing pool. He had a sharp intelligence which impressed a number of visitors who would drop by to check in with Patti and end up spending hours talking with Allen.

Tom Verlaine was the opposite with the all-important crooked teeth and big hands like Rimbaud. Terry Ork, whose Ork records would put out Television's response to 'Piss Factory', 'Little Johnny Jewel', probably had a better view than anybody of the two sides of the Smith–Verlaine affair:

They were very competitive in a way, just two kids madly in love, the same physical body type, the same kind of hunger for success, also I have a real theoretical thing about the whole period. The sixties were about five years dead, but here in the mid seventies was a kind of us against them mentality. They were both very paranoid about the establishment and I guess Wartoke was a go-between, a liberal public relations for the heads of the off-boat people. But I think that Patti and Tom both played this dialectic, this us versus them thing; they could use it to their advantage if they wanted to and they could drift into this snobbish attitude which would take them into the mainstream themselves; it was a dangerous line. There was a lot of that kind of politics that would unite them. They would talk to each other about their careers and what this whole thing was about. That was a strong element too. They were very exhibitionistic, fall down on the floor and mock sex.

'Tom was very paranoid,' said Terry Ork. 'I spent hours trying to get him to deal with people because he was very uptight. It's sort of symbolic that after her break-up with Tom, Patti went back to Allen, the Blue Oyster Cult mainstream rock guy, music that was selling and making money. You can see how Tom has struggled ever since.'

Once *Horses* took off, the first punk-rock album to cut into the big time, Verlaine was intent on making his own album, *Marquee Moon*, and going out into the world and putting his big hands to other uses, playing great runaway guitar in seedy underground clubs. Television already stood out as the most brilliant and beautiful bunch of boys on the block. Hey, Danny Fields creamed in his jeans every time he saw Television live. As an auteur, Tom was as driven as Patti, and success was not going to wait forever.

For Patti, what was most important was that unlike Allen or Tom, Fred was stronger than her. Even though professionally she had a more promising future than Fred, Patti found in him a strength that was all-compelling. The MC5's 1969 debut album *Kick Out the Jams* was a sourcebook for punk, and Fred could certainly still be seen as a hero in 1976. From Mapplethorpe through Carroll, Shepard, Neuwirth to Rundgren, Lanier and Verlaine, her boyfriends had been a veritable supermarket of sang-froid successful guys who were champions in their respective fields. Fred was married to a woman called Sigrid in Detroit, fronting the Sonic Rendezvous Band, scuffling to get by, while Patti was about to take over the world. But love would find a way. Though they would not get together for two more years, they began a secret telephone courtship as they both worked on a way out of their personal situations.

Years later, Thurston Moore reminded Patti of an item in *Creem* back then about a love letter she had sent to Fred. 'I sent him a telegram: "Light and energy enclosed",' said Patti. 'I couldn't believe they found out about that.'

Fame would mean that 'they' would find out about everything. An underground paper, the *Daily Planet*, hit the street that spring with a few pages of nude photos of Patti taken three years earlier, using Patti's remarks in her *Penthouse* interview in large type next to the pictures. 'I don't feel exploited by pictures of naked broads. I like that stuff. If it's a bad picture or the girl's ugly, it pisses me off. Shit, I think bodies are great,' the captions crowed, making it seem as though Patti endorsed the pictures, which were obtained without her knowledge or permission, infuriating the singer. They also published the address of the apartment Patti shared with Allen Lanier and accused her of union busting for crossing picket lines at NBC to perform on *Saturday Night Live* during a workers' strike. The magazine's reporters followed Patti, staking out her apartment and harassing her in the street in pursuit of a story. 'I want you people to stop bothering me!' Patti yelled as she jumped into the chauffeured black Cadillac that waited for her on MacDougal Street. She was beginning to pay the price of fame.

By the time she finished her first US tour, Patti was gearing up for the conquest of Europe, where she was booked to play eight cities in seven days in May 1976. Not a week passed without some interview or review of Patti in the British rock papers. On 8 May the *New Musical Express* had a short phone interview in which she told Charles Shaar Murray: 'I ain't afraid of the Parisians, man ... I know how to handle the French. I've done so much time in Paris, I've done so much spiritual time, I feel like I'm part French.' Patti's sets now consisted mainly of new material. She was looking ahead to the all important second album. This, she was determined, would be a Patti Smith group album, not just Patti Smith.

The European tour climaxed with two performances at London's Roundhouse on 16 and 17 May. Like many powerful artists Patti polarized the British rock press, which at that time comprised three weekly newspapers, the *New Musical Express*, the *Melody Maker* and *Sounds*, which published detailed accounts of every facet of the British music scene. At the time they were ahead of the American rock press not only in the amount of space they devoted to it but in their stable of writers, which included Nick Kent, Charles Shaar Murray, Miles, Mick Farren, Julie Burchill and Tony Parsons. The idea was to be as opinionated as possible and to stir controversy. They all had a go at Patti Smith.

Miles went to see her in her hotel before the first Roundhouse show. 'Patti and the band had played the Paradiso in Amsterdam the night before – one of those clubs where hashish is legal and handed round in huge bins and the "Summer of Love" still exists in a time-warp,' he wrote.

A few hours' sleep, airports and a hassle with customs and here she was, traces of that nervous energy still there, abbreviated stabs at the air while she talks, a highly expressive set of mouth muscles. 'Miles knew me when I was just a nobody,' she told Lenny. But now she has fame. A huge black limo takes her to the gig, Patti looking tiny and regal in the back while curtains twitch in the street as people peer out to see who it is.

The audience are regular Sunday night Roundhouse crowd, stoned and shaking sack-loads of dandruff over their

Levi's, part Patti Smith cult fans, including a large number of women delighted to have someone female do for rock what David Bowie did for the males. There are also a few fungoids and weirdos who have come to check her out. She comes bouncing on stage like Muhammad Ali jumping up and down on the spot, punchy and laughing, grinning, over-joyed at the cheering applauding audience who are all clapping with their hands over their heads. Lenny Kaye adopts the classic stance, legs wide apart and then that familiar New York music begins. And they are very New York. Patti doesn't mess around. Just grabs the audience and takes them up there. She has tremendous stage presence, not showbiz, not glitter, just a personal magnetism which keeps all eyes beamed straight at her. Patti is not a woman rock and roller as such. There's plenty of sex drive in her act but it's not specifically male or female by any usual arche-types, it's just a stack of burning energy bursting through. Not even so much sex as love because for all the sullen street punk imagery she is really warm and friendly.

The constant fuzz roar of feedback guitar, the sound of New York City, of the IRT subway taking a curve, the screech of tortured metal, iron on iron, trucks rumbling over the cobbles in lower Manhattan, transformed into music, organ-ized by the regular no-frills drumming of Jay Dee Daugherty, always on top of it, kicking it into shape. The band eschews solos, functioning very much as a unit to punch out pure positive street energy, raw, bare, naked. Lenny and Patti crouch at each other like playful lion cubs. Patti relates to him a lot on stage. They've been together now for six years and the chemistry must be just right because the strain of playing together in a band is heavy. A rambling spoken intro led into 'Horses' and the evening made that magic flip over from being a concert into being an event. I've not seen such audience appreciation in a long time. She returned and encored with 'My Generation'. They made her come back again and she ended with the very appropriate Stones number 'Time Is On My Side'. As she left the stage after the second encore she shouted to the audience 'Remember Keith Relf' but it was lost in the cheers. Backstage afterwards she was exhausted but very up. A roomful of rock press congratulated her. Even later at the Hard Rock Café she was still jumping, cruising the aisles, talking to fans, waiters, friends.

Other members of the band, who received less attention than Patti, were less inclined to accept victory so easily, feeling that this first of two nights in London was, in fact, one of the worst shows of the tour, primarily because they were exhausted. Despite this they soon became aware of the influence the show had on the English scene, when the majority of other musicians and critics they met during this first groundbreaking visit to the UK were outspoken in their praise. Chrissie Hynde (still two years away from forming a band) and the Clash's Mick Jones and Paul Simenon (with whom Patti was rumoured to have had a brief affair) were particularly friendly, the latter even joining them on stage, taking Cale's place on 'My Generation'. Some people went so far as to say that seeing Patti that night changed their lives.

'The crowd just went crazy, it was fantastic,' Jay Dee remembered.

They just went nuts and we ended up smashing up the instruments . . . The next night some friend of Lenny's said, 'You guys should come down to this club on Oxford Street and see the Sex Pistols.' It was like, The Sex Pistols? What a wacky name, yeah, okay, let's go. So we get down there and it's this dive and the floor's swimming in beer. This band comes on and before they even say anything Johnny Rotten's onstage, going 'And in we go to the Roundhouse the other night, see the hippie shaking the tambourines, Horses, Horses, HORSE-SHIT.' And I was thinking, 'Fuck, that was a quick fifteen minutes. We're over, we're fucking over already!'

'I don't like Patti Smith,' Johnny Rotten told Mary Harron, the British correspondent for *Punk* magazine. 'Just a bunch of bullshit going on about – "Oh, yeah, when I was in high school!" Two out of ten for effort. I used to hang around the hotel where she was staying. The last night they had to carry her up the stairs. I liked her for that. She was such a physical wreck.'

On 22 May the *Melody Maker* had a review of the Sunday Round-house show by Michael Watts, who called her a 'poetess' and sneered a lot, but concluded: 'At last there is a rock star who looks like Nick Kent and not the other way around. But Patti Smith is for those who like the idea of rock and roll, rather than its perfect execution.'

Steve Lake from the *Melody Maker* thought Patti's music was 'loathsome'. He viewed their stance as entirely manipulative and calculating. This was a time when punk rock was a real movement in England. Punk really meant something to a lot of people, including journalists. Patti was defensive in her conversation with Lake after one of the shows:

I've been a committed artist since I was a child. I do art every day. To me, rock writing is one of the highest professions. Such a high profession that I chose a rock writer to be my lead guitarist. Now, you're a rock writer and you question my integrity. Well, my integrity remains constant through everything I do. Look, I've read *Melody Maker* for years and it's like a lot of rock magazines, it takes a very hard line. It has a very self-important attitude, and rock and roll isn't the property of *Melody Maker*. Rock and roll belongs to the people. The album isn't recorded well. I'll grant you that. It doesn't sound good. We all know that. It's badly recorded. It sounds lousy on the radio. But it's cool, because it's a document of how it was. I mean, I know a lot of famous people. I could have had everybody in rock and roll on my fucking record. But I wasn't interested in that. I wasn't interested in any big star syndrome thing. You can call the record fucked up technically. You can call it a piece of shit.

I call it a naked record. Naked and exposed. And I really don't feel that I have to defend it.

Jane Suck, a writer who covered the punk scene for the *NME*, harshly criticized Patti's Roundhouse show. The next week the paper received a flood of responses to her piece which illustrated the level of Patti's fans' devotion, and the way in which she mesmerized her audience. 'I went to see Patti Smith and I have never been through a more ultimate experience in my whole life,' wrote Phil Neale of Woodingdean, Brighton.

She is the true Mona Lisa of rock, the real Joan of Arc, the battling crusader who has won. I was one of those stranded outside at 12:30 in the morning after waiting for her to come to the stage door. I had to walk home and I got there at 7:30 in the morning. I came back Tuesday and it was even better, I'd walk a million miles to see Patti. I'm no sycophantic college kid, I work in British Home Stores doing the washing up and I'm 17.

Patti Smith had definitely created a stir in England. She inspired at least one group of girl punks to put together a band of their own right away, the Slits, and many more would follow. The writer Mick Farren made the interesting observation that punk produced a larger and better group of writers than came out of the hippie movement. Writers like Lester Bangs, Andrew Wylie, Julie Burchill, Nick Tosches and journalists like Mary Harron and Jon Savage played seminal roles in the creation of punk: Wylie, for example, had been in a poetry group with Richard Hell who later changed his name from Meyers. Wylie introduced Hell to Smith as well as published her first book. Many of the New York contingent such as Hell, Verlaine and Smith thought of themselves initially as writers, and even those without pretensions to aligning themselves with the great French symbolists were outstanding lyricists, like Johnny Rotten and Debbie Harry. It's enough to make one wonder if a rock poetry magazine might have been as influential as *Punk* magazine. Punk and *Punk* magazine produced many wildly enthusiastic writers and artists.

The literary output of the relatively short-lived punk movement has been largely ignored. No one came close to Patti Smith at the time in terms of her recognition as a writer. In 1976 alone, her collaboration with Sam Shepard, *Cowboy Mouth*, was included in his collection *Angel City and Other Plays* (Horizon Books, New York) and her poetic collaboration with Tom Verlaine, *The Night*, perhaps her rarest publication, was released in London (Aloes Books) and Paris (Editions Fear Press). This book was given all the attention to detail usually attributed only to the most collectable poets. Twenty-five copies of the UK edition were signed and numbered. And the French version, though two pages shorter than its British counterpart despite containing the poems in both French and English, was beautifully designed to look like a folded road map.

Another sure sign of Patti Smith's stature in rock and roll was the number of bootlegs of her band from the beginning of their career. In the years before punk, according to Clinton Heylin in his history of rock bootlegs, the expansion of the bootleg market was mainly due to a lack of new music from certain artists whose fans demanded a constant flow of new material. It was by going back to 'lost' recordings or live performances of their favourite artists via bootlegs that fans could reconnect with their original feelings about the music, about rock and roll. At the time of the punk movement, many fans felt that rock had sunken into mediocrity, that it was self-indulgent and complacent, far from its incendiary roots. Apart from the pubs, where the bands played traditional rock and blues, there were no venues for original live music. Most bands that toured America were playing large stadiums where they seemed inaccessible to their fans.

Two exceptions in the mid-seventies were Patti Smith and Bruce Springsteen. Both artists had risen to popularity through the support of die-hard fans who saw them live in small venues, and both artists were heavily bootlegged on both sides of the Atlantic. As Heylin pointed out, Patti encouraged her early bootlegs, sometimes introducing 'Redondo Beach' as a song from

The Field Marshall of Rock and Roll: 1976

Teenage Perversity, the first Patti Smith bootleg from a landmark *Horses* show at the Roxy, Los Angeles, in January 1976. Lenny Kaye explained, 'It's easier to bootleg a band earlier because they're much more prone to do oddball radio broadcasts, or they'll just show up someplace and it's easier to go into a club, and you get a little bit better sound and it's a little bit better as a moment.'

In July, back in New York, Patti played a pivotal concert in Central Park. She introduced 'Radio Ethiopia', her most extreme statement. The song made clear the group's intentions to go in a new direction. Despite the group's technical limitations, they certainly seemed capable of interpreting and expanding on Patti's musical ideas. To deflect attention away from herself as 'the poet-performer' she changed the name of the band from 'Patti Smith' to the 'Patti Smith Group'. This was reminiscent of Chrysalis Records' vain attempt to draw attention away from Debbie Harry as the focus of her band by issuing the promotional slogan 'Blondie is a group'. No one was fooled.

In July Patti went into a New York recording studio to make her second album, *Radio Ethiopia*. Any second work can be particularly difficult for a creative artist who has poured into the first work all the dreams, plans, ideas and schemes of the previous twenty years. It is even more difficult in rock where the artist has been frantically busy since the success of the first work, and has had little or no time for introspection or digestion. In Patti's case the pressure was increased by acute personal problems. She was in the midst of breaking up with Tom Verlaine. Terry Ork was smoking pot with Patti one night just before the sessions began when her intercom went off at One Fifth Avenue. It was Verlaine dropping by for a visit. 'When she heard his voice on the intercom Patti just flipped out,' Terry recalled. 'It was way toward the end and she was clearly back with Allen.' Ork made motions to leave, but Patti grabbed his arm, going, 'No! Don't leave!' She begged me to stay. She didn't want to be alone with him. She was very uncomfortable around him, because he was still carrying a heavy load for her. It got very bitchy and I know there were some hard words before they finally separated.'

For the all-important, supportive role of the album's producer Patti chose the middle-of-the-road Jack Douglas. He was a good technician and proficient worker, but without Cale's artistic edge. She wanted somebody who would leave her art alone, leave her alone, and work with the band to get the required sound. Having said that, Patti proceeded to turn in a set of vocal interpretations that sounded on some tracks like the howling of a wounded animal. On others her lyrics were barely decipherable, because Patti had chosen to have the band's single unique instrument, her voice, mixed down into the music. *Radio Ethiopia* grew increasingly experimental and ended up being more of an 'artistic' album than *Horses*.

At a press conference after the album was released Allen Jones of *Melody Maker* asked Patti why she had chosen Douglas as her producer. Her reply is as good an explication of *Radio Ethiopia* as the hundred odd reviews the album received: 'I wanted to do a record that wasn't just a cerebral experience – it was more of a physical record. If everybody's hung up on poetry there's a big f****** poem in the record. Tell them if they're hung up because there's no poem in the record, that when they buy the record it's got the longest poem in the history of man. [Presumably she is referring to the ten-minute Radio Ethiopia cut.] It took me four months. The poem, I don't say it . . . everything you don't hear on the record because of the bass and drums . . . I've written the poem. In other words, it's like when you listen to *Madame Butterfly*.'

By now, Patti had taken on a new persona. She called herself the 'Field Marshall of Rock 'n' Roll'. 'I got a Marshall amp when we went to Europe, so I started calling myself "Field Marshall". I had a very romantic idea about having a network of people working with me. I thought of it more as a military regiment. I liked to read books about General Patton, Alexander the Great and T. E. Lawrence, and I had this view of people who worked with me as troops.'

The Field Marshall of Rock and Roll: 1976

Craig Gholson, from *Punk*'s competitor *New York Rocker*, described Patti as she sat in Jane Friedman's office: 'There are two basics to her uniform – the colour black and the perfect pair of sunglasses. She's wearing black leotards and T-shirt (with a long brown cotton shirt and knee-high suede boots) and the sunglasses, the Wayfarers, are tossed on the desk. ("My sunglasses are like my guitar. I keep wantin' to say Fender Wayfarers.")' The writer made note of the inclusion of the words 'Ali is still the champ' on the liner notes to *Radio Ethiopia* and saw Patti's recognition of herself as 'a heavyweight contender'. The boxing metaphor was one that Patti constantly used. Talking about the importance of her technical crew, she said, 'It's what helps a performer stay on top, like a boxer with a trainer. You have to know that these people are behind you. Then, when you really start to break and it's happening, a whole new kind of energy is created around you.'

Patti wanted *Radio Ethiopia* to achieve several goals for her and the band. She hoped it would provide a link between the live shows and the record, especially with the inclusion of the more experimental, improvisatory tracks that she knew would evolve over time, and that it would help to forge an even stronger group identity and consciousness within the Patti Smith Group. She hoped the band would become 'a great band, to become as big as possible, and to gain power'. For Patti, the key line in the album was where she speaks of turning God in another direction. Patti told one interviewer that it was the greatest lyric in rock and roll. 'It's a challenge to God,' she said. 'I wanna be God's daughter. No ... I wanna be God's mistress. I'm not willing to witness one miracle and believe. I wanna be fucked by God. Not just once, a thousand times.'

'If Jesus was around, if I was a groupie, I'd really get behind that guy,' she told Lisa Robinson. 'That's why I think Mary Magdalene was so cool, she was like the first groupie. I mean she was really into Jesus and following him around, it's too bad she repented: she could've left a really great diary. All this stuff about Jesus, how wonderful he was, and how he was gonna save us. All

I'd like to know is if he was a good lay. That interests me.'

That month, almost one full year after *Horses*, *Radio Ethiopia* was released. The album was anxiously awaited by her fans, as well as those who were now curious about just who this Patti Smith was. Arista's president Clive Davis was disappointed with the record, fearing it had little or no commercial potential. The cover photograph for the album, taken by Patti's friend, the photographer Judy Linn, was unmemorable.

The release of *Radio Ethiopia* coincided with a tour. Only one show was in the US, in Chicago, after which the group took off to Europe. Two days before leaving for the European tour, the group learned that Richard Sohl would not be able to tour owing to personal problems caused by the endless grind of touring and studio work. Patti was very close to Sohl, and later said that losing him felt like being dropped by a boyfriend – something that had brought her near to suicide more than once in the past. A replacement was found in an old friend of Lenny's from Boston, Andy Paley. Paley would later gain fame as the man who pulled Brian Wilson out of retirement, and fortune as a songwriter for Madonna, among others.

Response to the album was not good even by the critics who had long supported Patti. Charles Shaar Murray wrote in the *New Musical Express*:

> The selection of Douglas as replacement for Cale would suggest what a study of the album bears out: that *Radio Ethiopia* operates according to a significantly different aesthetic to its predecessor. Kral, Kaye, Sohl and Daugherty riff and solo in an approximation of the manner of the conventional hard rock band. Smith's songs are cast in various recognizable moulds (though her diction and delivery have, if anything, grown more extreme) and the instruments and voices are processed and balanced in such a way that an unkind listener might suggest that Douglas had set up the board for an Aerosmith session and then gone out for dinner. The implication would seem to be that picking up

on what Patti has to sing/say is fairly low on the listener's priority list.

The problem is that in the move from the uniquely personal and exhilaratingly unconventional territory staked out on *Horses* to the familiar ground she treads on *Radio Ethiopia*, she has not so much brought the qualities of imagination, perception and emotion displayed on the previous album into the hard rock mainstream, but simply allowed the limitations of the genre to dictate restrictions to her.

Her most important critic in the US, John Rockwell of the *New York Times*, agreed.

The level of songs seems lower than on *Horses*, and the shift away from declamation and minimal instrumental support to basic rock and roll robs Miss Smith's art of some of its individuality. It also leaves what's left sounding slightly gimmicky. Fine and good, that her band is improving technically and that Miss Smith is evolving an act that will channel her eccentricity into a form that can be marketed to the millions. But recent journeyman rock is no substitute for what she is capable of at her best.

That autumn Patti once again moved back into the loft with Mapplethorpe. She needed time to think. Her affair with Tom Verlaine was over but she was unhappy with Allen Lanier and unsure about how to handle their relationship. Her feelings for Fred Smith were growing but Allen provided her with the security she needed. She soon purchased an apartment with Lanier at One Fifth Avenue in the same building as Mapplethorpe's patron Sam Wagstaff, and moved in.

The Patti Smith Group spent part of October in Europe. Patti's 'Field Marshall' diatribes were becoming more intense. In London Patti shouted from the stage of the Hammersmith Odeon, 'Yeah! I'm a genuine starfucker! I ain't never gotta sell out because my old man is Allen Lanier and he makes the bread in our house! He don't care if I never make a cent! He hopes I don't make a cent!'

The Sex Pistols had just released their first single, 'Anarchy in the UK', and the punk movement was reaching fever pitch in England. The difference between English and American punk was beginning to appear extreme, and while Patti tried to be supportive she could not have known what she was dealing with. However, the British critics were not kind to Patti this time around. 'Neither Smith nor her band had progressed beyond the totally inept musical standard displayed at London's Round-house in May and on *Horses*,' wrote Maureen Paton of Patti's Hammersmith Odeon shows in October.

> The same embarrassing clichés were still handed out like food parcels to a largely bemused crowd. A lot of women present clearly got off on the idea of having someone up there to identify with. But it's precisely this kind of freak originality that Smith exploits so mercilessly by playing a rock and roll hero. The guitar that she hadn't even bothered to learn to play properly was toted around the stage as a symbol, nothing more.

The negative British reviews angered Patti. They may also have given her an adrenalin rush because the majority of the European dates, particularly the French and Spanish shows, were well received and she felt good connections, picking up a lot of energy. A repeated refrain in her interviews, that her job had been to incite people, to shake rock up, was coming true now as she applauded the explosion of British bands from the Pistols to the Clash. It was, she said, like CBGBs all over the world now, not just in London but in Brussels, in Copenhagen, in Berlin.

The journalist Julie Burchill attended a Patti Smith press conference in London. Burchill was then at the very beginning of her career. (She would later write a controversial book with Tony Parsons called *The Boy Looked at Johnny*, a vitriolic – and hysteri-cally funny – diatribe against everyone in rock and roll.) At the press conference, Patti lost her temper when asked why her tickets weren't selling, screaming, 'Fuck you! You're a drag! Get out of here!' according to Burchill. Patti then reached into a large plate of food and began to fling it around the room. Taunted by a journalist – 'Which Beatle newsreel are you acting now?' he sneered – Patti quit flinging food and climbed up on a table. 'For a two-year-old it would have been a very impressive performance; from the Queen of Rock and Roll it was like watching God jerk off,' said Burchill later. Before stalking out of the room, Patti declared, 'I'm the Field Marshall of Rock 'n' Roll! I'm fucking declaring war! My guitar is my machine gun!'

'Julie just burst into tears, she just collapsed. Patti was her hero,' remembered Miles, who had taken Burchill to the press conference.

Julie thought Patti was a lesbian. Confronted by her heroine – who she obviously had fantasies of going to bed with – she was horrified, just horrified, to see this person behaving in this incredibly egotistical, stupid way. I thought the best thing was to take Julie out of there. I took her around the corner to the Hard Rock Café on Piccadilly and gave her a large brandy, which made her cry even more!

Meanwhile, Patti cut short her European tour because Andy Paley had other commitments and could not continue. They badly needed to find a new, permanent keyboard player. Patti was disappointed in the interruption, but she was not worried. She was strong in her conviction about what she had achieved. An element that stood her in good stead through this period was her strong female following. In 1976 one critic wrote in *Urban Soundscapes*:

Sexism did not magically disappear. Punk continued to present itself in masculine outlines. Still, its reactive style, working on an unlikely amalgam of glam rock ambiguities, stylized differences, and not unaffected by distant echoes of Women's Liberation, also shocked into life a new conflictual female image within white pop. Emerging out of a collection of old school uniforms, dustbin liner skirts, stiletto heels, cosmetic masks and defiant vocals, a space for women as active protagonists within the production of the music appeared. The slightly earlier, largely isolated, example of the American Patti Smith was now replaced by a more collective reconstruction of the white female voice. The disturbance of the 'unnatural' voices of the British Siouxsie Sioux, Poly Styrene, and the Slits, shattered the existing mould of female singing in pop. This new figure did not fit easily into the traditional iconography reserved for women in pop.

Soon after the band's return to New York, Bruce Brody was brought in as the new keyboardist, and the new Patti Smith Group gave a three-hour-long concert in Central Park to unveil their new incarnation. The concert was a rousing success but no amount of audience enthusiasm could make up for the fact that *Radio Ethiopia* was far away from its projected sales and there seemed no way to turn around the bad publicity and the negative reviews. 'Everybody thought we sold out. They thought we had turned heavy metal. They found lyrics like ''pissing in a river'' offensive, they found experimentation offensive, definitely too sonic,' said Patti.

At the end of November, when the band played a week at the Bottom Line in New York, Patti was in what Lenny called 'full confrontational mode'. Her performances were getting increasingly chaotic, even self-destructive. 'I remember each show getting crazier and crazier,' Lenny said. 'At one point during ''Ain't It Strange'' I ran out into the audience, and Patti chased me and dragged me back, and we were walking on tables. It was just a lot of this adolescent energy and anarchy, and there was something very liberating about it because we were pushing the edge of the envelope.'

Bruce Springsteen joined them on stage a few times. Patti had been introduced to Bruce at the Record Plant studios by the producer Jimmy Iovine during the making of *Radio Ethiopia*. 'That was the period when Bruce was having his legal problems and couldn't record,' Patti recalled. *Born to Run* the previous year had made him a star, but he would not be able to record again until 1978. 'He was drifting around. We probably did "Because the Night" together, and some English Invasion covers. One night we did this thing where Bruce played piano and I just improvised, sorta sang and talked while he played. That was an especially memorable night.'

On 29 November Patti got herself banned from New York's most powerful alternative radio station, WNEW. Responding to the show's host Harry Chapin, who had asked Patti not to use any four-letter words since they didn't have a time delay, she let loose a long rant:

> How alternative is this radio? I want to know how alternative this radio is. The first thing that happens when I walk in is that you tell me you don't have a bleep machine and to watch what I say, that's no alternative, that's the same old stuff. You notice I said stuff, being completely professional at this moment, but we have the total alternative to like your alternative radio. The radio that I represent . . . it's like we're outer space people we're gonna zoom like a leech . . . gonna come in like right on a hand . . . take over WNEW right now!

Patti continued her tirade for several minutes, and any sense she might have been making was lost in her rambling.

> Rock 'n' roll is being taken over by the people again, by young kids again, who don't want to hear about your digital delay. They don't want to hear about any of this stuff. They don't want to hear that they can't do an Eric Clapton solo. They just want to get out there and just get down on a rhythm. They want to crawl up like a dog or they want to rise up. They just want to feel something.

> Harry Chapin was a tireless fund-raiser for world hunger, and Patti offered a suggestion:

What we should do is just take over the wheat . . . we should look at our power, relax, understand that rock 'n' roll is becoming more and more powerful . . . it like indirectly helped elect some guy into the presidency of the United States and we should like really exonerate and be happy about this power and do it for the good of mankind, take over the wheat and give it to the people for free. If Ethiopia calls up and says we need wheat, we don't ask them what colour they are or what their favourite A – what they're listening to on their radios . . . they don't have to have an AM station . . . or any particular station . . . 14 stations of crosses . . . they don't have to do nothing but be hungry and if they're hungry, you feed the people, that's all.

Chapin was speechless. The interview did not help world hunger or the sales of *Radio Ethiopia*. In December the album peaked in the US charts at number 122.

On New Year's Eve, Patti Smith gave a concert at the Palladium in New York. WNEW refused to air the concert on their station because she'd used the word 'fuck' on the Harry Chapin broadcast, a violation of Federal Communications laws, making the radio station liable for huge fines. Upon hearing of the station's decision, Patti wrote a heavy condemnation of 'progressive' rock radio in general (and WNEW in particular) called 'You Can't Say "Fuck" in Radio Free America' which was distributed as a pamphlet at her shows. It read in part:

We believe in the total freedom of communication and we will not be compromised. The censorship of words is as meaningless as the censorship of musical notes; we cannot tolerate either. Freedom means exactly that: no limits, no boundaries . . . rock and roll is not a colonial power to be exploited, told what to say and how to say it. This is the spirit in which our music began and the flame in which it must be continued.

They are trying to silence us, but they cannot succeed. We cannot be 'trusted' not to pollute the airwaves with our idealism and intensity. W(New) York radio has proved unresponsive at best to the new rock and roll being born under its ears . . . a music having worldwide cause and effect . . . injecting a new sense of urgency and imperative. Radio has consistently lagged behind the needs of the community it is honour-bound to serve. We do not consider paternalistic token airplay and passive coverage to be enough. FM radio was birthed in the 1960s as an alternative to restrictive play-listing and narrow monopolistic visions. The promise is being betrayed.

We Want The Radio And We Want It Now 1977 . . . the celebration of 1776–1976 ends tonight . . . we end with the same desires of individual and ethnic freedom of concept . . . the freedom of art . . . the freedom of work . . . the freedom/flow of energy that keeps rebuilding itself with the nourishment of each generation.

While condemning one of the few radio stations to have given support to Patti and other new-wave artists, Patti neglected to target or send a copy of her manifesto to the real purveyors of censorship, the Federal Communications Commission.

Robert Christgau wrote of Patti's New Year show:

It went against habit for me to see Patti that night. Neverthe less, there I was at the best concert of the year, nursing a bad cold and a pleasant high and engulfed by Patti's 'kids', who looked to average out to college age, juniors and seniors rather than freshmen and sophomores. The crowd wasn't as loose as it might have been, but I liked its mix – a few arty types among the kind of intelligent rock and rollers who almost never came out in force anymore, a sprinkling of gay women among the hetero couples. When Patti came on, these sophisticates rushed the stage like Kiss fans, and eventually two women took off their tops and had to be dissuaded physically from dancing on stage. I hadn't seen the likes since a Kinks concert in 1973 or so, when such hijinks were already blasts from the past. And the climax was better, the true 'My Generation'. It began with Patti wrestling a guitar away from her female roadie, Andi Ostrowe, and ended with Patti – joined, eventually, by Ivan Kral – performing the legendary guitar-smashing ritual that the Who had given up by 1969 or so.

After the same show, John Rockwell, her most penetrating American critic, wrote in the *New York Times*;

Patti Smith's performances are like some cosmic, moral struggle between demons and angels . . . at one point she slumped to the floor and started banging her head against the organ. It was reminiscent of Iggy Stooge's self-mutilations or the excesses of SoHo performance artists, except that it had real fervour to it. She has always walked the line between genius and eccentricity, between the compelling and the merely odd, between art and insanity . . .

The Fall

1977

There was a moment when I had my fall that I felt I could have gone through the black tube. I felt myself disintegrating and I didn't want to go.

Patti Smith

The once adulatory music press was turning against Patti. This was especially true of the British music weeklies, well known for their pattern of building up and then tearing down the latest darling of the pop music world. In its 1 January 1977 issue, the *NME* made three mentions of Patti. She was listed as number two of 'Last Year's Things' and there was a photo of her at Jim Morrison's grave with the caption 'Patti Smith went from promise to dementia'. In another looking-back section, Charles Shaar Murray listed her Roundhouse appearance as a 'great gig' but said that *Radio Ethiopia* was the 'most disappointing album of the year'. Tony Parsons, in the same section, cited 'the Roundhouse rise and Hammersmith fall of Patti Smith', as if her career was over. Patti's response? 'Listen, I'm over thirty. Nobody tells me if I can spit on stage or not.'

The New York press was more sympathetic but acknowledged the problems she faced at this juncture of her career. Robert Christgau published a piece in the *Village Voice* entitled 'Save

This Rock & Roll Hero'. In it he describes Patti as being 'caught in a classic double-bind – accused of selling out by her former allies and of not selling by her new ones'.

In the last week of January 1977 the Patti Smith Group began a long tour of America to promote *Radio Ethiopia*. The tour involved playing much larger venues than previously and they would also be opening for other acts, which they had rarely done. The second date on the tour was 26 January in Tampa, Florida, at the Curtis Hixen Hall, a 6,000-seat sports arena, the largest hall the band had ever played. The headliner was Bob Seger and the Silver Bullet Band. The previous night's gig in Hollywood, Florida, had been in a smaller arena and it had not gone particularly well. Bob Seger attracted a more mainstream crowd who wanted to hear 'that old time rock and roll' and his audience probably didn't know what to make of the spacey, punky New York poet. Moreover the Smith band was confined to using only a portion of Seger's stage and couldn't use his lights (standard procedure for the opening act). In Tampa the band was determined to win over Seger's fans. Unfortunately Patti began the show with a vitriolic harangue against the people and the marijuana of Florida.

Although the band played hard and strong, deafening silence greeted the opening number. 'They went over like a lead balloon,' observed Jim Marshall, a fan and friend who was at the show. Lenny Kaye, however, felt that the band were beginning to move the crowd as they went into their second number, an intense version of 'Ain't It Strange'. During this song Lenny and Patti would interact in a sort of dance, 'a ballet', Lenny called it, until they came to the part in the song where Patti would challenge God, saying something like 'c'mon, God, make a move'. Then she would start spinning as the musical intensity built, spinning and spinning until she reached for the microphone to continue the verse. That night there was a monitor on the stage near Patti's feet. It was painted black, making it impossible to see on the darkened stage. As Patti lunged for the mike, she fell backwards over the monitor and off the front of the stage, plunging 15 feet towards the concrete floor below. Patti's brother Todd, who was the head of her stage crew, attempted to catch her. From his drum seat at the back of the stage, Jay Dee Daugherty thought, 'Oh, my god, she's either dead or she's gonna jump back up on the stage'. If he had seen the fall from the audience, as Jim Marshall did, he wouldn't have expected her to get up. 'She hit the base of her neck on some two by fours in the [orchestra] pit, then flipped up and hit the back of her head again on the floor,' according to Marshall. 'She was twitching and there was blood everywhere, and it looked like she had broken her neck.'

Paramedics were called and an ambulance rushed Patti to Tampa General Hospital. 'It was like a Bugs Bunny cartoon,' she chuckled later. 'When he walks over a cliff into mid-air and just keeps on walking until he realizes there's nothing there.' Patti's neck was not broken, but she was very seriously injured. She had cracked two vertebrae in her neck and had broken some bones in her face. Twenty-two stitches were required to close the lacerations on her head. Her immediate reaction was one of embarrassment. 'I looked like an asshole,' she told the band from the hospital.

After two days in the Tampa hospital, Patti was flown to New York to have her medical condition assessed by specialists. Glad to be home, Patti took to her bed, confident that two weeks of enforced bedrest would take care of any damage caused by the fall. But the injuries were more serious than she imagined, and she soon began having trouble with her vision, and difficulty walking. The doctors were not optimistic. Though she was assured that her vision would return to normal, she received conflicting reports about the paralysis in her legs and different recommendations about how to deal with it. One doctor told her she would not regain the full use of her legs without undergoing spinal surgery. Another doctor, from the Nautilus Sports Institute, felt that rigorous physical therapy would correct the damage.

The Percodan she was taking for pain made it difficult to think clearly, and finances were a problem. Like many musicians, Patti had no health insurance and she had just used up her bankroll buying the luxurious apartment at One Fifth Avenue with Allen Lanier. The upcoming tour, which she had hoped would refill her coffers, was now cancelled. The thought of major surgery on the delicate spinal area under full anaesthesia was worrisome and in the end Patti chose physical therapy. It was the more demanding course of action but the one where she would feel more in control of the outcome.

Forced off the road by her accident, Patti had time to work on new material for her next book, which would be called *Babel*. Earlier in the year she had signed a contract with Putnam for $5,000 to produce a collection of her poetry. Patty realized that the writing in *Babel* was influenced by the Percodan she was taking. 'I wrote a lot of it in a very unusual state of mind because I had special prescriptions from doctors, so I think it deals with a very subliminal landscape,' she told a journalist. The book was written from her sickbed, dictated to a new assistant, Andi Ostrowe. Ostrowe was a fan who had written Patti a letter. 'Everybody was standing around Electric Ladyland, just hanging out, and the secretary hands me this fan letter,' Patti recalled. 'The envelope had all this Ethiopian writing on it and a stamp of Haile Selassie so I opened it up and inside was this heavy letter. It was like a lightning bolt. It was like instant karma.' Ostrowe had worked in Ethiopia as a volunteer for the Peace Corps. Patti was obsessed with Ethiopia because that was where Rimbaud had done his early exploring, when it was Abyssinia. 'I needed a guide and I get this fan letter from a girl who can do all that stuff – a guide who can interpret, who knows the language fluently, who knows all the shortcuts and where to buy the dope,' Patti explained enthusiastically. She started her off as a roadie. After the accident Ostrowe offered to work for Patti without pay. She would stay with Patti through thick and thin until she retired in 1979, and resume working for her in the nineties.

'I was able to clean up a lot of loose ends and best of all, I wrote a book – which I'm really proud of,' she said later.

The Fall: 1977

I was able to do a lot of work I hadn't been able to do for
a long time . . . the other books were like very spontaneous
efforts . . . I haven't published anything since early '73,
because I was so intensely involved in performing and verbal
expression that I lost contact with the word on paper. *Babel*
is entirely different. It's mostly prose pieces, they're longer
and there's much more voyage . . .

Around this time Patti separated from her longtime manager
Jane Friedman. Friedman had been with Patti since the beginning of her career and the split was painful for both women.
Friedman was now living with John Cale as well as managing
him, and some speculated that Patti felt she would not be Friedman's top priority. Instead Patti hired a lawyer, Ina Meibach, to
handle her career. Once again Patti's willpower and ambition
kept her on track. The recuperation, rather like the pregnancy
ten years earlier, gave her a chance for introspection and study
and she seized it. One night Lisa Robinson came by. She had
just returned from Toronto where the Rolling Stones were
rehearsing for a live recording and Keith Richards had been
arrested. Lisa was laying the scene out and Patti was on every
word, but when Lisa started talking about Debbie Harry whose
Blondie had played Toronto at the same time Patti snapped,
snarling, 'That stupid bitch!' Lisa said, 'No, Patti, Debbie's really
nice.' *Punk* magazine's Legs McNeil, also visiting, saw Patti was
seething. It was ironic that Patti's fall came the same month
Blondie started their astonishing rise. One afternoon Bruce
Springsteen dropped by 1 Fifth Avenue and he and Patti played
each other old 45s. Both from New Jersey, the two songwriters
had a camaraderie touched with friendly rivalry, a relationship
that would later result in a hit single.

Patti began her rigorous physical therapy at the Nautilus Sports
Clinic in March. She set Easter Sunday as a goal for her 'comeback' performance at CBGB's. Patti took on her physical therapy
like an athlete in training, 'like Mr America or Muhammad Ali,
somebody who can't let a day go by that they're not rebuilding

or maintaining themselves,' she said. 'It has given me a new kind of discipline – it has put my life in better form.'

A show of her drawings at the Gotham Book Mart was scheduled to coincide with the release of *Babel*, which was now completed. Around this time Patti was offered another art exhibition at the new, prestigious Robert Miller Gallery on Fifth-Seventh Street which had a new owner. Patti decided to turn the show into a collaboration with Robert Mapplethorpe. The idea of doing an exhibition together had been one of their earliest dreams and now it would actually happen, and at a prestigious uptown gallery. Despite the accident, things were coming together in a positive way.

The first show after the accident happened was planned at CBGB's on Easter Sunday. Fans lined up around the block to see Patti's return. Her show followed a matinée performance by Cleveland's Dead Boys and the British punk band the Damned, the final show in a three-night stand. The house was cleared after the matinée and a separate admission was charged for Patti. William Burroughs was a special guest and a youthful Thurston Moore (who would later go on to form Sonic Youth) was in the audience. Now Patti gave a demonstration of how to turn weakness into strength. She made a theatrical event out of her neckbrace, wearing it on stage for the first half of the show, then dramatically ripping it off. In the end Patti made the fall work for her. In a later conversation with Burroughs, Patti was candid about her feelings about being on stage again, and even made reference to her drug use during her recuperation:

Sometimes, I need the audience's energy. When I was first trying to learn how to be on the stage again, I was not only afraid, but I was concerned about my energy . . . I couldn't really move around so much. I mean, you were at one of those performances when I started to get back. I hadn't been able to get out of bed for a few months, and I was addicted to pills, or whatever, and had to be carried on to the stage. And I had them put a chair on the stage. Well, those nine days that I spent with the people [the 'Out of Traction, Back in Action' shows], doing a couple of sets a night at CBGB's, around Easter time in '77, was the best therapy that I had. I took my [neck-brace] collar off by the end of it. I don't quite understand it myself, but I don't find it overtly mystical.

Jay Dee felt that Patti had gone through a change after the accident, coming to grips with her own religious or spiritual system. The band cut 'Gloria', with its line about Jesus having 'died for somebody's sins, but not mine', from their set. 'She changed,' said Jay Dee. 'She didn't feel that way any more.'

Patti continued to perform over the next few months, doing shows at CBGB's in June and at the Elgin Theater and Village Gate in July. The shows were becoming increasingly accessible, 'shorter and faster,' Patti said. 'It's still improvisational but it's shorter, stronger and it's not so much groping around.' She also appeared with William Burroughs and Allen Ginsberg for a joint book signing at the Gotham Book Mart. Before going into the studio to record her third album, Patti played a benefit for the Museum of Natural History at the Hayden Planetarium. She introduced two new songs, one of them 'Till Victory'. Despite the steep ticket price of $35 many of Patti's devoted fans showed up and cheered her on.

Patti chose Jimmy Iovine as the producer for her next album, to be titled *Easter*, continuing her theme of resurrection. The band was friendly with Iovine, having met him in the recording studio at the end of making *Radio Ethiopia*. Iovine had worked on records with John Lennon and Bruce Springsteen and had encouraged the band in their songwriting. Early on he'd had the idea of getting Patti and Springsteen together. Bruce had already recorded a demo of 'Because the Night' but there were no lyrics other than the chorus. He gave the tape to Iovine, thinking the song was perfect for Patti's voice. When Patti finally listened to the tape she was immediately struck by its commercial potential. She did question whether doing a song written by an established artist so different from herself would conflict with her band's vision, but the strength of the song itself won her over.

One night Patti was expecting another secret call from Fred Sonic Smith in Detroit. While she waited, she listened over and over to Springsteen's demo tape. The lyrics to 'Because the Night' were written that night. 'It was an easy song to write, and the easiest song we ever recorded. Bruce was right, it was written in my key and it suited my voice perfectly. I knew exactly what to do with it.'

Resurrection

1978

Being great is no accident.

Patti Smith

n January 1978 the Patti Smith Group mounted another American tour. They played in many of the same clubs the Sex Pistols would play a week later. The Pistols' incendiary tour and messy break-up in San Francisco would signal to many in the music business the lack of viability in punk rock as a commercial force, and few punk bands would be signed in the following years.

During this tour Patti's secret two-year telephone affair with Sonic Smith finally became public knowledge. Fred Smith was born in West Virginia, and moved to Detroit as a child. He met Wayne Kramer in junior high school and in 1965 they formed the MC5, with Rob Tyner, Mike Davis and Dennis Thompson. Fred Smith eventually became one of the best guitar players in rock and roll, a naturally gifted musician whose talent was never fully recognized. The MC5 were an influence on both punk and heavy-metal bands of the seventies, but commercially they went nowhere. 'The importance of the MC5 can't be overestimated,' Cub Koda of Brownsville Station told the writer Ben Edmonds. 'There would have been no Michigan scene without them. The Five brought focus to the whole thing, a sense that it meant something to be from here. They were the guys who chopped down the trees to clear the dirt roads to pave the streets to build the highway so the rest of us could drive by in Cadillacs.' But by

1976 the MC5 had long since broken up, and Wayne Kramer was in prison.

Fred Smith was married to a woman named Sigrid when he first met Patti. The couple soon separated, and he began spending time with Kathy Asheton, sister of Scott Asheton, who had been in the Stooges with Iggy Pop. They weren't a regular thing, but Kathy still thought of Fred as her boyfriend. Fred had recently formed a new group, the Sonic Rendezvous Band, and they had opened for Patti on several shows in the Detroit/Ann Arbor area. At first Kathy thought it was 'kinda cool' that Patti was interested in Fred's new band but less cool when she saw Patti moving in on what she considered her territory – Fred.

Patti told friends, 'I've found the man I love, all I've been looking for all my life.' In addition to her strong romantic feelings about Fred, Patti also felt that the two could collaborate on an artistic level. 'Fred and I had always worked together,' she later recalled. 'We wrote songs and pursued individual ideas. It had been that way since I met him in 1976. He instilled in me confidence and clarity, a calmness that made me believe I could do anything.' The relationship had a quality of inevitability, and shortly before the release of *Easter* Patti surprised everyone she knew by leaving Allen Lanier to live with Fred Smith in Detroit. 'She'd met God!' exclaimed one friend. 'It was as simple as that.'

In 1978 New York was in every way the cultural capital of the world, having undergone a rebirth of sorts after its brush with bankruptcy. Detroit had never fully recovered from the race riots of the sixties, and there had been a mass exodus from the inner city over the following decade. With the decline of the auto industry, by 1978 it was one of the most depressed cities in America, with a soaring crime rate. Detroit was not perceived by the outside world as a desirable place to live. It did, however, have a long and illustrious musical history, first as one of the hottest jazz spots in the country, and then as home to Motown in the sixties. Detroit rock bands of the sixties, such as the MC5 and the Stooges, would be models for punk rock, but none would have commercial impact. In 1978 there was a vibrant local music scene, full of energy and creativity, but it was self-contained, with musicians tending to keep their own counsel, avoiding the hustle of New York or Los Angeles.

Patti had left Allen Lanier, who was supportive, successful and financially secure, for someone who appeared to offer little. Fred Smith was an anomaly in the music business. He was not a driven self-promoter, but a talented loner who walked his own path, fitting more comfortably into the role of artist than rock and roller. And he looked cool. 'Fred was one of the classiest dressers,' noted his friend Freddie Brooks. 'Even if he was wearing jeans he always had a nice cotton shirt. He prided himself on looking neat.' The couple moved into the tony Book Cadillac Hotel to begin their life together. Although to the outside world Patti's move to Detroit defied logic, for her there was no other choice. Such is the power of love.

Always given to creating myths around her life, Patti would later describe her move to Detroit and especially her union with Fred in highly romantic terms. 'To leave New York was a very tough thing,' Patti told William Burroughs in 1979.

But it was a great joy, too – you know, like a pioneer. It's like you have to 'Go West!' I've always been a very East Coast girl. I was raised in south Jersey, Philly, Camden, all the coolest cities. Actually, though, when I was a teenager I thought that the coolest city wasn't New York, it was Detroit, because Detroit had Motown. But the thing is, I'm very happy because I have met the person in my life that I've been waiting to meet since I was a little girl. For the first time I'm not pursuing – the person has opened up to me another way to express myself truly, which is music.

'I always loved New York, and I did miss the light of the city and how good it had been to me and my friends,' she told Lisa Robinson. 'But I never for a moment had any regrets. I just felt I did everything I could have done in my twelve years in New York. It's my spiritual home, where I flourished as an artist and gained confidence as a person. But I've never been afraid of change.'

She told a Japanese television interviewer:

I'm not burnt out. I may be thirty-one years old but I've just begun. I feel like it's new and fresh . . . I'm just starting! I believe that we, that this planet, hasn't seen its Golden Age. Everybody says it's finished . . . art's finished, rock and roll is dead, God is dead. Fuck that! This is MY chance in the world. I didn't live back there in Mesopotamia, I wasn't there in the Garden of Eden, I wasn't there with Emperor Han, I'm right here now and I want now to be the greatest time. This is my Golden Age . . . if only each generation would realize that the time for greatness is right now when they're alive . . . the time to flower is now.

Babel, Patti's collection of poetry, came out and was reviewed in the prestigious *New York Times Book Review* by the critic Jonathan Cott. 'If Patti Smith lacks the range of poets such as Diane di Prima, Anne Waldman and Carolyn Forche,' he wrote, 'she must still be praised for her insistence that one "never let go of the fiery sadness called desire", for her striving to attain the kind of vision Rimbaud nicknamed "voyance" – and this at a time when many writers settle simply for being voyeurs.' Patti considered *Babel* to be 'an extension of what I used to do on stage. I used to improvise a lot of poetry, but in one way it's such a drain. I do want to have fun. My mental processes have become so complex that it would go on forever. It would be like a verbal network or trying to say a map.'

The ramifications of her new relationship for Patti's band were unclear, but they could not but hear the distant death knell for the group. They tried to make light of it with cracks like 'It must be love!' but inside they had to face the prospect of being out of a job. Their role had been to support Patti. She was their director, their inspiration, their leader. Without her, there would be no band. How long could they carry on with Patti a thousand miles away? How long could they write songs over the phone (the way Mick Jagger and Keith Richards had been doing for years with diminishing results)? The final break would not come for some time, but in a way the slow breakdown of a band that had been more like a family was scarier and sadder than a sudden break might have been. Patti's move to Detroit was hard on Lenny, Jay Dee, Ivan and DNV, whether he was in or out of the band.

Early in her music career, Patti had talked about the possibility of leaving the rock stage. She told Legs McNeil in an interview in *Punk* magazine in January 1976 that she gave herself 'one or two years maybe. I'll do as much rock 'n' roll as I can and I'll transcend to something else. I did as much painting as I could – I transcended to poetry – now I'm into this period of my life . . . I wanna keep transcending.' The liner notes to *Easter* would include a quote from the New Testament: 'I have fought the good fight, I have finished my course . . .' (2 Timothy 4:7)

In March, *Easter* was released. For the first time the cover, by Lynn Goldsmith, was in colour. The image of Patti was softer and more feminine than the stark androgyny of *Horses*; and the lyric of 'Because the Night' which implored her lover to 'come on now, try and understand / how I feel under your command' foreshadowed her deferential relationship with Fred Smith. Allen Lanier, who had been badly hurt by Patti's abrupt departure, was ever supportive. In the 4 March issue of the *New Musical Express*, he praised her album in an interview. '*Easter* goes right at you. It has none of the idiosyncrasies which prevented people from deciding whether they really liked her or not. Her band is so improved that the ambivalence has gone.' Unfortunately in the same issue the writer Paul Rambali was less enthusiastic. 'We find Miss Smith still plagued by the problem of getting her stream-of-consciousness raps in synch with the hard pumping rock of her band, and of getting it down with the ferocious energy it possesses live,' he wrote in his review.

In the US reviews were generally more positive. 'Christ gains admission to Smith's eccentric pantheon of "Rock n Roll

Niggers'', beside Jackson Pollock, Jimi Hendrix, and unless my
ears deceive me, Smith's grandmother,' wrote Ken Tucker somewhat sarcastically in the *Voice*.

But even though 'Rock n Roll Nigger' has pretty silly lyrics,
it's also the album's best rocker, with a sublime found guitar
riff that Lenny Kaye and Ivan Kral throttle with skill and
delight, and Smith's most concise, magnetic hook yet: the
refrain 'Outside of society', sibilants exquisitely hissed by
Patti and Lenny. Other pleasures include 'Ghost Dance'
and an American Indian chant that is every bit as haunting
as it is meant to be.

Tucker compared Patti to Willem de Kooning, Neil Young and
the Three Stooges in her ability to 'pile everything on too thickly'.

'Musically, this is Smith's best album,' wrote Daisann McLain
in *Crawdaddy*. 'What was implied on *Horses* is filled in on *Easter*,
and improved.' But McLain found Patti's religious preoccu-
pations unsettling. 'It's as if any minute she'll come out with "I
am the way and the truth and the light" over the E chord.'

Patti was determined to re-establish herself and began an
extensive tour but again a critical backlash followed her. At least
some of it seemed to be provoked by Patti herself. At a New York
press conference, she exhibited some of the in-your-face punk
behaviour that she was soon to deride in others, such as Sid
Vicious. She entered the room 'from the back to the front',
remembered Bebe Buell.

She walked across tables to get to the stage, and in the
process anything in her way – human, glass or alcoholic –
ended up on the floor, so it was just a shocking moment,
truly shocking. Now when somebody does that you go 'Oh,
fucking asshole, go back to Des Moines.' But on her part it
was definitely rebellious, she was the real thing, and you
truly wondered: Could she snap? Could she hit me? Maybe.
You weren't sure. In Patti, there was some real element of
danger that's not present any more.

Resurrection: 1978

In 1975 Patti had impressed Clive Davis by being aware of how little time she had to make it. Now that she had she was not sure she could sustain it. 'This line of work is tough,' she admitted in a radio interview with KSAN. Like Keith Richards, who kicked heroin at thirty-three, she could not help identifying with the ultimate rock star's paradigm: 'Look at Christ – he only lasted thirty-three years!'

The European tour began in March and the writer Chris Brazier spoke to her in Berlin just before she took the stage. He asked about *Easter*'s intimate relationship with Christianity, Patti replied:

> The myth of Christ is still exciting and stimulating to me, and whether he's a real guy or not doesn't really matter any more. I did say 'Jesus died for somebody's sins but not mine', and I still believe that. I wasn't saying that I didn't take responsibility for the things that I do – I didn't want some mythical or ethical symbol taking the blame or the credit for what I do. When I steal, if I commit murder or adultery, whatever I do – I believe that the crime goes hand in hand with art. It's bad enough being a Smith, 'cause the word Smith means Cain, and being a true Smith means I came on the Earth marked anyway, and marked once is enough. Also, I'm a very Old Testament kind of person and in the Old Testament man communicated with God directly; in the New Testament man has to communicate with God through Christ. Well, I'm a one-to-one girl and I have always sought to communicate with God through myself.
>
> And I feel that was one of the reasons I fell off stage. I'm re-evaluating my state of being, I'm learning to accept a more New Testament kind of communication. So as part of that acceptance I have to re-evaluate exactly who Christ was. And that's why on 'Till Victory' it says 'God, do not seize me, please, till victory' because I felt like my work wasn't done.
>
> To me, the greatest thing about Christ is not necessarily Christ himself but the belief of the people that have kept

him alive through the centuries – the guy must have had powerful magnetism. I mean to me, Christ, Jimi Hendrix, Brian Jones, Jim Morrison, they're all the same. All great men. I'm into the war manoeuvres of Alexander the Great, I'm into Popeye, I'm not just into neo-Christianity. Right now I'd rather be a little less satisfied 'cause I really love being an earthling. But like Alexander, I'm gonna go after all the territory I can.

Even with the help of Alexander and Popeye, Patti's march on Berlin was of mixed success. The audience was silent and still during most of the set, which made the band uptight. Patti was frustrated and she took the offensive: 'I ain't impressed with you,' she taunted the crowd. 'I sang in front of 14,000 people so 2,000 don't mean shit to me!' Luckily, most of the German audience had no idea what she was saying, and at the end of the set they applauded for over fifteen minutes, demanding an encore. The manager of the theatre told Patti there would be a riot if she didn't return to the stage, and the mystified group returned for an extended version of 'Land'. The British critic Paul Morley described one of her performances in Germany as 'a mesmerizing, sucking hole in time . . . honouring the vibrant spirits of destiny, anarchism, surrealism.' He felt the band was strong as well: 'The Patti Smith Group have grown – matured as their audience has expanded. The group played strong rock and roll, and Smith is finding her way back into performing. They are at a transition period: one more effort and they are truly great, truly special. Classical.' The Berlin paper (whose writer perhaps spoke English and had heard Patti's insults) was less kind. He complained about the hype, said the music wasn't much 'fun' to listen to and the lyrics were indecipherable, but that Patti 'had a good voice'. Berlin was a good example of Patti's ability to confound, infuriate and mesmerize all at the same time.

During her European tours Patti performed one of her rarely publicized acts of charity when she ran into a down-and-out Nico in Paris. 'Patti was very kind to me,' Nico recalled.

....Reading... February 10... 8:30... 1971
Gerard Malanga: POETRY.
patti smith: WORK—
St. Marks Church-on-the-Bowery... 2nd Ave. + 10th St.

Flyer for poetry reading at St Mark's Church on the Bowery. (GERARD MALANGA)

Portrait of Arthur Rimbaud (1854 –1891), taken in 1870.

Patti across the street from the loft she shared with Robert Mapplethorpe.
(GERARD MALANGA)

Patti and her younger sister, Linda, at a Saturday afternoon party hosted by
Terry Ork in 1971. (GERARD MALANGA)

'I'll be your mirror.' Patti and Robert Mapplethorpe on the fire escape of their apartment at 208 West 23rd Street. (GERARD MALANGA)

Femmes fatales: Patti with fellow cast members Jackie Curtis and Penny Arcade in 1971. 'Patti always got raving applause at the end of the show.'

'We wrote one play, **Cowboy Mouth**, together on the same typewriter like a battle . . . and took it straight to the stage. It was the true story of Sam and me.'
— Patti Smith (GERARD MALANGA)

Patti Smith, Victor Bockris, Andrew Wylie and Gerard Malanga in front of
Kensington Church in London, the morning after the Better Books poetry
reading of 3 February 1972. (GERARD MALANGA)

Two people — two big dreamers: Patti with Sam Shepard outside Kensington
Church after their secret liaison. (GERARD MALANGA)

Patti reads from her first book of poetry, **Seventh Heaven**, while Jay Dee
Daugherty sips lemonade in the background. (DANNY FIELDS)

Enjoying the good life after a Rod Stewart concert: Patti (centre) with Lenny Kaye
and her boyfriend, Allen Lanier. (LEEE BLACK CHILDERS)

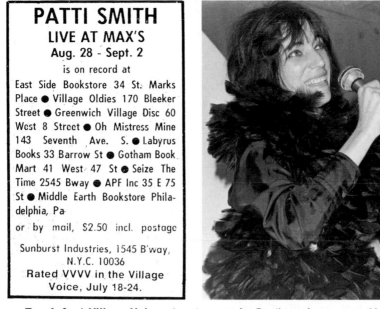

Top left: A **Village Voice** advertisement for Patti's performance at Max's.
Top right: Appearing at the trendy downtown cabaret Reno Sweeney, Patti mixed her poetry with Cole Porter and Frank Sinatra songs. (DANNY FIELDS)

Patti debuts at the Whiskey a Go Go in LA in the autumn of 1974 with Richard Sohl and Lenny Kaye. Many thought the group was at its purest when it was a trio, a perfect balance of communication and trust. (JOE STEVENS)

Top left: Downtown at Mickey Ruskin's Ocean Club in 1975. Patti was already wielding her guitar. (DAN ASHER)
Top right: Patti, wearing her Keith Richards T-shirt, works the crowd at The Other End while Bob Dylan sits unobtrusively at the bar. (DANNY FIELDS)

Backstage at The Other End in Greenwich Village in 1975: the first time Dylan saw Patti live. Patti joked with the photographers: 'Hey boys, why don't you take **my** picture!?' as Dylan genuflected. (DANNY FIELDS)

'Secretly I've been trailin' you, like a fox that preys on a rabbit . . .' Patti sings The Marvellettes' 'Hunter Gets Captured by the Game' in 1975. Later she would record it for the **Ain't Nothing but a She Thing** album. (DAN ASHER)

Richard Sohl, Ivan Kral, Patti, Jay Dee Daugherty and Lenny Kaye at Mickey Ruskin's Ocean Club, 1976. (ROBERTA BAYLEY)

Patti appeared on the cover of the second issue of **Punk** magazine, March 1976.

Patti with Allen Ginsberg and William Burroughs at Gotham Book Mart, 1977.
(JOE STEVENS)

Patti's first show after her accident, at CBGBs on Easter Sunday, March 1977.
(GODLIS)

Fred Sonic Smith with the MC5s. The MC5s 'were the guys who chopped down the trees to clear the dirt roads to pave the streets to build the highways so the rest of us could drive by in Cadillacs' – Cub Koda of **Brownsville Station.** (JOE STEVENS)

The 'Field Marshall of Rock 'n' Roll' salutes. Patti with her producer, Jimmy Iovine, and Bruce Springsteen backstage at the CBGBs 2nd Avenue theatre, 27 December 1977. (JOE STEVENS)

At the Nova Convention honouring William Burroughs, Patti appears wearing a
$10,000 mink coat she had recently purchased. (MARCIA RESNICK)

Fred and Patti backstage at the Masonic Auditorium, Detroit, July 1978.
(ROBERT MATHEU)

Above and below: Fred and Patti playing at Ann Arbor's Second Chance, March 1979. (ROBERT MATHEU)

Fred and Patti at Second Chance, 1979. (ROBERT MATHEU)

Patti waves goodbye, 1979. (GODLIS)

Top left: Patti back home in New York, 1995. (BOB GRUEN)
Top right: 'I'm going to get into all the magazines when I grow up,' Patti told her childhood friends in South Jersey, and in 1998 she's still gracing magazine covers around the world. (GODLIS)

In 1997 Patti appeared with Oliver Ray at the Hoboken Street Fair, New Jersey. (GODLIS)

Resurrection: 1978

Early in 1978 my harmonium was stolen from me. I was without any money and now I couldn't even earn a living playing, without my organ. A friend of mine saw one with green bellows in an obscure shop, the only one in Paris. Patti bought it for me. I was so happy and ashamed. I said 'I'll give you back the money when I get it', but she insisted the organ was a present and I should forget about the money. I cried. I was ashamed she saw me without money.

As good as the European shows were, many observers saw the toll that touring was taking on Patti. Dave Ramsden of the *Melody Maker* saw Patti's show at the Rainbow in London and noted that even though the fans loved her, Patti was exhibiting signs of rock-and-roll burnout. 'She has none of the bounding excess of energy, the sheer childlike exuberance that used to crackle through her performance,' he wrote. 'She often stands stock still or goes through stagecraft motions where before she'd leap up and down excitedly. Hand in hand with that is a drastic reduction in her communication with the audience – she seemed unable to think of anything more to say than "I'm really happy to be here."' The writer Paul Morley commented that 'she looked weary, was in fact very ill and running to a tight doctor-imposed schedule . . . the bubble was soon to burst.'

Patti herself had no use for most rock critics and instructed them to 'put more integrity into your writing' instead of 'writin' a bunch of gossip and bullshit of [your] own twisted ideas of what we're doin' . . . I think a true hero can only be criticized by himself. A true hero is his own highest critic. What he needs is support, he needs confidence, he needs the energy and the strength of the people. He doesn't need criticism.'

'She's a very strange woman,' Paul Morley wrote, 'hopelessly impractical, breathtakingly wise, energetic, polite, mentally acrobatic and perversely perceptive. Crudely, she had a vision and rock 'n' roll was best equipped in terms of its endless range of emotions, its potential audience, its ecstasy factor, its possible pureness.'

Tony Parsons in the *New Musical Express* criticized Patti's guitar playing, describing her as 'crouched over her dull axe like Quasimodo on a Bert Weedon course for butter-fingered beginners'. He wished that a few more people had 'the common sense to call her out when the going gets unbelievably corny'.

'Because the Night' was the first single from *Easter*, released on 29 March while the band was on tour in Britain. The track was immediately picked up by radio stations and was one of the signature songs on the airwaves that season, becoming the biggest hit of Patti's career. In the UK the single went to number 5 while the album went to number 16. In the US the single peaked at 13, the album number 20. The band was finally succeeding in its mission to reach a large audience. Patti was thrilled:

> Charts are charts. Our whole point of doing work is to communicate ecstasy or joy, but now we're communicating to a lot more people.
>
> I think the reason we got such heavy airplay this time was mostly on our own steam. But the song is really good; Bruce gave me a structure that really fits the kind of singing I used to do when I was younger. Of course, I think that FM radio playing the single more than the album is pretty gutless. I think that it's taken a lot of guts and foresight for AM stations to play our single, because when you play something by my group, you're not just playing a piece of music that's abstract, but a whole political outlook. But FM. . . it's like they'll play the single so they don't have to deal with my saying 'fuck' or 'nigger'. I was banned for a year and a half on WNEW because one night I came on and criticized them for being pseudo-liberal.

Chris Brazier called 'Because the Night' 'the first entirely successful conventional rock song that Patti Smith has created – this doesn't carry her hallmarks of extremism or adventure, but it's so good that it doesn't matter.' Patti faced a catch-22 that all artists who achieve commercial success must deal with. Blondie's *Heart of Glass* would hit the same year, but Blondie had not been touted as an art rock band. 'Patti got a little frustrated when people thought of it as a total Bruce Springsteen song,' said Lenny Kaye. Patti also felt that all the attention to the single drew attention away from the album. She later told a longtime friend, the writer Ben Edmonds, '*Easter* was strong, and some recognition of that was lost. Also, people imagined that now we were really huge and hugely prosperous. But that never actually occurred. The Patti Smith Group never had much financial success. And the record didn't even go gold or anything.'

The popular success of the single placed enormous pressure on her. While she publicly ridiculed the song as 'commercial shit', it allowed her a measure of recognition that she had not previously had. And, though it didn't make her rich, it did allow her to fulfil one dream; to buy her father a car. 'He walked outside,' she told Edmonds, 'and when he saw the car – a shiny black brand-new 1978 Cordoba – he just sat down on the front step and stared at it . . . Is there a gold record in the world that can compete with a moment like that?'

For herself, Patti made the seemingly incongruous purchase of a mink coat, and wore it on stage at the 1978 Nova Convention which honoured William Burroughs. 'This coat cost $10,000,' she told the crowd. 'I sleep in it. I live in it.' Such a display cannot have endeared her to the wannabe Beats in the audience. But Patti's love of the finer things in life was nothing new. In 1973 she had done a fashion show at Saks Fifth Avenue for Revillon. 'I like Fernando Sanchez, who designs furs for Revillon,' she said at the time. 'He makes me feel like Anouk Aimée – I would love to dress in Balenciagas. When I was a kid and going nuts over Bob Dylan and Rimbaud, I was also reading *Vogue* and *Bazaar.* I thought the whole Saks show was an honour.' In 1976, the *New York Times Magazine* quoted a close friend describing Patti's secret love of 'Bergdorf Goodman and little lace panties'. But while her actions may not have been inconsistent, they annoyed those on the punk scene who had been her champions. Trashing Patti became an increasingly popular pastime. Given so much ammunition by Patti herself, it may have been like shooting ducks in a barrel, but that didn't stop anyone from taking aim. For somebody who had compared herself to Paul Revere to use the moment of her highest profile to date to prance around in a ratty looking fur coat belting out the refrain 'the night belongs to lovers, because it belongs to love' begs at best a surreal interpretation.

However, as it turned out either Patti had nine lives or she was very clever because the success of the Springsteen collaboration helped her escape the death of punk which came rapidly on the heels of the Sex Pistols' January to February rampage across the US. As bands with any of the punk stigma desperately scrambled to become new wave, *Easter* received terrific reviews in the American press. Dave Marsh's *Rolling Stone* rave titled 'Can Patti Smith Walk on Water?' best summed up what she was doing.

When she played her hometown's Palladium located on the great dividing line between downtown and the rest, Fourteenth Street, the answer was very apparently, Yes. 'Watching the crowd rise out of its seats when Patti walked onstage, you had to clench your fist for her,' wrote Fred Shruers. 'Patti Smith is the Gunga Din of a certain kind of rock magic, trumpeting so hard and bravely that even the false notes become poignant and powerful.'

When Patti appeared on Stanley Siegal's popular, controversial morning TV talk show and was confronted by a jittery host who could not figure out what was supposed to be threatening about her, Patti came face to face with the conundrum she and other bands, like the Talking Heads, the Cars and most spectacularly Blondie, breaking out of the underground were in. Her decision to play it straight and charm her host was perfect.

Patti had graduated from being a punk rocker, if she ever was one, and was now, for the most part, treated as a popular entertainer. Not that she would never have another problem with an interviewer. In fact another TV spot on the *Today* show royally pissed her off:

I don't like people introducing me like they [the *Today* show] did, as 'outlandish' and 'crazy'. 'Cause it sets me up, like I'm a rat. They back me up against a wall, and I'm not really a hard person to get along with. By the same token, there's not much difference between being introduced as a crazy on the *Today* show and the rock press calling me 'the Queen of Punk'.

Steve Seimels of *Stereo Review* marvelled at Patti's 'unswerving faith' in herself and her work. 'Only a supremely confident artist could continue to maintain, as she does, that everybody's least favourite Patti Smith song, "Radio Ethiopia", represents her finest achievement to date in any medium.' He was also struck by her professionalism and ability to control her image despite 'the seemingly anarchic quality of her act on stage and off . . . she is thoroughgoing pro in the most traditional show-biz sense: she knows exactly how to present herself at all times.'

Patti did countless radio interviews that summer, wearing a polyester lizard jacket, a gift from Fred Smith who had worn it on stage in the MC5. 'I do everything with the same fervour, whether it's writing a poem, doing a drawing, or playing electric guitar,' Patti told a DJ.

Personally, I feel that playing electric guitar is the heaviest thing I can do; it's the most exploratory, it's the most daring, the most risky. And I don't feel that's opposed to Art. My definition of Art is much more advanced, I think, more futuristic than most critics. I said in *Babel* that in another decade rock and roll would be Art. But when I say a decade, I mean for other people. For me, since 1954 or something, it has been Art. Since Little Richard, Elvis Presley, Jimi Hendrix. I mean, these guys are masters. And I'm an illuminated apprentice who seeks to go beyond my masters. Being great is no accident. Little Richard wasn't an accidental phenomenon; he knew what he was after. He might not define it with intellectual terminology, but he was defined by what he did. I didn't think Jackson Pollock wrote a manifesto first and then did all his painting according to it. Now, as for what I'm trying to do as an artist . . . Well, the highest thing an artist goes for is communication with God. Which is universal communication. I've always spewed out my sub-conscious through improvising poetry, language. Now my language is being extended into sound, which I find much more universally communicative. People respond to it. I mean, what makes opera communicative?

'Y'know, the same girl that takes Jimi Hendrix as a master has learned a lot from Debby Boone this year,' she said to the Hong Kong based DJ and writer Gerrie Lim.

I've watched Debby Boone sing 'You Light Up My Life' maybe fifteen, twenty times. Each time . . . perfect. Each time with total, focused, concentrated commitment to delivering that song. Which I think is real good. Now I ain't a Debby Boone fan, specifically, and I ain't gonna start wearing chiffon tent dresses tomorrow. But I did learn some-thing by watching that. I've got to be able to deliver 'Because the Night' with all the strength and integrity and clarity that I was able to deliver it with in the studio. And if Debby Boone can do it, I certainly can do it.

And she did: Patti actually added 'You Light Up My Life' to her 1978 concert repertoire.

I have changed, though. I've learned to relax. When I first started performing, if it wasn't real every second, if it wasn't magic, I would get desperate. I didn't want to cheat anybody, that's my morality. I'm not moral in many ways, but I'm a very responsible person.

It's very hard to peg me down because my body encases a soul split and contradictory, I run, like Leonardo da Vinci, on many rhythms, good and evil, disciplined and maniac. I offer no excuses or explanation, I am still a physical archi-tect. Building a temple of experience. I am not dead, finished, or nearly finished.

Asked her opinion of her peers, she replied, 'I love the Clash, and I really love the Sex Pistols' (who had broken up but were still the most famous punk group).

> I think Johnny Rotten's great, I have a real crush on him. All those kids were my friends before they had bands, so it's real gratifying to me to see them up there. I don't like Elvis Costello. If you ask the fan in me you're gonna get a pretty narrow view. Basically, if there isn't somebody I want to fuck in a band, I couldn't care less. Unless it's such great abstract music it carries me away. Otherwise, if it's a rock and roll band, there better be somebody fuckable or forget it.

'We're not all one, we're not equal, who wants to be equal?' she told a fifteenth DJ.

> That's a totally absurd idea, it's against creation, against sexual tension, against seeking of wisdom. Nobody wants to be equal. But there is something that makes us not equal but of one great rhythm and that's our most ancient source of communication which is belief. I'm sure the ultimate way to get to it is relaxation but me being a true American the only way I can get there is to first blow myself out, which is why I play electric guitar . . . I feel like Ernest Hemingway.

Andy Warhol had known Patti since 1971 when she appeared in the Tony Ingrassia plays with Jackie Curtis. By 1978 he viewed Patti with some distaste, mainly because of what he saw as her blatant social climbing. Patti in turn was suspicious of Warhol because of the way he had treated Robert Mapplethorpe in the past. In his diary entry of 29 May 1978 Warhol wrote:

> I walked over to have lunch at One Fifth [a fashionable restaurant located on the ground level of Patti's apartment building] and on the way I saw Patti Smith in a bowler hat buying food for her cat. I invited her thinking she'd say no, but she said, 'Great.' When we walked in, there was the number-one bestseller Fran Lebowitz sitting with Lisa Robinson.

Patti didn't want to eat too much, so she ate half my lunch. She said she only loves blonds and that she wanted to have an affair with a blond. All I could think about was her b.o. – she wouldn't be bad-looking if she would wash up and glue herself together a little better. She's still skinny. She's with a gallery now, doing drawings and writing poetry. The Robert Miller Gallery. She reminds me a lot of Ivy [Nicholson, a Warhol superstar from the sixties] – everything was put on. She said she didn't take drugs in the sixties, that she'd only started recently, and just for work.

On 12 June she opened for the Rolling Stones in Atlanta, Georgia. 'One of my dreams,' she told Nick Tosches. 'Now all I wanna do is open for Rimbaud. Why don't the Rolling Stones play the Apollo? We could play it together. I'll call Mick up. We're friends now, ya know. He's a really great guy. I mean, he's really a nigger. If anyone qualifies to be a nigger, it's Mick Jagger.' This casual use of the word 'nigger' would cause Patti some problems later on.

In June, the Robert Miller Gallery presented Robert Mapplethorpe and Patti's joint exhibition, 'Film and Stills'. The opening was a bona fide media event, with overflowing crowds and television news cameras. Patti and Robert arrived together, obviously ecstatic to be finally realizing their long-held dream of 'making the big time' together. Reviewing the show for *Art in America*, the poet and critic René Ricard wrote:

> Their friendship is their masterpiece. What's on show, the works, is documentation or artefact; its importance is that it was made by these people. This works doubly. Mapplethorpe photos are always beautiful, but a Mapplethorpe photo of Patti Smith is, well, history. By the same token even if Patti had no talent for drawing (it's only gravy that the drawings are fine) the lovely drawings of Rimbaud in the show would be something to have, the way a Verlaine or Rimbaud would be something to have ... Verlaine, Rimbaud, Smith, Mapplethorpe: we are dealing here with a network of homage

and swapped destinies, like Piaf and Cocteau, people who would die within minutes of each other.

Patti Smith had returned with a vengeance from the setback of her accident seventeen months before. In July, she made the cover of *Rolling Stone*, a striking photo by Annie Leibovitz of Patti standing in front of a wall of real flames, wearing a see-through white blouse revealing a black bra underneath. The story by Charles Young was titled 'Patti Smith Catches Fire' and was the most widely read piece on Patti yet. 'This woman can sing rock & roll,' Young wrote. 'Power, passion, sex appeal, unique style, enough control for professionalism, enough lack of control for suspense – it's all there. She is, at the age of thirty-one, a star.' However, the article turned out to be highly ambivalent.

> Her personal charm, when she wants it to be, is enormous. Her followers are increasing every day, and they are among the most ardent anywhere. She is a poet for the people. Patti Smith's detractors think Radio Ethiopia, a loosely defined organization of her supporters, amounts to a Kiss Army for intellectuals who like to be mystified by poetry without capital letters. They think she is a fool. Because she cultivates the look of a possessed poet, she can say things like 'the word art must be redefined' and get away with it. Her fans, in fact, eat it off a stick. And she is happy to feed them, so long as they don't question the menu too closely.

Young asked Patti about her earlier comments to Nick Tosches about Mick Jagger.

> The other day you said that if anyone was qualified to be a nigger, it was Mick Jagger. How is Mick Jagger qualified to be a nigger?

> SMITH: On our liner notes I redefined the word nigger as being an artist-mutant that was going beyond gender.

> REPORTER: I don't understand how Mick Jagger has suffered like anyone who grew up in Harlem.

SMITH: Suffering don't make you a nigger. I mean, I grew up poor too. Stylistically, I believe he qualifies. I think Mick Jagger has suffered plenty. He also has a great heart, and I believe, ya know, even in his most cynical moments, a great love for his children. He's got a lot of soul. I mean, like, I don't understand the question. Ya think black people are better than white people or sumpthin'? I was raised with black people. It's like, I can walk down the street and say to a kid, 'Hey nigger.' I don't have any kind of super-respect or fear of that kind of stuff. When I say statements like that, they're not supposed to be analysed, 'cause they're more like off-the-cuff humorous statements. I do have a sense of humour, ya know, which is sumpthin' that most people completely wash over when they deal with me. I never read anything where anybody talked about my sense of humour. It's like, a lot of the stuff I say is true, but it's supposed to be funny.

REPORTER: You were quoted in [*Rolling Stone*'s] 'Random Notes' as saying you jerk off to your own photograph. I'm trying to figure out if you're actually that sexually attracted to yourself.

SMITH: No, it was just one of those moments, ya know? It was the photo for the cover of *Easter*. I thought if I could do it as an experiment, then fifteen-year-old boys could do it, and that would make me very happy. Ya know, people say to me, 'Aren't you afraid of becoming a sex object?' Especially a lot of writers are obsessed with making you feel guilty or upset because you might become a sex object. Well, I find that very exciting. I think sex is one of the five highest sensations one can experience. A very high orgasm is a way of communication with our Creator.

REPORTER: You jerk off to the Bible too?

SMITH: Definitely.

Patti's comments in the *Rolling Stone* article about redefining the word 'nigger' incensed many of the magazine's readers, as well as its editors and writers. The magazine's own review of *Easter* questioned her appropriation of the inflammatory word. ' "Rock 'n' Roll Nigger" is an unpalatable chant because Smith doesn't understand the word's connotation, which is not outlawry but a particular kind of subjugation and humiliation that's antithetical to her motives.' This controversy would dog her throughout the year. 'If I wanna say nigger, I'll say nigger,' Patti proclaimed. 'If somebody wants to call me a cracker bitch, that's cool. It's part of being American.'

On 4 August the Patti Smith Group released an EP in the UK that was a mixture of old, new and live material. It led with 'Privilege (Set Me Free)'. The song was originally recorded by Paul Jones (former lead singer of Manfred Mann) for the movie *Privilege* (starring sixties supermodel Jean Shrimpton as a journalist) and 'Ask the Angels' from the *Radio Ethiopia* album. The flip side was a live version of '25th Floor' and a poetry reading of 'Babelfield' from her new book. It peaked at number 72 in the UK. On 27 August, Patti was back in England to headline the Reading Rock Festival in Berkshire with the Tom Robinson Band, John Otway and Sham 69. Ian Birch reviewed the show in the *Melody Maker*:

> Gradually the sound improved and the band tightened, but Patti increased her unsettling line in chat between numbers. Maybe it was designed to be acidly witty, but it didn't come across that way to me. Rather, it lay somewhere between the infantile, the slightly removed and a nascent showbiz stance. All this wouldn't have mattered so much if she had appeared to be as intent on entertaining as the rest of her band, who worked and worked and worked . . .

Graham Locke in the *New Musical Express* thought her show was lacklustre. 'She never gave the impression that her heart was totally in it . . . a thoroughly entertaining, if surprisingly unadventurous, hour and a quarter.'

At a press conference in London in September to promote

Babel's publication in England, Patti admitted, 'I spew out a lot of stoned spaced-out meanderings of the sort I'm well known for spewing.' Later, talking to Paul Rambali of the *NME*, she said 'While I'm very intelligent, I'm no intellectual. All my beliefs, political and otherwise, are very romantic. It's like me having a crush on Prince Charles. I don't know anything about him, I just think there's something sexy about him.'

Explaining the unevenness of the shows to Rambali, she said, 'We're not like a male band either, in that the male process of ecstasy in performance is . . . building and building until the big spurt at the end. We're a feminine band, we'll go so far and peak and then we'll start again and peak, over and over. It's like the ocean. We leave ourselves wide open for failure, but we also leave ourselves open to achieving a moment more magical.'

Ian Penman reviewed *Babel* in the *NME*:

> Most of us were writing better than this in the lower Sixth, with or without expensive drugs, friends or book deals. I hate this book, actually. All it'll ever give people is confusion and ignorance. This is self-conceit, and it should have been burnt out or burnt years ago. This is semi-literature, and I hate it even more when I realize that it's probably the only book of 'poetry' a lot of impressionable young people will buy this or any other year.

'I was surprised by Patti Smith's rise,' said Allen Ginsberg.

> It's sort of heartening to see how somebody else could get ahead. I wonder how she'll do. I was reading Rimbaud's last letters, when he was dying, about how miserable life was and 'all I am is a motionless stump' and I'm wondering how she'll deal with that aspect of heroism.

After the British publication of *Babel*, Patti withdrew to work on songs for her next album, *Wave*, and to be with Fred. She obviously found the transition hard, as she told many of her New York friends, but when Legs McNeil found himself visiting friends in the same building, he knocked on Patti's door only to be faced with a surly Fred Smith, who said Patti was not in. Legs left a message, but never heard from her. It would turn out to be hard for her band to communicate with her too, separated as they were by a thousand miles. It was the beginning of the end for the Patti Smith Group.

It's All Over Now

1979

Pull the chain on Buckingham,
The drain calls you Ma'am,
BUGGER THE QUEEN.

William S. Burroughs
(Lyrics given to Patti Smith
for a possible song)

Everything Patti now did had to be approved by Fred. In retrospect it is easy to see how each of her choices put distance between her and the boys in the band. First Patti and Fred decided Todd Rundgren should produce the next album, *Wave*. This made sense but it also meant the group and their entourage of assistants, roadies, and family had to move to the hamlet of Bearsville in upstate New York, where Rundgren had built a world class studio. Patti told Todd that this was to be the last Patti Smith group album, but swore him to secrecy, not even informing the loyal Lenny of her intentions. When the band arrived they were surprised to discover that the pre-production period, in which the band get to know the producer and he gets to know their music, had been cut and they were to start recording right away. It was as if Patti did not want to spend an hour longer than she had to with them. Next, just as they were getting into a groove, word came from New York that ex-Sex Pistol Sid Vicious had slashed their road manager, Patti's little brother,

Todd's face with a beer bottle. Luckily he was not seriously injured and the recording sessions contined efficiently.

In between the album's completion and release they played a few warm-up shows and Patti did some very select interviews.

On a cold night in early March 1979, Patti visited William Burroughs at his famous residence, 'the Bunker', to be interviewed by him for *High Times* magazine. The two were alone for the interview, and though Patti had always professed to idolize the esteemed 64-year-old writer, Burroughs, a world-class raconteur himself, barely got a word in edgewise that evening. Patti had a lot to say.

I look to my future with so much joy, because I am in the most wonderful position. When I entered rock 'n' roll, I entered into it in a political way, not as a career. After the death of a lot of the leading sixties stars, and after the disillusionment of a lot of people at the end of the sixties and early seventies, I felt that people just wanted to be left alone for a little while. But when '73 and early '74 came around, it was just getting worse and worse, and there was no indication of anything new. I felt that it was a time for me to do something. All I really hoped to do was initiate some response from other people. I didn't have any aspirations of a career. I look at the world, I get very broken-hearted about what happens in the world. I hate to see people hurt. I see what's happening with Iran, and I'm mostly worried that Iran will lose its culture, or that somebody will destroy [the Sufi poet] Rumi's grave. I worry about things that are not, I suppose, really so important to anybody. But the things that I was involved with politically in America were very simple things having to do with the minds of teenagers, and how they were being shaped. I feel that in my own way, I was able to at least put a stick in the coals a little. Now it's 1979 and I'm still involved in this thing, but it's come to a point in my life that, like you said, I have to stop and say, 'What am I doing?'

I was actually very heartbroken in the last few years, because I had to accept a lot of things about our planet and about, you know, realities. But still, like I said, just as we have the temptation to be corrupted, we have the strength not to be corrupted. I like to think of those forty days when – I've talked to you about this before. The idea of Jesus. I haven't completely accepted that thing in my mind. The day that I totally accept him is going to be a very wonderful day, if it happens, but I have to think about it still. I'm still exploring that guy. But one of the stories that I really like is when he, just at this period of time, went into the desert for forty days and wrestled the Devil, you know, when they actually had a verbal and physical battle. Forty days of someone woodpeckering your spirit, is pretty . . .

BURROUGHS: Yeah, it's pretty harrowing.

PATTI: And he came out of it. And so for me, whenever I think that I have it tough because I have to fight radio stations, or a record company or anything, I get pretty ashamed of myself when I think that this guy had to spend forty days without food or drink in the middle of a desert with the Devil. But it does get to you.

Initially, all I wanted out of life was to do great work, and thus communicate with myself, but most of all, to be able to honestly, totally communicate with another person, totally. Telepathically, or whatever. I've no desire to be like some movie star and leave a trail of husbands behind me, you know?

Our credo was, 'Wake up!' I've said this before, but just to tell you, in case you haven't read or anything: I wanted to be like Paul Revere. I didn't want to be a giant big hero, I didn't want to die for the cause. I didn't want to be a martyr. All that I wanted was for the people to fuckin' wake up. That's all I wanted them to do, and I feel that that's what happened.

BURROUGHS: Well, as you say that this is what happened. You have the whole punk generation, essentially, who are anti-heroes. See, they're rejecting the old values, because having been woken up, they realize that all this nonsense that they've been brought up on is nonsense. And all these standards. And they're rejecting those standards. So we could regard them, if you will, as something that you have been instrumental in creating.

PATTI: I don't agree with these kids. I believe in heroes. See, I love these kids, but I think they've spawned a lot of little monsters, though, sometimes. Because I don't feel the same way they do. I don't think it's cool to shoot yourself up with heroin at 21 years old and die. I don't think it's cool to die at 21, you know. I don't want to be dead. I would exist forever.

What's important is that there are, I hate to call it this, more imposters, than ever. I never think that anybody should do art unless they're a great artist. I think that people have the right to express themselves in the privacy of their own home, but I don't think they should perpetuate it on the human race – at least in a pleasurable kind of manner.

It used to be that art was unquestionably art. And I think that we have to get back to that frame, but that can only happen again by the eruption of like at least ten great people at once. I want to live in an illuminated time.

I wouldn't talk to you about gender, if we were talking about performing properly, or the act of doing work. I understand that it's important to go beyond your gender in that process. I know that women, by the basis of our make-up, we perpetuate civilization, and we have to be optimistic. We have to believe in the future, or else . . . since we're the ones who bear the children of the future, we have to feel we're not setting them to light on a volcano. You don't want to bear a child and then drop it in a volcano. You want to bear a child and put him in paradise.

I don't believe in having nine kids at this point. I'm not a Mexican Catholic. You know, I desire for the planet to go on, and not see swans go extinct, and all that stuff . . .

Wave was released on 27 April. Fred Smith's influence on Patti can best be traced in the two areas which she had previously made her domain – the interview and the stage. Reporters trying to pin Patti down were given the runaround and finally put away with the line, 'Could you come back later, or call me tomorrow 'cause it's all up to Fred and he's busy.' Any intrepid scribe who attempted to breach this line was met with a firm rebuttal. When Patti played New York's Palladium in May, John Rockwell reported that her performance was not up to her greatest but was more controlled and effective than many recent efforts. He withheld his praise for an encore on which Patti was joined on stage by Fred. 'Lots of rock performers play self-indulgently with the mind-blowing aspects of feedback,' Rockwell wrote. 'But what Mr Smith wrought in that regard – soft bending filigrees of sound alternating with rich grating onslaughts – was the most interesting use of feedback this writer has ever heard.'

Robert Christgau was one of the few critics to defend the album:

A lot of folks just don't like Patti anymore, and so have taken to complaining about the pop melodicism ('AOR sellout') and shamanistic religiosity ('pretentious phony') she's always aspired toward. But this is an often inspired album, quirkier than the more generally satisfying *Easter* – especially on the sexual mystery song 'Dancing Barefoot', quite possibly her greatest track ever, and, yes, the reading for the dead pope that she goes out on.

More typical were Simon Frith and Julie Burchill. Frith wrote in the *Melody Maker*:

The crucial component of *Wave* is Todd Rundgren's productions. He had his own theory of rock, a technological, engineer's theory, and it's his sound rather than Patti's that dominates this LP. Now they're an American rock band – double guitar breaks, synthesized sustenance – and she is an American rock singer, filling in the spaces the musicians leave.

Burchill was merciless:

Her story is that of the Emperor's New Clothes in reverse; Patti has the gear, but there's nothing inside it. Is this the blandest record in the world? Even old Todd's lack of talent in the production can't be blamed. I thought Patti Smith had got what she wanted, but she is obviously a very disappointed person. She had babbled and jived herself into a corner where two mirrors meet and seems set to stand there examining herself for the rest of her career, wishing that she could be like Stevie Nicks.

Wave reached 18 in the US Top Twenty, while reaching number 41 on the UK chart. On 16 May Patti publicly announced plans to stay in Detroit with her new man, Fred Smith. Unfortunately, she had agreed to do a long US and European tour, but in the interim had lost her enthusiasm. She turned on her closest associates, including the devoted personal assistant Andi Ostrowe. For Ostrowe the tour marked the low point of her relationship with Patti, whom she had virtually deified. As the tour neared its end, the two women were not even on speaking terms.

The stress of being on the road was taking its toll on everyone, especially Patti. As the frontwoman, the focus was always on her. Constantly doing interviews and going to radio stations, being constantly catered for by an ever increasing entourage of employees and hangers on, it became increasingly hard for Patti to remember her original motives for performing. On top of everything else she was plagued with recurrent bronchitis throughout the tour. In the beginning there was the novelty of it all, but after she met Fred and decided to move to Detroit, things changed.

'In the seventies I actually enjoyed the privileges and the excitement and some of the danger of being a rock 'n' roll star', Patti later remembered. 'It was intoxicating. But it wasn't enough. Basically I had fallen in love with Fred and I didn't like being parted from him. When we [the Patti Smith Group] started performing, I really gave everything to it. I gave my time, my energy, my love. But my feelings for Fred were so strong that when I was on tour and away from him it didn't mean anything, and I felt extremely false being on stage.'

'Actually, when I think about it, my happiest memories of that time weren't about performing,' she said many years later. 'I think about sitting on the edge of the stage at the end of the night, talking to the kids who don't leave and answering their questions or listening to their philosophies.'

The *Minneapolis Tribune* described Patti as 'dispirited'. She told the crowd, 'If you don't like the tired aspect of it, go get your money back and leave me the fuck alone. I am extremely tired.' In Europe the reviews were, if anything, worse. *Sounds*' Phil Sutcliffe reported:

Atrocious axewomanship! Patti Smith is a wonderful gift of the late seventies, an inspiration to me, but this is the wrong time and the wrong place. I could only think that after a lot of experience and intellectualizing she still doesn't know why she goes on stage and so her efforts are rather aimless and dependent on the prevailing winds for their success or otherwise . . .

The summer shows in Europe were mostly in large arenas. The band had prepared a set for those spaces which included Dylan's 'Mr Tambourine Man', John Lennon's 'It's Hard', the Who's 'The Kids Are Alright', Manfred Mann's '5–4–3–2–1', Elvis's 'Jailhouse Rock', and Phil Spector's 'Be My Baby'. The set had been organized so that each member of the band could take a vocal to give Patti some rest. 'Radio Ethiopia' had been dropped. The chaotic final shows in Italy were emblematic of the whole experience. It was the closest Patti came to her own

Altamont. In Bologna the concert promoters had been forced to accept the 'protection' of the Italian Communist Party. However, there was no 'protection'. Many fans were breaking down the barriers and getting in for free. There was also no protection backstage, for the band. Attempting to take the stage, the band lost themselves in a maze of corridors, occasionally confronted by threatening-looking 'guards', who instructed them to obey their orders. When they finally got on stage they were in a state of fear hardly conducive to playing music to 80,000 people, the largest audience they had ever confronted. The first Italian show was little different from its predecessors, except that it was the second-to-last show and they were all exhausted, particularly Patti. The band did their best, each taking a turn at the mike so that the whole burden of singing would not rest solely on Patti. As the concert neared its end, what appeared to be a full-scale riot broke out, as overeager fans broke through the flimsy barricades and charged towards the stage. It was an extremely frightening moment. It turned out, however, that Patti's Italian fans were simply so enamoured of her that they just wanted to sit on the stage, to be as close to her as they could.

After this happened in Bologna, Patti's manager, Ina Meibach, confronted the promoters, demanding protection and insisting that nothing like this assault on the stage could be allowed to happen again. The Italians assured her that everything was under control. The following night in Florence was a carbon copy re-enactment of the previous night's show, and it unnerved everyone in the band.

Afterwards, back at the hotel, Patti told the band that she had had it, that this was it, that the Patti Smith Group was over. Ivan and Jay Dee were devastated, feeling that after working their way from the bottom of the barrel to almost within reach of the pot of gold, to quit now was insane. Despite Patti's claims that she was going to settle down with Fred in Detroit and devote herself to having a family, she was a star, and there were many ways that she could have continued to have a career. Whereas, apart from Lenny, none of the other band members stood a chance for this level of success on their own. Lenny defended Patti to the hilt, and they all told themselves this might be a temporary decision anyway, brought on by exhaustion and the craziness of the last two nights. Like Dylan after his motorcycle accident, maybe Patti would return.

Dream of Life
1980 – 88

I was immersed in writing, study-ing, raising our children. I had a completely different life that was task-oriented. I did not listen to [my own music], and I really did not think about it that much, because my life was so full at the time.

Patti Smith

J ust how private Fred and Patti wanted to keep their lives was illustrated by their wedding on 1 March 1980. In a country where rock stars are treated like nobility, the marriage of the house of Smith to the house of Smith could have been a big story in the media. Instead they had a surprisingly tiny, private wedding, inviting only their parents.

At first Patti's life in Detroit was fun. Despite a poor economic standing because of the decline of the auto industry, Detroit had a rich cultural heritage and Detroiters possessed their own blend of toughness, battling hardships with humour. 'Detroit people are my favourite people in the whole world,' Fred stated. 'They have good hearts and feelings. Europeans are always interesting, but nothing like here. I always want to get back. It's more than just home.'

In June 1980, the Patti Smith Group, which had not yet been formally disbanded, performed at a benefit for the Detroit Symphony Orchestra at the city's Masonic Temple. 'I love classical music,' said Patti, explaining her reason for doing the benefit,

> but it always seemed inaccessible. And then we started watching the Beethoven series on television and listening to Antol Dorati [the conductor of the Detroit Symphony] talk. We started looking forward to it the way we might have looked forward to a Rolling Stones concert. Having lived in New York where the orchestra is very aggressive and flamboyant, there was something inspiring for me about the way Dorati presented the Symphony. We just want to help support the Symphony and get more people to share the experience of listening to the Symphony play. We care about the Symphony a lot and just want to help in our own way.

Fred concurred: 'It makes you feel good, the music. It inspires you. It extracts the feeling out of you, and we want to help pay back the Symphony for that enjoyment.'

The show Fred and Patti put on together had enough different angles to confuse anyone trying to analyse the message. First, Patti took the stage alone and gave an inspired poetry reading. Then she was joined by the angelic DNV, who accompanied her on a big pipe organ for an outstanding rendition of 'Hymn' from *Wave*. No sooner had that number ended than a screen was lowered behind her and Patti was joined on stage by Fred. While a silent black and white film of the great abstract expressionist painter Jackson Pollock (after whom they would name their son) doing one of his famous action paintings played behind them, the Smiths improvised a soundtrack, Patti on clarinet, Fred on sax, and a Fender duo-sonic guitar leaning against an amp on feedback. Next Fred left the stage and Patti was joined by Lenny, Jay Dee, Ivan and DNV. They started with three jazz-influenced oldies, taking Patti back to her childhood. Next, harking back to the days of *Radio Ethiopia*, they launched into an experimental improvisation pointing to an excursion into the heady avenues of 'Afghanistan'.

In an interview he gave shortly after the show, Lenny sounded as if he believed they might develop in this direction. In that case he must have been as upset as Jay Dee and Ivan when that same month Patti called a business meeting of the band in New York and formally told them it was over. Considering how hard they had worked for six years and had just started making the big money, they were to say the least, frustrated by their benevolent despot of a leader. 'The official end of the band came when we were in our accountant's office,' reported Jay Dee.

I don't think Richard was there, I guess he already knew. It was me, Lenny and Ivan. Patti basically said, 'The group is no more. We're going to go out gracefully – we're not going to announce that the group is breaking up.' I know that it was very hard for her, and I know that she probably thinks that we think badly of her. Deep down inside, I hope she knows we don't. I wasn't angry, but I was devastated. I mean, for like the last year of the Patti Smith Group she was living in Detroit with Fred, so it was something I had feared might happen, on a purely selfish kind of level. But I didn't realize at the time that the group was my identity. That's who I was – I was the drummer of the Patti Smith Group. I wasn't anything, I wasn't me, I was a thing. So it was just like, 'Wow. Now what?'

'We started out playing in front of 250 people at St Mark's Church, and finished up in front of 70,000 in a Florence soccer stadium,' concluded Lenny Kaye years later.

You can't invent a better narrative that that. Patti was extremely inspirational. She had a great enthusiasm for the creative energy of art. There was the personal side of her, which was very warm and funny. We used to giggle a lot and tell jokes and sit around and have good times. There was something very little-girlish about her. She also had very set ideas about pushing herself and making sure that neither she nor anyone else she was working with was content with what was. She was working for what could be. That's why the band split up. When there was nowhere else to go we decided to go on to new things. I first got into Patti as a fan when she was an actress in a Jackie Curtis play at La Mama. I still remained a fan throughout my association with her. She's one of the great creative minds of our generation. Music was not the foremost thing on her mind right then, I supposed, but I was sure we had not heard the last of Patti Smith.

When asked what she thought of Patti's decision to withdraw from the field, Debbie Harry, the lead singer of Blondie, who were at that moment the number-one bestselling pop group in the world, answered wisely and without malice that she thought it was probably the most sensible thing that Patti had ever done. Debbie, after all, was in a better position to judge the dangers of the game both she and Patti had been playing. Of course, Debbie did not know Fred, or Detroit, or what strange engines ran Patti's emotions. Though Patti and Debbie had emerged from the same scene and had travelled a lot of the same terrain, like Elvis and Jerry Lee Lewis they never had been and never would be friends. But Debbie was the more generous of the two, and she understood the wisdom of Patti's decision.

The end of Patti's rock and roll career is as much a part of her legend as her beginning. Patti had always wanted to be a shaman, but she had never wanted to be a sacrificial victim like Brian Jones, Janis Joplin, Jimi Hendrix and Jim Morrison, four of her heroes, but not role models.

Looking out at those 70,000 people in the vast arena of Florence, little different except in size from the Roman arenas in which gladiators cut each other to pieces, or lions ate Christians alive for the amusement of the mob, Patti faced for the first time a crowd she could not tame. The concert had run its course, building until that moment in the last three songs when, if she'd succeeded, the crowd was on the edge of madness. Suddenly she felt a foul, uncontrollable force driving the fans to that edge which the Greeks call *Sparagamos*: the rending to pieces of the hero limb by limb. To take an audience to this height is an extraordinary achievement. Elvis could do it. Jagger could do it. But Patti was facing something she had not encountered before – the knowledge that the crowd could have gone either way, and it was no longer up to her. That was the last time Patti Smith would confront a rock audience for sixteen years. The next time she went out, the single most pronounced aspect of her shows would be control.

Patti's retirement took most people by surprise. The year before she had enjoyed a hit single and had reached a whole new level of popularity. 'I didn't even think of it as retiring,' she said.

> I mean, I've read everything – that I burned out, that I was on drugs – which was totally untrue. I was actually at the top of my game. But the reason I left was because I had met a man who I deeply loved. Who had been through all of that. Who wanted a quiet life, to raise a family. I found it really unacceptable to be parted from him. And everything lost its meaning. When I began to perform, I did my work with my group with all my heart. It took all of my energy. I put it before everything. And I could no longer do that. And so when I worked, I felt – not like a phony – but I just felt like I wasn't giving what the people deserved to have. And I just didn't want to be parted from Fred. I felt good when I left because I felt my initial reason for being involved in that world was hopefully to create space and inspire others. I was intentionally trying to create space for some kind of idealistic minority. You know, if you felt like an alien, whether that was a black, a homosexual, a thief, a female. I know we made a certain difference, we had an effect on people and it was positive. The idea is to create a

space for yourself and leave one for the people coming. You want to leave room for other people to work, not to plant a flag and say, 'This is mine.' I feel that my group achieved that goal. And we didn't start work to achieve fame and fortune. That wasn't supposed to be our goal. And that was where it was heading. So I felt it was an honourable leave taking.

Fred had broken up his Sonic Rendezvous Band in 1979 when Patti dismembered her own group. Patti constantly referred to starting a family with Fred, but she also believed that they would start a band, or at least make music together. John Lennon was making a big comeback in 1980 with his wife Yoko Ono, after his withdrawal from the music business in 1975, the same year Patti stepped on to the rock-and-roll stage. Given her flair for timing and attaching herself to the mythos of rock legends, it was not surprising that rather than wearing the widow's weeds that she had handed to Lenny, Jay Dee, Richard and Ivan, Patti would take her chance to grab the gown of matrimonial rock and become the new-wave John and Yoko, or Yoko and John. It made sense in a lot of ways. Yoko was an oft-cited influence on some of the first female punk and new-wave singers, influencing groups like the B-52's, and was finally coming into her own with her tracks on the *Double Fantasy* album. Patti booked herself and Fred into a Detroit studio and started working on a new album, tentatively titled *Dream of Life*. She was going to show everybody back in New York just who the real queen of punk rock was. Lydia Lunch and all those no-wave jerks who were already putting her down had better watch out. Patti was hot as a pistol. She would redeem Detroit! She would make it the Motor City again! Before the end of the year Patti and Fred had recorded five songs but soon after, they suddenly dropped the project.

After her stint as a 'big star' Fred thought, according to Patti, that she needed humbling. Her everyday existence in Detroit, cleaning and doing laundry, was certainly that. 'I didn't do it for that reason, but Fred knew it was necessary,' said Patti. 'I learned all those things from him, and I'm extremely grateful to him. It wasn't an easy task to teach me, either.' Patti confided to friends that she deeply missed New York and that the transition to life in Detroit was difficult. Rumours floated back from Detroit that Patti had retreated into the arms of Morpheus, that she was taking refuge with the Chinaman, that both she and Fred were junkies. Since they were out of the studio and not seeing anybody or doing anything, to a lot of people that was the only explanation that made sense.

William Burroughs's amanuensis James Grauerholz made an intriguing point when he said that Patti had pulled off the all but impossible feat of having died a rock 'n' roll death without having had to actually die. The truth, which nobody appeared interested in at the time, was that Fred and Patti were more than happy. In the carefree early days of their marriage they dreamed up a paradise. Completely free of any demands and financially independent as long as they lived frugally, they set themselves tasks and aided each other in their completion. Patti wanted to learn how to write prose. Fred wanted to learn how to fly and get a private pilot's licence. In time they both succeeded. Since Patti wanted to write about a man who explored beaches, Fred plotted his flying lessons at small aerodromes near the great lakes of the region. Packing lightly they would take off on these adventurous trips, staying in cheap motels. When Fred got his pilot's licence he was able to take Patti flying in a small two-seater plane for an exhilarating view of the earth. The outcome of Patti's task, *The Coral Sea*, was not published until two years after Fred's death.

Patti had by this time achieved enough notoriety to be a reference point in the mainstream press. When Cher appeared on Merv Griffen's television show in 1980 wearing her version of the punk look, the *Los Angeles Herald Examiner* commented that 'when Cher talked, she mumbled incoherently, sort of like Patti Smith, but as if she had paid Patti Smith a huge weekly salary to teach her these mannerisms'. Meanwhile, outside the island of self-imposed exile in Detroit, the music world was rapidly changing.

In October U2 released *Boy*. It was compared to the best debut albums of all time, including *Horses* and *The Velvet Underground and Nico*. Patti Smith was already a part of history. According to Nico, it was not the music world that changed, but Patti. 'She became boring and married,' Nico complained, offering her own surreal take on Patti's choice. 'She should have married John Cale, and they could have lived in a gingerbread house and made gingerbread children.'

Opinions on Patti Smith's role in the rock-music world were divided. In a book on women in rock, Lucy O'Brien mused: 'Was she a rock 'n' roll saint, an asexual hero, or a feminist sell-out?' There was no consensus on that question, but in the eighties a panel of British female punks, including members of the Slits, the Raincoats and the Au Pairs, concurred that Patti Smith was more of a threat to feminism than women who openly sold their sexuality in rock music. According to the Passions' Barbara Black,

> Patti actually denied she was a feminist. She said, 'Oh yes, it's over there somewhere, but it's nothing to do with me. I'm here because of my merits.' That is simply not true. When Patti Smith came to the UK, there were thousands of women who went to see her because of the way she was, her way of performing. And to deny her association with them, to me, is cowardly. I think she's lying to herself when she says the women's movement has nothing to do with her.

Patti had always described herself as someone who didn't like movements. 'Part of the reason I was so obsessed about women, and acting so like a snot all the time, saying "Women are stupid, I don't like women's lib" was because I was afraid of the woman in myself,' she told Nick Tosches. 'And I didn't want to admit to myself that I really didn't know nothing about how women are held back. I never felt held back. I was like a little animal all my life. I was given free rein.'

When Patti walked off the stage in June 1980, one of the strongest reasons was the fear of being consumed by her fans, of becoming a creature dependent upon their approval and vulnerable to their madness. John Lennon's murder in December 1980, outside his apartment in the Dakota in New York, confirmed her worst fears. Patti knew she could have died at her show at the soccer stadium in Florence. The writing she wanted to do about her experiences would not come, and she was not making music either. For the first time since she left New Jersey for New York, Patti was definitely, in the words of Carlos Castaneda, 'off her spot'.

Meanwhile, in New York, people heard from her less and less. Penny Arcade came back to the city in 1981 and heard that Patti had gone into virtual seclusion. 'Everyone who ran into me thought that I was in touch with Patti, that I could get a message to Patti. It was bizarre. I would say, "Look, I haven't been close to Patti for years. I don't have her phone number, I don't talk to her, I don't write her, she doesn't write me."'

Although Patti had by now apparently cut herself off dramatically from the scene that spawned her, the ambitions she had clarified in her final interview of 1980 – when she had said that the band's aim had been to make a place from which others could take off, a rock-and-roll launching pad – came true on 18 June 1981 when Sonic Youth, formed by Thurston Moore and Kim Gordon, took their name from an amalgamation of Big Youth, a late-seventies reggae band, and Fred Smith's Sonic Rendezvous Band. 'Fred loved that,' Patti recalled. 'He always said, "They got that from me!" I'd say, "Well, you don't know that." It was a source of pride for him. He was sonic.'

An indication of how quickly even the most compelling figure can disappear from rock's memory came like a spear shooting through the roof of Patti's brain when in the 1981 readers' poll in the *New Musical Express*, Patti Smith wasn't even mentioned. To make matters worse, during this tough transitional period Debbie Harry, whom Patti hated, was at the peak of her popularity; Elvis Costello, whom Patti also hated, was at his critical and commercial peak; and Chrissie Hynde, the tough, talented guitarist and band leader, made her debut, and would take Patti's place as rock's leading female singer-songwriter of the eighties.

It must have been difficult for both Patti and Fred, proto-punk innovators, to stay outside the action. The American rock scene continued to change beyond their comprehension in the eighties with the advent of MTV. Debbie Harry's dramatic fall from grace must have given Patti a little satisfaction, but she couldn't have taken much pleasure in the inexorable rise of the Detroit native Madonna Ciccione. If indeed Patti thought of these things at all.

In the art world there was a new explosion of work by young artists who had been partly inspired by Patti and the punk or new-wave music of the preceding decade. Artists like Keith Haring and Jean Michel Basquiat sold internationally and became major stars in the art world. Patti's old flame Sam Shepard became a fully-fledged movie star in such films as *Days of Heaven* and *The Right Stuff*, and Jim Carroll was recognized as an influential and original writer and signed a contract with the Rolling Stones' record label to make an album of his music.

Patti put a positive spin on her life in Detroit with Fred. 'Fred and I always worked together,' she said of these transitional days.

By now Patti had settled into a comfortable collaboration with Fred. There can be no doubt that the most enjoyable thing they did together regularly was play music. Fred taught Patti guitar, encouraging her to play and they spent hours together improvising. There was never any doubt that Fred and Patti were gearing up to record an album together. Patti's ex, Tom Verlaine, made the curious observation that the majority of female musicians he knew appeared to share a desire to find the man with whom they could make music and love, adding that he had rarely found similar twin desires in men. In retrospect this sounds more like a confused take on the intense physical emotions that pass between two people playing rock and roll. It would be harder to find a stronger bond than Lennon–McCartney or Jagger–Richards. Male–female collaborations are rare because what makes them work in rock appears to be the tension between the opposing natures of collaborators. Two people who loved each other with the commitment of parents, for example, would be unlikely candidates. As Patti noted:

We write songs together and pursue individual ideas. It's been that way since I met him in 1976. We have been writing and working on songs together for ourselves. I never stopped writing. Working with Fred is very important to me. We have a lot of other ideas and songs we haven't done yet. Many songs. We're looking to the future with some other works. What we wanted to do was a piece of work together that addressed the things we care about.

In late 1981, Patti became pregnant. By the time she gave birth to her son Jackson in 1982, the phone calls to New York had stopped completely. When friends tried to reach her, they discovered she had made sure they could not. Her number was unlisted, and when she moved out of the Book Cadillac she left no forwarding address. To her friends it seemed as if Fred could not afford to share any of her. Along with the rumours of drugs, there were rumours of domestic violence. Fred had been known to be violent with Sigrid, and some friends theorized that the couple's isolation was a result of Patti not wanting people to see her bruises. 'Fred was beat as a kid,' Wayne Kramer asserted.

He was an abused kid. His dad beat him pretty good. Lots of times Fred didn't come to school because of it. Sometimes I'd go over to his house and he'd have black eyes. His dad was from the South and had that kinda down-home ignorance – you beat your wife, you beat your kids, when they don't do like ya say. That syndrome gets passed from generation to generation, unless you interrupt it with a lot of hard work.

But all the rumours were speculation. No one knew the truth. The writer James Wolcott interviewed Patti around this time and remembered having 'a spooky vibe about Fred and Patti's relationship'. Patti phoned Wolcott the day after the interview asking him to omit any mention of her affairs with Tom Verlaine and Sam Shepard. When Wolcott reminded her that these relationships were a matter of public record, Patti replied, 'I know, but Fred gets upset when he reads that stuff.' She also requested that Wolcott omit other facts from the interview. 'She didn't sound like a considerate spouse trying to spare her husband's tender feelings; she sounded nervous, fretful – cowed,' said Wolcott.

In 1982, after Jackson's birth, the 1980 *Dream of Life* sessions were scrapped and new recordings were begun. These sessions, too, were scrapped. Those who knew Patti didn't think it was ever her intention to let her career lapse for so long. Patti was also not the easiest person to work with, especially for a perfectionist like Fred who couldn't stand sloppy playing or moving tempos. In some people's opinion Fred suffered considerably for problems caused by Patti. 'Patti drove Fred crazy with frustration half the time with the way she works,' said one. 'But who has a perfect relationship? John and Yoko?' In addition Fred's stomach problems, combined with his drinking, had rendered him incapable of performing. Getting him into a studio was a major production, and then, when he got there, he would insist that without just a little taste, he couldn't play. When he had consumed the two bottles of wine he required before playing a note, the truth was he couldn't play. Patti, who used to kick Lenny in the ass if he repeated the same solo twice on a song, was understandably frustrated.

In the Alcoholics Anonymous jargon that would become so prevalent in the eighties, Patti could be called an enabler, one who was in deep denial herself, maybe even a co-dependent. She loved Fred and couldn't help deferring to him. She could not stop his drinking, yet by allowing it to escalate she made it impossible for him to collaborate with her. 'It's really easy to blame the guy,' said one friend, 'but sometimes people can push you a little too hard, and Patti knew all the buttons to push. But the fact that Patti and Fred chose not to do the rock-star thing is what really makes people mad, because most people would sell their grandmothers for that.'

And so it was that *Dream of Life* would take nine years to see the light of day. Despite the obviousness of the problems, as early as 1982 when the second series of recording sessions were scrapped, Patti seemed paralysed by her dilemma. She turned her attention towards bringing up Jackson, who would see his mother change over the next ten years from a vibrant 36-year-old to a careworn, grey-haired mirror image of her 'old man', whose decline was so marked that his former bandmates from the MC5, meeting up with him in the early nineties, would hardly recognize him. Patti had a close relationship with a pet fish called Curley, and took pleasure in watching television, which she called 'studying'.

> I went through different phases, such as a *Kung Fu Theater* phase – it aired every Sunday on the USA Cable Network. Everybody had to be quiet so I could have my cup of sake and sit there and watch it. And I used to watch the original *Route 66* at night. When they took both shows off the air I was brokenhearted.
>
> It was hard to stop working in public. But I balanced myself in the early eighties. It was slow in coming at first but very rewarding. I had never been much of a drug taker but I did smoke a lot of marijuana. I gave that up and was drug free, which required a lot of concentration. I had to learn to work again, find my own time, usually before 6 a.m. when my baby woke up. Eventually, I found that my facilities had really sharpened. I find that the things I did in this period are far more extreme than the things I did in the seventies.

To succeed in the family way Patti had to build a whole new set of processes. At first she and Fred had done everything together, but five years into the marriage it became evident that, much like Patti's parents, they were polar opposites. Whereas Patti thrived on a communal environment and working in collaboration while creating songs, Fred needed isolation to do his work. Furthermore, Patti's work methods would have annoyed Fred because he was a stickler for hitting the exact note at the exact time. Patti was all over the place, more interested in the feeling than the technical proficiency. 'She coulda driven him crazy a lot of times,' commented one engineer who had been in the studio with both of them. 'She can be a very frustrating person to work with, asking for something and then by the time you get it for her she's changed her mind and wants something different. She can really piss you off.' For somebody who had been allowed to be a benevolent despot for so long it was hard to accept other musicians as equals.

As of 1983, neither Patti nor Fred had released anything to the public, and they had virtually become recluses. Learning new rhythms and ways of working would dominate the next few years. Motherhood, much more than marriage to Fred, would change Patti's day-to-day existence. Even from the relative isolation of Detroit, she was able to dedicate time and energy to her artistic pursuits. With Jackson's birth, late nights sitting at the typewriter vanished as she was forced, like any new parent, to adapt to the demanding schedule of an infant, rising early and being available for his every need. Raising a child is both physically and mentally demanding, requiring, above all, patience. Patti rose to the challenge, focusing on staying healthy and maintaining her flexibility as she grew into her new role as mother. Fred was a devoted and caring father. Old priorities evaporated for the couple as Jackson became the centre of their existence.

Keeping up with current trends in music was of little interest to Patti. What she heard on the car radio was the extent of her exposure to new music. At home Patti and Fred tended to listen to classical and jazz, exploring Beethoven and Puccini, Coltrand and Ayler. There was always some new gem from Bob Dylan to treasure, but for the most part music ceased to be the compelling force it was in Patti's life in her teens and twenties.

Patti and Fred rarely went to the movies but they rented films to watch at home on the VCR. They found inspiration in the works of such master directors as Kurosawa, Bertolucci and Godard, as well as Woody Allen. 'I saw the *Purple Rose of Cairo* ten times,' said Patti.

Dream of Life: 1980–88

Patti evinced little interest in the world outside her door in the chic suburb of St Clair Shores, Michigan, some forty miles outside of Detroit, to which she had moved her family. The new house that they had bought was large, comfortable, almost luxurious, and located half a block from Lake St Clair. Unlike any other house in the suburban neighbourhood, it looked somewhat like a small castle, made of dark-brown brick and wood, and topped off by a small turret. It sat on an acre or two of land and even had a small swimming pool when they bought it. Not being swimming-pool types, Patti and Fred broke up the pool, hauled out the concrete bottom and sides and filled in the hole so you couldn't tell a pool had ever been there. There was a picnic table in the garden, a symbol of the family life Patti was now living.

St Clair Shores is an extremely peaceful place. Just sitting on the edge of the lake gives a feeling of centred solitude which may have helped Patti through the hard times later on. There may have been more bumps in Patti's life with Fred than she had originally expected, but for the most part Fred, Patti, Jesse and Jackson lived a calm family life in this home.

Friends wondered how they were supporting themselves since neither Patti nor Fred was doing work that was producing money. Patti continued to receive regular royalty payments on her albums and publishing rights as various new bands began covering some of her songs, and Fred collected occasional minor royalties from MC5 re-releases. Though the Smiths owned a brand-new sedan, Patti remained one of the few people in Detroit without a driver's licence, which trapped her at home and made her completely reliant on somebody to drive her wherever she wanted to go. 'I'm the only person here who doesn't drive,' she admitted. 'But I am getting such a multifaceted education from Fred because I am privileged to learn so much of what he knows – which is a million things.'

Fred's longtime friend, the producer Freddie Brooks, confirmed Patti's view of her husband. 'Fred was a really smart man,' said Brooks. 'I just basically soaked up whatever knowledge I could from him. We were equals but I was totally under him –

it was like a study programme. If there were two options for a way to do something, Fred would always come up with a third way, he would just invent a whole new thing. I was just in awe of him. Fred was a great guy.' Like the Rolling Stones' Brian Jones, Fred had the capacity to quickly master almost any instrument. 'Fred played the piano and he played the saxophone,' said Brooks, 'Fred could play just about anything, he could figure anything out. He was a real musical guy.'

In 1985 Robert Mapplethorpe became the most famous artist in the world for a brief moment when a portfolio of his pictures of black male nudes became a bone of contention on the floor of the US Senate. Mapplethorpe became the goad of the Reagan administration, the quintessential 'rebellious artist working outside society' and a target of born-again Christian conservatives. His cause was taken up outside the art world, becoming the subject of countless editorials defending him under the First Amendment. Robert became everything Patti had wanted to be. Ten years after Patti had been featured in the *New York Times Magazine* with *Horses*, Robert Mapplethorpe made an even bigger splash with the *X Portfolio*, hitting the headlines and editorial pages around the world.

Meanwhile, Patti Smith seemed as forgotten as Memphis Minnie. But when the *NME* critics compiled a list of their all-time top 100 albums, they had *Horses* at number 18. In 1986, Patti and Fred went back into the studio for the third time for another shot at *Dream of Life*, this time in New York with Richard Sohl, Jay Dee Daugherty, the producer Jimmy Iovine and a revolving team of bassists, including Utopia's Kasim Sulton. (Utopia were Todd Rundgren's band.) Lenny Kaye was conspicuously absent, apparently at Fred's insistence. When Patti wrote *Cowboy Mouth* with Sam Shepard, she had been the equal of her male collaborator, but now she deferred to Fred in every way, seemingly incapable of doing anything without his okay. To her old friends she seemed to be a different woman. The question was: who or what changed her? Was it her devotion to Fred? The isolation of life in Detroit? Was it the slavelike servitude of being a mother? 'Fred was a real traditionalist, he wasn't into "modern" relationships,' said Wayne Kramer.

He was a 'You're my wife, and the wife does this and the man does that' kind of guy. As much as Patti eloquently repainted him as a gifted artist and a saint of a man, he had his roots in this Kentucky redneck attitude, and I think that fed into their disconnection with the outside world. The wife's job is to stay home and raise the kids – keep 'em pregnant and barefoot.

But Patti insisted that she was happy in her life with Fred. 'Fred wanted a family, a son and a daughter, and that's what I gave him,' said Patti. 'He was a great father, a really loving, compassionate father. He was a complex man: warm, generous, and gentle. He was extremely soulful, but he was also exacting in his philosophies about relationships, marriage and work ethics, and he was extremely private. Our communication was limitless and if we had difficult times, we rode them out together. Sometimes it felt like we were together in the same car while it was crashing, surviving it together.'

Patti had nothing but positive comments to make about the recording experience.

Jimmy Iovine was wonderful to work with as producer. Fred and him really collaborated well on this project. The important thing is that all the musicians were properly represented. It was a real collaboration on everyone's part. Everyone really did their part, from Richard Sohl to the assistant engineer.

They finished laying down the tracks and were slated to record the vocals when Patti discovered that she was pregnant. The project would have to be put off for almost a year.

It seemed only fitting that Robert Mapplethorpe would do the cover of this all-important album. Robert and Patti had not seen each other for several years when they met in the coffee shop of the Mayfair hotel on Sixty-Second Street and Central Park West in New York to discuss the image. Both of them had gone through enormous changes in the interim. Robert had contracted the AIDS virus. Patti had been married for seven years and given birth to two children. However, judging by appearances you would have thought Patti the ill one and Robert in his prime.

Mapplethorpe's worldwide fame, his, albeit unwitting, political effect and the money they had brought had given him everything he had ever wanted. Apart from the fact that he was dying, he could not have been happier or looked better. Patti, on the other hand, who had withdrawn from fame and lived a life that some friends would later characterize as a complete nightmare, looked it. Her hair, which had always been the crowning glory of her image was now straggly, unwashed and streaked with tired grey. Her face, an icon of rock, looked gaunt, pale, battered. Her eyes stared out from behind schoolmarm glasses, frightened. She was no longer in control of her life. Robert was profoundly shocked, not to say insulted by the way her children demanded her attention when she was trying to talk to him. Worst of all for Robert was the fact that she was forbidden to make any decisions without getting permission from Fred. That Patti Smith had to get permission from Fred Smith for the way in which Robert Mapplethorpe was going to take her photograph was not only another insult to Robert, it was also an unworkable set-up.

It was no surprise then that getting a successful image took three sessions. Finally, on the day the art department demanded the cover art Patti received by Fed Ex an image from Robert that everybody accepted.

Patti and Fred continued in the studio until it became too much for the pregnant Patti. The sessions went on hold until Patti's second child, Jesse Paris, was born in 1987.

I actually worked harder in the eighties than I ever had. I finished about five books that will soon be slowly published [only two have been published as of this writing]. I spent time as a wife and mother, bearing and raising two children. There's a lot of sacrifice and very intense responsibility. I've grown and expanded as a human being in that way. That's permeated into the work. And a lot of the other work I've done over the past years hasn't been shared yet. I think it's some of the best work I have ever done. It's the most articulate, and I'm pleased with it. Fred and I have done a lot of work together. A lot of writing and exploring in a lot of different areas. It wasn't like we sat at home not doing anything. Working with Fred is very important to me. Our album represents us working together. We have a lot of other ideas and songs we haven't done yet. Many songs. We're looking into the future with some other works. We have achieved what we wanted with this album.

In the spring of 1988, Patti and Fred finally finished *Dream of Life*. Patti downplayed the length of her time away, saying there was no special difficulty about communicating with her audience for the first time in nine years.

Dream of Life had taken so long to make because of the children, but neither Fred nor Patti would have had it any other way. As its title suggests, it had been an organically made album, growing out of the life they shared. 'I really love my kids,' Patti said.

I love having them around even though they are a big responsibility and can drive you nuts. But one of the plusses of advancing through life is how your spectrum widens. In being a parent your spectrum widens even further. You become real aware of how everything affects your child. I know Fred and I, individually and mutually, have always been concerned about the state of the planet, but somehow when you have children, it becomes even bigger.

What interests us most in the entire process is the work aspect. For me, releasing an album is never as exciting as working on the music. We strive to do the work that we want, and we don't want any outside type of pressure or motivation that could shift the quality or direction of our work. Ever.

Released in the summer of 1988, the album was greeted warmly by rock critics, who all bought Patti's mythologizing about her new mature, married self: 'Patti Smith's nine-year absence from the music business has been a positive experience for her, a time of emotional healing and personal growth,' wrote Mary Anne Cassata in the *Music Paper*. 'She spent most of her time raising her two children, Jackson Frederick (now five) and Jesse Paris (now two), drawing much inspiration from them. *Dream of Life* is a celebration of family unity and of the love Patti and Fred share for each other, their children, and the world.'

'*Dream of Life* is an inspiring piece of work,' wrote Brett Milano in *Pulse!* He also observed that

the phrase 'Fred and I' turns up often in conversation – that's who wrote the songs, that's who made the record, that's who's in for the long haul. Most of all, she emphasizes that the Patti Smith of the Patti Smith Group and the Patti Smith of 'Fred and I' are two different animals. 'People Have the Power' caught a lot of Patti Smith's old fans by surprise. The hippie-ish sentiments were odd enough, but the kicker was that Smith expressed them convincingly. 'That's a gift type of song,' she said. 'I meant it to give some kind of positive energy and hope to people in a very difficult time. The song addresses itself to the various dreams that mankind has and reminds us that perhaps we can achieve those dreams if we work together. It's not intended to incite so much as to remind people.' Asked if she would have believed those sentiments at the time of *Horses*, Patti replied, 'Sure. I was never a pessimistic person. I questioned many things and had a growling nature, but that doesn't mean pessimism. Art is by nature optimistic. If one keeps working one has hope for the future. If one didn't feel that, one would crawl into an opium den and pull the covers over their heads.

'It is time to make things better. We have to help our fellow man, we have to address problems like AIDS, we have to amass the money to find a cure. We have to make people aware of the dangers, we have to clean up this world. I mean, every time I fill a water glass for my son, I'm thinking, is there too high a lead content in this water? We need to get a great cosmic broom and sweep up the planet. I've had millions of dreams of the great collective, of the whole planet ringing in prayer.'

Some of Patti's old friends were amazed by her apparent transformation. Reading a piece on Patti in *Vogue*, Penny Arcade was shocked.

I just wanted to kill her. I'm reading this thing, and it was very reactionary. She struck me as a reactionary person. I didn't know where her politics were and then towards the end of the article she says this thing about, 'Well, I'm a married woman and I would always change my name to my husband's name and the only reason that I didn't change it is 'cause his name is Smith, too.' I was like, what is this? That article probably really coloured my not wanting to see Patti. I don't understand her and I don't understand who she became but on another level, I feel like, Patti became a fantasy, as opposed to becoming who she was gonna be.

In New York doing publicity for *Dream of Life*, Patti visited Robert Mapplethorpe, who was now in St Vincent's Hospital. Patti continued her relentless promotion of the album, giving interview after interview, reinforcing her new persona as New Age mom and benefactor of the planet.

The first rule of the comeback album is you must tour to support it. Patti flatly refused to tour or play any dates in public, using her children as an excuse. However, as any number of critics pointed out, they could have played one date on the east coast, one date on the west coast and one date in between, filmed it for HBO and publicized the album that way. Unfortunately by now it seemed more likely that Fred was not up to the hard physical demands of touring. He was beginning to age dramatically in appearance.

Patti had been gone from the music scene for nearly a decade, and even though she was idolized by many younger bands, and generated a lot of press, she was unsuited to contemporary radio and was a nonentity as far as MTV, the main promotional tool of the moment, was concerned. On its own, a seventies cult reputation just wasn't enough to generate record sales. *Dream of Life* was a commercial failure. Patti had envisioned *Dream of Life* as the pinnacle of her long collaboration with Fred, yet when the record failed it was Fred who was the most affected. 'The fact that the album was not successful was very depressing to Fred,' said Freddie Brooks. 'I think breaking his heart would be the right expression, that's really what happened. It just broke his heart.'

Years later Marianne Faithfull spoke about *Dream of Life* and the limitations put on women artists in the music business. 'It made me really angry when Patti Smith's "Dream of Life" record was rejected,' she said. 'She changed her opinions and fell in love and got married and had kids and made a tender record and her record was rejected because she wasn't the raging junkie any more. I don't know her that well but I know she was incredibly hurt by that.'

Dreams of Death

1989 – 94

How will she deal with suffering?
How will she transcend suffering
and become a lady of energy, a
sky-goddess, singing of egoless-
ness? Because so far her prop-
osition has been the triumph of the
stubborn, individualistic, Rimbaud-
Whitman ego: but then there is
going to be the point where her
teeth fall out and she's going to
become the old hag of mythology
that we all become.

Allen Ginsberg

Robert Mapplethorpe was dying. He called Patti in Detroit in February 1989 to tell her he was going to Boston for a series of special treatments. Fred drove Patti to New York so she could spend some time with him. Though Robert maintained a cheerful stoicism, Patti knew he was very ill. The two spent a long afternoon together. Patti remembered them looking at a photograph of a desert scene that graced the cover of an old *Life* magazine which bore the date of Mapplethorpe's birthday, a gift from a friend. 'We stared at the picture for a long time,' Patti told Patricia Morrisroe. 'It was like the photograph had opened up and we had entered the scene.' After a time Robert began experiencing severe gastric pains and had to be helped to the bathroom by his nurse. He was in bad shape. When he emerged he looked at Patti. 'I'm dying,' he told her. Patti began to cry, sobbing and sobbing until finally Mapplethorpe was able to calm her. In their last conversation, he made her promise that she would write the introduction to his forthcoming flower book. Even in the face of death their artistic collaboration was the thing that mattered most. Robert rested his head on Patti's shoulder trying to ease her pain and her tears, but after a few minutes she realized he had fallen asleep. For the next two hours she sat with him, quietly listening to the beat of his heart.

The doctors in Boston were unable to administer the special treatments Mapplethorpe was hoping to receive because of other infections he was experiencing. On 9 March 1989, Robert Mapplethorpe died of AIDS at the age of forty-two. The moment she got news of his death, Patti began a portrait in prose of him that would be published as *The Coral Sea*.

> I wrote that the same day Robert died. He was in Boston and I had my children and I couldn't go. I was sitting up all night in vigil because I knew he was dying and his brother called me at 7:30 in the morning to tell me that he had finally passed away. I wept for him so much while he was still alive that I found when he died I was unable to weep. And so I wrote. Which I think he would have preferred anyway, because Robert liked to see me work.

Patti's foreword to Mapplethorpe's *Flowers* was published in 1990, and was the public's first glimpse of Patti's calm and magical mature style. It was followed by *The Coral Sea*, a special tribute, enhanced immeasurably by the scattering throughout of Mapplethorpe's pictures. The title of the book is taken from one of these: a grainy photo of a huge grey sky pressing down upon a bristling, streamlined aircraft carrier, *The Coral Sea*. Patti imagines Mapplethorpe as a sailor taking passage on a ship, 'venturing to Papua to secure for his soul a legendary butterfly, which he would tack to his chest as [Peter] Pan had attached his shadow to his wild little feet'. This hero, M, is 'destined to be ill' and is feverish, prone to hallucinatory reveries and recollections. 'Art, not nature, moved him. Nature, he had boasted, was meant to be redesigned; opened and folded like a fan.' Patti weaves herself into the story and, as she has said, 'the Uncle who appears is a little homage to Sam Wagstaff' (the influential curator and photo collector who was patron to Mapplethorpe and had also recently died). Though the writing's near-biblical formality, old-fashioned usages and relentless mythologizing can get over-rich, many thought the book one of her most beautiful and moving works, feeling it truly 'rings the bell of pure poetry', as William Burroughs quoted from Tennessee Williams.

Then, on 3 June 1990, just over a year after Mapplethorpe's wrenching death, the 37-year-old Richard Sohl, who had most recently worked with Patti on *Dream of Life*, was suddenly killed by a cardiac seizure in Long Island, New York. 'He was wonderful and I was actually quite heartbroken,' said Patti.

Later that year, Patti, in her first public performance of any kind since the Detroit Symphony benefit in 1980, performed with Fred a moving acoustic version of 'People Have the Power' at an AIDS benefit at Radio City Music Hall. Again, in May 1991, she made a rare public appearance at the Nectarine Ballroom, Ann Arbor, Michigan, for the Wellness Networks fight against AIDS. She was joined by Fred, Lenny Kaye, Jay Dee Daugherty and Scott Asheton. The crowd adored her. Fred, however, did not look well.

According to Freddie Brooks, who had been estranged from Fred for ten years, Fred was in bad shape at the Nectarine Ballroom. 'He did not seem all there.' Brooks also remembered Fred's almost complete lack of recall of the MC5 material. 'I'm not putting Fred down or anything,' said Brooks, but they were playing some of his old songs and he just didn't seem to remember them. Some people attributed it to his being drunk, but it was obvious to me that it wasn't just drinking. I know that for a fact. I attribute it to health problems. The drummer in the Sonic Rendezvous band said Fred was always taking Rolaids. [His condition] was probably pretty painful, and when things are that painful it's conceivable that you might be doing something to try and alleviate the pain, whether it's the right thing to do or not. His whole family had illnesses that passed through their lives. You don't go from being a powerful guy like Fred to looking as frail as he did at the end for no reason. He had bad stomach problems all his life. I think there was something going on there that no one will ever know because they didn't delve into it when he died.

Added to Fred's health problems was the stress produced by having two bands savaged by the music business. To make a record as strong as *Dream of Life* and have it fail was the final straw. *Dream of Life* wasn't just a Patti Smith record, it was also in large part a Fred Smith record, and its rejection broke him.

In late 1991, the MC5's vocalist, Rob Tyner, died of a heart attack in Detroit at the age of forty-six. In the aftermath, Wayne Kramer had his first close dealings in many years with his old bandmate Fred Smith.

'Rob didn't have any insurance and he had left three kids and of course being in the MC5 had not left any of us independently wealthy,' Kramer recalled.

So they started to get this whole thing organized in Detroit – it was gonna be a four-day tribute to Rob Tyner in four different clubs all over the city, climaxing with this big tribute show at the Michigan Theater. I didn't wanna go up there and jam, I wanted to rehearse and have something together but Fred was being real obstinate about it.

Kramer was shocked at the changes in Fred, one of his oldest and closest friends. It was almost impossible to get Fred to do anything, and Kramer felt a lot of it had to do with drinking. Whatever the reason, Fred had become a recluse.

He doesn't go anywhere, they [Patti and Fred] don't talk to anyone. I don't know that they have any friends. They don't hang out, he doesn't make records. He looked like his skin had drooped down like he had palsy and all his teeth were rotted. He looked scary, man. Afterwards, me and Michael [MC5 bassist] went out to dinner together and said, 'Man, did you see Fred's face, oh Jesus, man, what happened to the guy?'

Determined to pull off a good show for the Tyner benefits, the other musicians set up a rehearsal. Dennis, the MC5 drummer, was first to show up and then Wayne and Michael arrived. Two hours passed. 'We jammed and we were having fun, and finally Fred showed up,' said Kramer.

The roadies scurry out and they carry in his gear for him and here comes this frail old guy and he sits down. These other guys are tuning his guitar for him and plugging everything in. He sits down with two bottles of wine and commences to knock one off before we start playing! And then we start to rehearse what we're gonna do and he can't play his guitar, he don't remember the parts! 'Wayne, what did I play? You know what I used to play?' 'Yeah, I think it went like this, it's seventh fret, doo-do-da.' He said, 'Oh, oh, I don't remember anything, after the band broke up I, I don't remember anything.'

Fred just commenced to get plastered. Dennis got so angry at one point he said, 'Come on, can we get on with it? I have more fun at the dentist.' Finally we finished the rehearsal. We might as well not have rehearsed for what good it did. The next day we got to the gig and everyone's waiting for Fred to get there. He arrived late and then it was time for us to play. The stage was dark and the gear was ready and we were waiting, sitting backstage and Fred would not go on. Fred was drinking more wine out of a coffee cup, and waiting. Michael and Dennis both kept coming in saying, 'Come on, let's play, let's play, let's play,' and Fred wouldn't play. Then at one point they left the room and Fred looked at me and said, 'Fucking amateurs,' which was an old joke. We went on and played. Fred told the audience, 'Well, if we know anything, we're only here for a minute and you've got to make your mark and Rob certainly made his mark.' Patti was not around at all. She never showed up, not even for the gig.

The benefit would be Fred Smith's last public appearance.

In the midst of all this death, and Fred's appalling plunge towards illness and alcohol poisoning, Patti continued her public artistic rebirth with the publication of *Woolgathering*, a pocket-size volume of new writings in a chic and handsome series from Hanuman Books that included volumes by Bob Dylan, Allen Ginsberg and Richard Hell. *Woolgathering* is a collection of nine short poetic prose pieces, most of which are evocations of the poet's child-hood in rural New Jersey. Like her other published writings of the nineties, it presents a serene and meditative Patti, seemingly far removed from the aggressive, wilfully provocative rebel of her youth. The book is wistful, sweet and pure, per-meated with marvellous insight and imagery. 'The mind of a child is like a kiss on the forehead – open and disinterested. It turns as the ballerina turns, atop a party cake with frosted tiers, poisonous and sweet,' she writes. As the book's title suggests, the work is a kind of daydream, and memory-shapes, fantasy-shapes, glow and shift inside it with the compelling beauty of the passing clouds the writing directs our attention to over and over again.

The only music Patti and Fred released in 1992 appeared in September on the soundtrack album for the Wim Wenders film

Until the End of the World. The song they contributed, 'It Takes Time', was largely written by Fred. In December, Patti's picture was included on the cover of *Life* magazine in a collage of the history of rock. While this spoke well for the public perception of her importance, the only reference to her in the accompanying text is the following snide comment: 'Patti Smith, who didn't shave under her arms, was a punk goddess.' At least REM's leader Michael Stipe was quoted in the issue saying, 'Patti Smith was the one who said anybody could sing . . . and I thought, yeah, I can do that.'

Patti was cropping up a lot in the media. *Rolling Stone*'s twenty-fifth-anniversary 'Portraits' issue featured her nude in a famous seventies Mapplethorpe photo, and additional shots of her were referred to as pictured in 'Rimbaud Manqué menswear'. In *Spin* magazine's cover story on the Band of the Year, Nirvana, Courtney Love said, 'Patti Smith saved my life', and in a *Details* magazine article on Sonic Youth, Patti was named as one of the band's idols.

'I realize that I first heard Patti Smith out of context, and was very lucky that way,' wrote Kersten Hersh of Throwing Muses, who first heard Patti's voice blaring from her father's turntable as a child, and then later rediscovered her, listening to a tape on her long walks to rehearsal as a fledgling musician. 'It was her bubble I heard. I didn't hear it as seventies' rock, or as coming out of a scene. I just heard a voice. It didn't seem so much of a "fiery rebel" thing to me, and by the time I grew up I'd seen so many "rebels" that it'd stopped meaning anything any more. She was so delicate, and her voice was so thin. She seemed kind of breakable, which is great. I mean, that's a planet!'

When Lisa Robinson quoted Cocteau's statement that 'domesticity kills art', in a conversation in New York, Patti replied, 'It doesn't matter, because if you're a real artist nothing can kill it. Genet wrote his great works in prison.' Was Patti comparing domestic life to prison? 'No, no! I just mean that if you really have the calling, you'll do it, you'll find a way, and I feel that my work's flourished. It may be slower getting out to the world, but I'm not concerned about that. I'm concerned about the quality of the work.'

Cover versions of her songs appeared too, though none became hits. The Springsteen collaboration, 'Because the Night', was the most often covered; 'Dancing Barefoot' came in a close second with at least seven versions. U2 and Johnette Napolitano were two of the notables to record 'Dancing'. 'I found it very wonderful to hear different interpretations,' Patti said. 'It helped keep the music alive.'

In early 1993 a short essay by Patti, 'February Snow', memorializing Andy Warhol, Mapplethorpe and Richard Sohl, appeared in *Interview* magazine. The piece was requested to accompany photographs of winter scenes by Bruce Weber, Kurt Markus and Margaret Durrance. It was a moving piece, something Patti had written years before and never finished. She reminisced about the night in 1987 that Warhol died, when she was recording *Dream of Life* and pregnant with her second child, and mused on the elusiveness of life. 'Everything dissipates, commingles with dawn,' she wrote. 'First Andy died. Then Robert. And then quite suddenly without a word, Richard followed. It is time, I think, to walk across the field. The snow falling very fast fills my steps. No one will know I passed over. For there is none but a shroud of snow stained in memory, graced with mourning light.'

On the hot steamy evening of 8 July 1993 in Central Park, Patti Smith gave a remarkable public reading. Though nervous and uncertain of how she would be received, she gave a convincing comeback performance. 'It was one of the happiest nights of my life,' she would say. 'I couldn't believe how great these people were. The whole atmosphere – not just the audience, but I had my brother there, and Fred was there, and so I have really happy memories of it.'

In a highly unlikely but fitting development, where the *Dream of Life* album had failed to find a receptive audience, her writings and readings made her realize that it was this talent she should pursue. Patti was still a little uncertain about her subject matter.

She had mixed rage and love, but as soon as she connected with her audience she found her subject. Patti had been out of the loop when the grim reaper had descended on the gay community, systematically demolishing its most talented groups in San Francisco and New York, the capitals of AIDS. Now she realized that it was this subject and death in general that her audience expected her to confront. 'A lot of people in that crowd have all gone through that,' she said, 'and all the rough experiences in the past decade still join us together.'

Another death affected Patti deeply, the suicide of Nirvana's leader Kurt Cobain in April 1994. She wrote a song, 'About a Boy', in his memory. 'Fred and I wept when that kid did that,' she recalled. 'I loved that *Unplugged* record, but we didn't weep for him like fans. We wept like parents. We mourned the loss of someone who was so gifted and obviously in so much pain . . . and we all know there are lots of kids in that same pain.' Patti expressed admiration and concern for Cobain's widow, Courtney Love. 'I think she's done really good work . . . I just think it's important that for even artists that move toward the edge, you have to maintain some balance or you won't live. I hate to see anybody throw their life away, so I hope that a lot of these younger people will try to keep some balance.'

One of the few bright occasions in 1994 was the publication by W. W. Norton of *Early Work, 1970–1979*, a selection from Patti's poetry. It made generally available, in elegant form, the writings that first brought Patti acclaim. Sadly, while Patti seemed to be gradually returning to her audience, Fred sank more deeply into passivity and wine.

Wayne Kramer had heard from his friend Joe Hurley that Fred had been hospitalized for stomach trouble, and Ben Edmonds, who was writing a book about the MC5, told him it was still 'drinking central' at Fred's house in St Clair Shores. There was talk among Fred's friends about doing an 'intervention', a practice where on medical authority, the person with the problem is suddenly whisked off to hospital. There, friends and family members confront the drinker in an attempt to get them to acknowledge and deal with their problem, and get treatment.

'One of the Hurley brothers was involved in therapeutic community work, he was a counsellor or something. They loved the guy [Fred], so they're saying he don't need to be on stage, he needs to be in the hospital. They were going to pull an intervention,' said Kramer. But there was a fear that Patti would not allow it, so the idea went no further. It looked to him that Fred might be the next to die.

No one can know what would explain Patti's apparent acceptance of Fred's self-destruction. Perhaps she was just tired, and didn't see any way out of the situation but to let him die. And he did indeed appear to all who saw him to be dying.

On 4 November 1994, which would have been Robert Mapplethorpe's forty-seventh birthday, Fred Smith died in a Detroit hospital. The cause of death was listed as heart failure. He was only forty-six. A memorial was held for him on 8 November, at the Mariners' Church, where the couple were married. Fred's parents Dewey and Kathleen, and two sisters, Margie Provan and Pat Halett, attended.

Friends who remembered him most fondly claimed that he could have made a career in music with his charismatic wife but that he put his family first. 'That's an important thing to say, because everyone seems to think rock 'n' roll people are irresponsible idiots, and they can't put one foot in front of the other,' said a member of his Sonic Rendezvous Band. The Reverend Richard Inglass of Mariners' Church, who had married Patti and Fred in 1980, remembered Fred as 'gentlemanly and decent. There was a sense of values . . . when the pull was so strong in other directions.' Another friend said, 'I always remembered him as a really solid guy. The stuff he did with Patti Smith, "People Got the Power", was brilliant. My only wish was I could have gotten to hear more of that. If they would have ever gotten out on the road, it would have been great.'

Fred had not lived long enough to prove his talent to the public. 'That was the genius and the tragedy of Fred Smith,' said Freddie Brooks. 'Most artists want to be ahead of their time just once in their life. Fred was ahead of his time at least three times that we know of. His career ended only because he died.'

'It wasn't important to Fred to be a big deal in rock 'n' roll,' said Wayne Kramer. 'He was always looking for truth and value. He cared about his family. No one could write a song like Fred. He was a bad motherfucker.' But Kramer did not romanticize Fred's death. 'I believe Fred drank himself to death, and I also believe Fred never recovered from the loss of the MC5. I know what a big issue surviving the MC5 has been for me, and what I've had to go through to make peace with the loss of my band and to reclaim my lost brothers,' said Kramer, who had got deeply involved in drugs after the band's break-up in 1971, before getting his life together and returning to music in the eighties. 'I know that Fred Smith never went through any of that process. I actually asked him at Rob Tyner's funeral if he'd ever grieved about the loss of the MC5 and he said, "Oh no, I just got busy with other things." But the reality is that it doesn't just go away. I believe he carried that anger and bitterness with him. And I think that was his undoing.'

There had been some talk in the Smith household that year of a comeback with a loud and heavy guitar album by the husband and wife. After his death, Patti said, 'Fred and I had planned to record this summer, not only as a means of self-expression, but as our livelihood, to take care of our family. We had a lot of plans to do things.'

At the end of that same November Patti returned with her kids and her brother Todd to their parents' home for the Thanksgiving weekend, just as she'd done with Fred for each of the previous sixteen years. Todd tried to console her, urging her to start performing again. 'When I saw my brother, he took me for a drive, and he had the soundtrack to *Natural Born Killers*,' Patti remembered.

> My song 'Rock n Roll Nigger' is on it, and he put it on really loud, and we drove around. I was just totally desolate, and he said, 'I'm going to get you back on your feet. You're

going to go back to work. Working will help you.' He said, 'I'm going to be right there with you.' We talked about it for days, and I felt that with his help I could do it.

One month later, utterly without warning, Todd Smith died of a stroke. He was forty-five.

On 30 December, Patti turned forty-eight. 'I was writing a book of poems and stories and things that pretty much surrounded a lot of people that I had lost,' Patti recalled. 'And also people that I admired – I wrote a poem for Nureyev and Genet and Audrey Hepburn, just different people that I really liked that influenced me. But since I lost my husband and brother – I haven't been able to write much, so I've just set it aside for a while. But when I feel stronger I'll get back to it.'

The Return of Patti Smith
1995

I am an American artist and I have no guilt.

Patti Smith

The year 1995 would be Patti's comeback year, but it would not be without difficulties. The deaths of Fred and Todd had made a profound impact.

Freddie Brooks began to see Patti after his old friend Fred's death. 'I had been out of touch for a long time,' said Brooks,

> but after Fred died I went to the funeral home and saw Todd, who I was close to since we'd been on Patti's road crew together. A month later Patti called to tell me Todd had passed away. I started going by her house in St Clair Shores, and we started talking about doing a record of Fred's music. I have tapes of all the Sonic Rendezvous' stuff. I started going by every so often and she was just grieving really badly, I would play a certain tape and she would just break down. So I started to try to get her out of the house, just take her out for a drive, get coffee someplace, anything, just to get her out of the house. It didn't seem to be healthy for her to just stay home. I had been trying to figure out some way to get her doing some music and I ended up working up a version of 'Hunter Gets Captured by the Game'. I knew she had done that previously, so I put a version together with Luis Resto. One day I went over to

207

her house and the tape fell out of my pocket. She said, 'What's this?' – I had been trying to think of some way to ask her to do it – and I said, 'It's something you might be interested in', and she says, 'Well, I can do that.' She did a totally great version of it, in the studio, me and the engineer just looked at each other. We couldn't believe how good her voice sounded.

Fred and Patti had planned to return to the recording studio and make another album in order to pay for their children's education. So in that sense she was carrying on with the plan she and Fred had made. This gave her a sense of continuity and purpose. As for her voice, everybody noticed how it had improved. Patti's belief that she had somehow internalized Fred and was singing for both of them helped focus her drive.

On New Year's Day 1995 she made her first public appearance since 1993, reading poems and singing 'Ghost Dance' at the St Mark's Poetry Project where she had begun her career in 1971. "Ghost Dance" is a song about the Native American uprisings of the late 1800s,' Lenny explained. 'They believed the ghosts of their ancestors would follow them into battle and toss the white invaders off their lands. It's a song about resurrection. When we played it was incredibly emotional for the audience, for her and for me. It was a great moment.' During the set, Patti broke down once for less than a second. The large, adoring audience hardly noticed. Time and tragedy had endowed her with a messianic aura, many of her admirers thought. It was a brilliant performance and Patti bathed in the glow of applause that followed it.

'Ms Smith appears to be taking on a new image in the nineties, that of an extremely empathetic and compassionate woman pushed back into the public eye by the hand of death,' wrote Neil Straus in the *New York Times* that month. 'I've seen a lot of death lately,' Patti noted.

When we did *Dream of Life*, I had a child, the engineer had a child, and Jimmy Iovine, one of the producers, had a child. Three children were born in the process of making *Dream of Life*. Since then, Richard Sohl, my keyboard player, died, Fred died and Robert Mapplethorpe died, all had key roles in creating that record. Three children were born and three men died: that's the beautiful way of life.

In February Patti accepted poet Allen Ginsberg's invitation to appear with him at the Hill Auditorium in Ann Arbor. The event was a benefit to raise funds for the Tibetan Buddhist group Jewel Heart. Ginsberg had sold out the 4,000 seat event on his own before Patti accepted, so it was clear that he was not 'using' her to sell tickets but rather it was an example of the poet's generosity and compassion. He knew of Patti's recent tragedies and perhaps wanted to use the event to coax her back into the spotlight as a form of healing. He had always been supportive of fellow poets. 'Allen is such a good man,' said Patti before the benefit. 'Look at what he did for the Beat movement. He made sure the work of Burroughs and Kerouac wasn't lost in obscenity, or a heap of vomit. He's so unjealous, he wanted all of them to do well. He doesn't want to be a big kingpin writer. He just wants everyone who deserves to, to excel. He's so generous.'

Ginsberg opened the show with a brief selection of songs, backed by a trio of musicians. Before the intermission he announced that the second half of the show would include 'an important rock-and-roll poet who took poetry from lofts, book-shops and gallery performances to the rock-and-roll world stage. We're really pleased and happy that Patti Smith is able to join us.' Despite having sold out the show himself he said generously, flattering Patti: 'I see we have a full house, and I think that's due to her charisma, glamour and genius'.

Patti began her performance with a poem she had written after reading the Dalai Lama's autobiography. Jewel Heart is an organization dedicated to preserving Tibetan Buddhist culture, a subject that was of particular interest to Patti since the age of twelve when she did her school assignment on Tibet. She finished by saying, 'As unfortunately I did live to see Tibet taken from the Tibetan people, I do hope that I will live to see it returned.'

Her children Jackson and Jesse, thirteen and eight years old respectively, were in the audience, seated in the front row. Patti's performance included a selection of her poetry and prose culled from her long career. There were no Patti Smith songs, but she included the poem 'Florence' written after the last performance of her band. 'I travelled with a rock and roll band in the seventies,' she said. 'And the last job we ever played was in Italy in a big soccer arena. I'd like to read this in memory of my brother Todd.' Patti's voice broke as she read from the dedication: 'Brother when you were six I rescued you from the enemy and you pledged allegiance. Now you are free and I realize that I shall never again experience such selfless devotion, and singular care.'

Near the end of her set Patti announced that she would 'like to sing a little song for my husband who many of you loved as Fred "Sonic" Smith.' Backed by guitar, bass and viola, she sang a haunting version of the Johnny Mathis song 'The Twelfth of Never' with its refrain: 'I'll love you 'til the poets run out of rhyme/Until the twelfth of Never/And that's a long long time.' Her performance that night included moments of humour and warmth as well as pathos, and she closed with a poem from *Woolgathering* called 'Cowboy Truths':

Standing there, squinting in the sun; everything so damn beautiful, enough to make the throat ache. He scans the terrain, the palm of his hand and that golden nuisance for one small moment.

Allen Ginsberg, who had been a world-famous poet for forty years and was a genuine admirer of Patti's, came out and read his longest and greatest poem *Kaddish*, a prayer in memory of his mother Naomi Ginsberg. As he entered its last long breath bardic stanza, 'Caw caw caw crows shriek in the white sun over gravestones in Long Island,' his voice, trembling with emotion yet powerful and measured, lifted the entire audience, the way a good rock concert can, for a few moments into that place of emotional reality called Art.

Patricia Morrisroe's biography of Robert Mapplethorpe was published in the US by Knopf in March 1995. Patti had given Morrisroe several lengthy interviews for the book, which was written with Mapplethorpe's cooperation. Morrisroe's portrait of Mapplethorpe's controversial life disturbed many of the people who knew him best, and none more than Patti.

'I gave [Morrisroe] what I thought was a good sense of what it was like to be an artist,' said Patti.

> I saw Robert go from an extremely shy misfit to an extremely accomplished person. The years in between were represented in the book as one hustle after another. We were all poor and humble. When I think of those times, I think of the joyfulness, the youthful fervour. We weren't plotting and planning to be famous. We just had a million ideas and lots of energy. Innocence prevailed. If Robert was part hustler, or whatever, fine. But he did his work. Taking photographs as an openly gay man was a revolutionary concept when he began. This book has him screwing all the time. But he worked until the day he died.

Patti's remarks are somewhat at odds with Mapplethorpe's own statements about himself. He boasted of having had literally thousands of sexual partners, and though he certainly had a work ethic, it was not quite the one Patti describes. He told one writer in 1977 that his life consisted of going 'from being very social to going to leather bars to working. Those are the three things I do. If anything could be my downfall it could be [sex]. I could just let myself get into sex considering it's the most exciting thing in the world to do.' Mapplethorpe felt his work ethic came from self-imposed guilt, but he solved the problem by defining both the 'social thing' and the 'sexual thing' as work. By that definition he was indeed a dedicated worker.

'Some days I'm happy to talk about Fred and I can do it without any problems at all,' Patti told friends that spring. 'But there are days when just the mention of his name is almost too much to handle. Without getting too deeply involved in it, when Fred died I went through a really tough time. I felt completely desolate. From him I learned a more compassionate view of the general populace. He was much more compassionate about those who will inherit the earth than I. I had no idea how I was going to apply myself musically any more. But with the warmth and camaraderie of Carolyn Striho and her band, with whom I played some warm-up gigs in the Detroit–Ann Arbor area, and her husband, my sometime producer Freddie Brooks, I started doing the best work I've done in fifteen years. The quality of my singing has strengthened. That's my legacy from my husband. I feel some of the best strengths of Robert Mapplethorpe, Richard Sohl and my brother Todd as well, I find myself gifted, enhanced, a richer person because I have magnified aspects of them within me.'

Fred's last gift to Patti was a series of nightly guitar lessons: 'Fred was a private man who could be difficult,' Patti admitted.

> But he was a really wonderful father and though he kept to himself he was extremely kind. I wanted to learn chords so I could sit down and write melody lines. So he gave me guitar lessons every night after the kids went to bed. I was slow but he was very patient. He taught me chord after chord and how to structure songs. He used to tease me and tell me I wasn't allowed to tell anybody! I'd play a song really poorly and I'd say, 'I can't wait to tell people my guitar teacher is Fred Sonic Smith, and he'd say, 'Don't do that Patricia!

On 8 April, Patti performed at a tribute concert for Fred at the Ark in Ann Arbor, Michigan. She had not toured since 1979, and she told friends she was not planning to tour formally again, apart from special dates. She recorded a song for a compilation album called *Ain't Nuthin' but a She Thing* to benefit organizations working on women's isssues. The song she chose was the Nina Simone standard 'Don't Smoke in Bed', produced by Freddie

Brooks. She began planning a new solo album – her first in seven years – to be recorded in New York.

On 5 July 1995, Patti moved out of the club circuit back on to the rock and roll stage, at the Phoenix Concert Hall in Toronto, Canada. Her show was electrifying, and she totally captivated the audience from the moment she walked on the stage. After doing a searing, unaccompanied reading of 'Piss Factory', she read her old poem about Bob Dylan, 'Dog Dream', in her 'Dylan' voice, and a ferocious version of 'Babel Field', which ends with the lines 'I step up to the microphone/I have no fear.'

'I never left,' she told the audience. 'I was never gone. I was with you always. When I was cleaning my toilet, I thought of you. When I was changing my children's diapers, I thought of you. Do you believe that? You may.' Her audience may have felt uncomfortable about the fact that Patti thought of them mainly in such situations, but it may well have been that it was at these gruesome moments that Patti most longed to be on a rock and roll stage.

Joined on stage by her new Motor City protégés Carolyn Striho and various members of the Detroit Energy Asylum, she launched into the musical segment of the show, playing the 'Jackson Song' from *Dream of Life* and 'Don't Smoke in Bed'. Patti did not try to contain her delight at being in front of her fans once again. 'I'm sorry if I'm not cool enough to pretend that I'm not loving every minute of this,' she said. The show would foreshadow the persona that she would develop over the next year. There were elements of the rebellious punk poet, the grieving widow and sister, caring single mother and committed (a)political activist.

As would be the case in a number of these comeback shows, Patti broke down momentarily when a reference to 'daddy' came in the 'Jackson Song'. If anything the emotional moments were what fuelled the shows and made them unique. On this occasion the show was lifted to yet another level of wonder when Lenny Kaye and Jay Dee Daugherty joined her on stage to close with 'Ghost Dance' and the Fred Smith penned tune that was becoming an anthem, 'People Have the Power'.

On 27 July, Patti played her first New York show since 1993, choosing Central Park as the venue. Patti opened the 'family night', as she called it, with a reading by her old friend Janet Hamill. She then read her own poems and sang a few songs accompanied by Lenny Kaye and her youngest sister, Kimberly. 'I've always liked collaborating with friends,' she said in an interview, explaining why she has set up her SummerStage appearance as a reunion of family and comrades. 'And I've lost so many of them.'

The rest of the summer was spent recording. Although Patti was reluctant to talk to the press, she did give interviews to Lisa Robinson and Evelyn McDonnel for a cover story in the *Village Voice*. She also gave a long interview to a Chinese writer, Gerrie Lim. *Horses* had been voted the number one rock album of all time by a major Asian rock magazine, *Big O*. The interview was conducted at Electric Ladyland, where Patti had recorded 'Piss Factory' and *Horses* and was now recording her new album. The choice of studio had been Lenny's suggestion. Patti told Lim:

It's an inspirational thing. Everybody's been so great here. It's wonderful to walk in because the room we're in has huge murals of Jimi Hendrix and all of Jimi Hendrix's gold records, and it has a really great spirit.

I don't have fears. For myself, spiritually, I look at death as a continuing journey. I don't wish to die, especially being a parent. I wouldn't want my children to be left without a parent. And I love life, love being on the planet. But I really think of death as part of a continuum. I think it's more of a Buddhist point of view. That's the way I feel. Sometimes I just feel ecstatic to wake up. I'm so lucky.

I read in a magazine recently that a writer was really surprised because Michael Stipe had said that I was a viable model for him, and they thought it was unusual coming from a guy. I think that in our time, as we move into the future, future generations will be less prejudiced about gender, race, colour and things like that.

The Return of Patti Smith: 1995

'It actually makes me feel like crying when people tell me I influenced them,' she remarked on another occasion.

Patti Smith seemed content to be in New York City. 'I'm really happy to be here, even in the heat,' she said. 'My kids love it here, and I'm happy walking in the streets. People say hello to me wherever I go. A guy in a sanitation uniform said, "Hey Patti, I'm a sanitation worker, but I'm a poet, too," and he wished me luck. I feel like I'm back home.'

Patti told Lim about the personnel on the new album.

I have a new keyboard player who plays very similar to Richard [Sohl]. He's from Detroit and his name is Luis Resto. And Lenny's playing guitar and a good friend of Lenny's [Tony Shanahan] is playing bass. And we'll have other guitar players on this record – my old guitar player Ivan Kral and perhaps Tom Verlaine and certain other people might be guest-playing.

The alternative summer package tour, Lollapalooza, was playing Randall's Island, NYC that August. When its director heard Patti was playing Central Park he shot her an invitation via Jay Dee to do a one off surprise spot on Lollapalooza's Second Stage.

Dressed in a sweat soaked grey T-shirt and blue jeans, Patti tore into the music with a dynamism and flow that was a definitive jump back on to the rock stage. The planned thirty-minute set was thown away as Patti played non-stop for an hour. Needless to say all the alternative bands on the tour watched in awe. Courtney Love of Hole was so awed she refused an invitation to meet Patti, saying she was just too scared and tongue-tied to meet a person she had credited with saving her life. By the end of the set members of the audience were literally in tears. The following day a great photo of Patti, her arms spread wide looking like Jack Kerouac's rail-thin sister, bounced off the page of the *New York Times*.

Patti really appeared to enjoy herself that day. She said she was going to take her energy from Lollapalooza back into the studio with her. Members of Hole and Sonic Youth, who shared a dressing room with Patti, stood in awe. 'The people were all ages,' said Patti, 'and very surprised. Many people have never seen us perform. All the bands made us feel welcome and special. It was a great feeling, especially after having this difficult year.'

According to a reporter from *Newsday*,

> Smith erased the memory of Thursday night's disappointing acoustic love-in at Central Park SummerStage by completely abandoning herself to the music in an electric – and elec- trifying – performance. Power flowed into her like lifeblood as Smith relocated her messianic muse in such songs as Bob Dylan's 'The Wicked Messenger', the Byrds' 'So You Want to Be a Rock 'n' Roll Star', and 'Ghost Dance'. She finished the inspired set with 'People Have the Power'. Smiling beat- ifically, her arms outstretched in both glory and need, she screamed her late husband's lyrics with desperate faith, ring- ing out their message of hope through years of pent-up fury.

Patti spent the balance of the summer completing the record- ing of *Gone Again*. She was pleased that the songs favoured for singles, 'Summer Cannibals' and the title song, had both been penned by Fred. In its structure and feel the album was equally influenced by Bob Dylan's lovely acoustic album, *World Gone Wrong*, which was Patti's favourite record that year.

After a summer in the studio, Patti filled herself with the posi- tive energy generated by the New York audiences and flew out west in September for a series of performances. 'The theme of Patti Smith's first southern California appearance in sixteen years was death, but the message was life,' wrote Robert Hilburn in the *Los Angeles Times*.

> Backstage before the performance, Smith spoke about the way the shows have lifted her spirits: 'Everywhere I go it's touching that people really want to comfort me,' she said. 'Sometimes these young kids will come up and you can tell that they don't even know what to say. They look at me and

I wind up telling them that things are OK. I can see in their face that they really feel bad.'

This show was in a bar dubbed the Belly Up Tavern. As Patti clambered on stage looking as thin and slick as a switchblade, cries of 'We love you!' floated up from the attentive audience. 'Patti was life itself when I was growing up,' the bar's talent booker told Hilburn. 'I listened to her music every morning through high school. It was a tension release. The music made me feel like there was someone out there feeling a lot of the things you were.'

Patti's set, which included covers of the Grateful Dead, Dylan and Buddy Holly was sheer joy for the audience and the singer.

The evening's most haunting number was the final one, 'Paths That Cross'. Though written for Smith's last album, its key lines express the optimism that comforts her now: 'All things renew / Paths that cross cross again / Paths that cross will cross again.'

Patti also performed a benefit in San Francisco and found

real positive energy. It made me feel connected with the world. I can lend a helping hand. And I am not ashamed or opposed to asking for a helping hand myself. We had two shows. And the first show was, I could say, conservatively structured. It was upbeat but more of a typical poetry reading with some music. And the second show, just an hour later, was kind of wild. The people were more energetic and interactive, and the show sort of lost its structure and it's like we were having a little party together with poetry and music.

I feel that the older we get, that all of our different ages come back in us. In my thirties, I felt completely different than in my twenties. But now, at this point, at forty-eight, I feel the same type of tension of adolescent rage is still within me.

In October 1995 Patti played some East Coast dates, the Lowell Celebrates Kerouac Festival, the Smith Baker Center, and she and

Kaye joined Janet Hamill at the Old Cambridge Baptist Church in Massachusetts, selling out the house. At the end of the month, it was announced that the Velvet Underground were to be inducted into the Rock 'n' Roll Hall of Fame in January 1996 and Patti Smith would introduce them.

In the *New York Times*, Patti spoke about her view of the future:

The future will be permeated by technology. And one may fear that works of art will reflect the bowels of a machine rather than the heart of man. I believe our duty is to be like John Henry [a mythical hero from American folklore]. He relied on himself, his own spirit, his own hand. He was a steel-driving man, driven from his craft by the terrible miracle of technology. But he fought it. He symbolizes the hand of man. For what I have found in my lifetime is that a John Henry always comes through: Jesus, Michelangelo, Picasso, Brancusi, Jackson Pollock, Bob Dylan, Kurt Cobain. There is always someone who will permeate a slack, complacent or convoluted surface; someone who comes through. We are the conscience. When things look bleak or seem decadent and jaded, someone will come through. John Henry's flight was a little reminder of the power of the individual. I think it's important to remember this as we move further into a technological society.

On 2 November (All Souls' Day), Patti led a dedication to her late husband at the Mariners' Church in Detroit. She had created the Frederick D. Smith Memorial Fund and chose the Mariners' Church as its beneficiary. The church had a history of being a beacon and comfort to weary sea travellers, and was Fred's favourite Detroit site. With the money raised by the fund Patti arranged to have an eight-by-eight-foot black granite marker depicting the church's logo, the three crosses of Good Friday grounded by an anchor, placed in the bell tower as a permanent memorial to Fred. 'Fred loved church bells,' said Patti. 'In fact he once wrote a song called "Bells of Berlin". It was never recorded, but his idea was for the music to be resounding church bells. For something to be in his name on a bell tower is just perfect.' The service was designed to be 'positive, upbeat and celebratory' and was open to the public. Oliver Ray, Patti's new friend and assistant, read a psalm at the memorial. Patti sang a song she had written, 'Farewell Reel'.

Patti constantly spoke of Fred and Todd in her interviews after their deaths. 'Fred was a great man,' she sighed. 'I'm trying to still do work on his behalf. We had a lot of plans to do things. And so I had to go and do them myself. But also I find the most positive way for me to restructure my life is to work. It also involves me with other people – reinvolves me with my friends – and that's comforting. A lot of it's the camaraderie.' That week's shows at the Theater of the Living Arts in Philadelphia – what Patti called 'my little guerilla warfare' – would have a special poignancy because she had done shows there the previous year when Todd was alive.

The year 1995 had been a good one for Patti. Nothing could have crowned it as perfectly as the shows she did in December. On 7 December, Patti performed the first of eight opening acts for Bob Dylan in Danbury, Connecticut, during the East Coast swing of his US tour. Given her roots and reputation, Patti could not have dreamed up more powerful and perfect reintroductions to the stage than those provided by Allen Ginsberg and Bob Dylan. 'The atmosphere was happy at our first show. I thought the audience was basically Bob's people, but they seemed real happy to see us because they know that I'm one of Bob's people, too.'

Patti added, 'As long as I think I have something worthwhile to impart on the people, I'll do work. Basically what I'm trying to say is, "Well, it's good to be alive."'

The tour went smoothly. Her band included her longtime collaborators Lenny Kaye and Jay Dee Daugherty, as well as Tom Verlaine. Michael Stipe of REM travelled with her, not to make music but to lend encouragement, and would later publish a book of his photographs from the tour called *Two Times Intro*.

Oliver Ray, who had been Patti's constant companion for some time, travelled with the band on the dates with Bob Dylan, playing one song with the band each night. He was the only musician to be introduced by name. Observers described Patti's relationship to Oliver at this time as that of an artistic benefactor. She encouraged the 22-year-old in his pursuit of poetry, music and photography. She even bought him a guitar of the same year and make as the Gibson six-string Sam Shepard had bought her in the early seventies. Some on the tour saw Oliver as a famefucker, only interested in hobnobbing with Stipe and Verlaine and ignoring the less stellar members of the entourage, but Patti seemed devoted to him. Oliver had previously been in a relationship with the actress Tatum O'Neal, and had worked as an assistant to the photographer George Dubose. At some point the nature of Patti's relationship with Oliver Ray changed and they became lovers, despite the twenty-six-year age gap.

'I'm working with some of the same people that I worked with in the seventies,' said Patti.

> There are new ones, too, and I feel that we'll do well. Things between us that are spoken and unspoken are very evolved. Tom Verlaine and I have worked back and forth since 1974. There's also new energy from Oliver Ray, who's twenty-three and in touch with a whole other area of knowledge. Oliver and I wrote the pivotal piece on the new record together. It's a ten minutes long track called 'Fireflies' and even though Oliver and I wrote it the most important interpreter of it is Tom. Tom is one of the greatest guitar players we have. I don't know how long we'll work together, but I think we have a good thing.

Dylan, in his generosity and wisdom, had invited Patti on the tour to reintroduce her to the heart of her audience, and got paid back in spades. Her charismatic sincerity and high aim inspired Dylan to do some great shows. Patti gave her finest performance on her last night, the third night in the Electric Factory in Philadelphia.

The Electric Factory has been in existence in one form or

another for almost thirty years. It consists of one rectangular space which resembles a large garage or small airplane hangar. The place is always either too hot or too cold and its grimy floor has seen a lot of vomit. Philadelphia is Philadelphia, but to make matters worse, it was a Sunday night, and everybody in Philadelphia gets the Sunday blues real bad. On the first night, even the second night, the place had been so full that it was impossible to move once the three-hour show began, but on Sunday the club was only half full. Perhaps one of the reasons Philadelphia is so infected by rock and roll is that everything happens there in extremes. When it's cold, it's ass-bitingly cold. And when it's hot, the heat flattens you on to the pavement like a shadow.

Patti Smith stepped on to the stage wearing an oversize Unabomber jacket whose hood completely engulfed her head. The only way you could tell it was her was from the unique sound of her voice and the distinctive syntax she used. She read the crowd to perfection from the moment she took the stage. 'I've been taking a look at your city,' she began in measured tones, with just the right edge of terror in them. 'Went over to the museum and saw the Brancusi show,' she continued slowly, settling the crowd down and setting it up perfectly, describing the exhibition in great detail. Then she sailed across the Schulykill River, taking the crowd to nearby Camden where, she reminded them, they could pay their respects to Walt Whitman, whose home has been restored. At this point some joker yelled out, 'It ain't safe in Camden!' (A racist remark, the majority of the population of Camden being black.)

'Then move there,' Patti countered, 'and make it safe.' Yanking off the hood, slamming her face into the microphone and crashing into 'Horses', she KOed the entire audience. With that one tremendous, sweeping move from which she extrapolated and extrapolated and extrapolated, she went on to enrapture the vulturelike, famished audience with a heavy dose of rock and roll iconography.

Patti showed she had a lot going for her as a rock and roll star. She had again reached the mountaintop and was able to sing with her hero and mentor Bob Dylan during his set. He brought her out for a beautiful duet on the little-known 'Dark Eyes' from his mid-eighties album *Empire Burlesque*. Patti found herself once again at a pivotal moment in American cultural history. What she has, perhaps more than any other female singer on the circuit at the moment, is the combination of an instantly recognizable, vintage voice and an equally recognizable face, which she uses in parallel with her religious voice to mirror the mood of the crowd or, as she once put it in a 1972 interview, 'marry the moment'. In juxtaposition to the iconographic micro-phone itself, her perfectly sculpted Mount Rushmore face flashed anger, flashed destiny, flashed famine, flashed despair, flashed beauty, flashed pain, flashed contempt and attitude in hearts. Once she hit the boards she never let up. It was relentless, freez-ing cold and skincrawlingly hot, sweaty and funky, muted and searingly intense. She took on the Liberty Bell and won hands down.

Patti gave a great show that night in Philadelphia, sharing her exultation with each member of the audience. By holding on to the music, following her through the swan dives, the Stuka bomber raids and the crashing assembly of great hooks, the drivelling, snivelling, fried-brain bombed and stoned carpet of a crowd were reunited with themselves as beautiful individuals struggling under the weight of the burden of life itself. Drunk and exhausted, they momentarily regained their dignity, their sense of humour and the self-respect that is the prize a ticket to a rock and roll show holds out but does not always deliver.

It was in Philadelphia, that sore thumb of a city, with its mur-dering pillhead police force and its stench of corruption, that this beautiful poet with her almost Russian sense of suffering rose from the ashes of her own haunted life, danced in Buddhist celebration on the buried bones of the men who had shaped her fate and sang in the sweet, wild, high mercury breath of ecstasy. She came back under the wing of the people's poet, the great spiritual captain of generations, Bob Dylan, but by the time she got to Philadelphia, she had taken flight on her own wings.

Gone Again

1996

**The Guardians of history are soon
rewarded with history.**

Motto of the

Patti Smith Group

The year 1996 could not have started on a more positive note. In their first issue of the year *Rolling Stone* magazine reader's poll voted Patti Smith's the comeback of the year. On 16 January she inducted the Velvet Underground (Lou Reed, John Cale and Maureen Tucker – the fourth member of the original band, Sterling Morrison, had died in 1995) into the Rock 'n' Roll Hall of Fame at a ceremony in the Waldorf Astoria Hotel in Manhattan. In a brilliant stream-of-consciousness speech, she said of them, 'They opened wounds worth opening, with a brutal innocence, without apology, cutting across the grain, gritty, urbanic. And in their search for the kingdom, for laughter, for salvation, they explored the darkest areas of the psyche.' She followed this with a keening rendition of their song 'Pale Blue Eyes' (written by Lou Reed), accompanied on acoustic guitar by Lenny Kaye.

After the ceremony, in which the Velvets performed a song in memory of Morrison written for the occasion, 'Last Night I Said Goodbye to my Friend', Lenny went looking for Patti to take her to the post-awards party in Allen Klein's suite. She was nowhere to be found. To his astonished guests Lenny had to explain that

Patti was still jittery after such an emotional public appearance because she felt the absence of Fred so intensely. As the Velvet Underground celebrated their induction, Patti was on a plane flying back to Detroit, blowing off a date with John Cale to record on his new album the following morning.

That spring, Patti, with her new band, played scattered US dates, mostly on or near the East Coast. They were gearing up for the release of *Gone Again*, recorded at Electric Ladyland, and for a summer tour of Europe. Patti was working with old friends, people she could rely on. She also introduced new blood into the band with the young guitarist Oliver Ray, who was to play an increasingly important role in Patti's return to form. She was very positive about her return to the studio, touring and her musical future.

> Now I'm working with some of the same people that I worked with in the seventies [Patti said]. Not all of the same people – there are new ones, too, and I feel that we'll do well. There are six of us at the moment. There is Lenny Kaye, Tony Shanahan and Jay Dee Daughterty – the only drummer I've ever had – so the things between us that are both spoken and unspoken are very evolved. Tom Verlaine and I have worked together back and forth since 1974. There's also new energy from Oliver Ray, who's twenty-three and in touch with a whole other area of knowledge. Oliver and I wrote the pivotal piece on the new record together. It's a ten-minute-long track called 'Fireflies', and even though Oliver and I wrote it, the most important interpreter of it is Tom. Tom is one of the greatest guitar players we have. Every time I walk out on stage these days, I feel like a lotus in a junkyard. It's like this huge flower just opens slowly through the night.

The rise of media interest in Patti and *Gone Again* brought Patti to a younger audience, many of them hearing of her for the first time. This would lead a new generation to the earlier works – *Horses*, *Radio Ethiopia*, *Easter* and *Wave*.

Gone Again: 1996

From 1993 to 1996 more of Patti's comeback appearances had been about poetry and writing than rock and roll. With the album coming out she had to shift the emphasis to playing rock and roll. However, she still made a point of fitting in as many good literary events as she could. On 1 June Patti made a quick trip to London to play and give a reading in the ICA's *Incarcerated with Artaud and Genet* series. The reception of *The Coral Sea* was typified by Robert Yates in the *Guardian*, who had also attended the ICA performance:

> Despite plenty of evidence to the contrary, Smith has gained a reputation as a fine wordsmith who happens to work in rock. The truth, however, is that although a great songwriter and performer, many of her words, naked on the page, have the gauche insistence of a fourth-former discovering self-expression.

In early July she paid another visit to London to read at Michael Horowitz's gallant attempt to repeat his famous Albert Hall Beat Summit reading. Unfortunately both the audience and the performers fell far short of his aim. Despite a feeling of dreary failure that hung over the whole event like a shroud, Patti managed to brighten the scene for a brief moment, kicking off her reading from *The Coral Sea* with the droll remark, 'Shall I count the audience?'

Gone Again was released internationally on 15 June. The sombre cover photograph of Smith deep in thought was by Annie Leibovitz. The album packed the punch of a good Lou Reed record, such as *Magic and Loss*. Both albums were about the death of loved ones, both drew an inordinate amount of press but were subsequently rarely played, largely because they were too depressing. Both artists would eventually be charged by sceptical critics with using their friends' deaths to further their careers.

At first *Gone Again* was greeted by predominantly positive reviews. Astonishingly, *Rolling Stone* described the album as 'the most focused and direct work Patti Smith has ever done'. *Newsweek* called it 'the best rock album of the year'. *Interview*'s editor,

Ingrid Sischy, wrote, 'Listening to *Gone Again* was an experience I'll never forget,' and *Spin* was diplomatic: '*Gone Again* is a forceful modern record that brings one of our most important voices back to centre stage.'

When the smoke cleared, the album was clearly dominated by two tracks, 'Gone Again' and 'Summer Cannibals', both originally written by Fred Smith and completed by Patti and the band. Originally, 'Gone Again' was not going to be on the album. Fred and Patti had worked on the song the summer before Fred died but the tape had since been lost. Lenny Kaye continued the story: 'At the last minute Patti was feeling agitated one day, walking around the house kind of restless. She opened up a drawer and there was the "Gone Again" tape as if by magic. We recorded it quickly, and all of a sudden it seemed to be the glue around which everything could find its place.' Patti noted, 'If there's anything negative on the album, it's that song. But it's got a sense of humour, in the way I sing it, because I survived it all. It didn't have an unhappy ending for me. It's a survival song.'

The rest of the album, except for the cover of Dylan's 'Wicked Messenger', was weaker, casting Patti in the role of the martyred widow.

Patti did not tour the US on the release of the album, but she gave a series of interviews on the radio and to a wide variety of magazines. She had not expressed herself so effectively since the release of *Horses* in 1975. Patti had given a number of interviews on the release of *Dream of Life*, but they were limited by the censorship of Fred Smith. He did not care for her to talk about her favourite subjects, Sex and the Men in Her Life. Now, with that constraint removed, she was the subject of at least fifteen outstanding, long interviews, read by more people than bought her records or saw her perform. In the course of these interviews she showed that she had lost none of her skills as an interviewee. The deaths of Fred Smith, Robert Mapplethorpe and her brother Todd dominated her thinking and her explanation of *Gone Again*. In all the interviews she played the widow and survivor, while emphasizing her other role as mother:

Fred and I had already started work on a new album. We are parents and we have financial concerns, we have to make a living as well as express ourselves as artists. And we had a lot of things we wanted to express, I, Fred, wanted to do another rock album. He wanted to do a very globally concerned album. And also, it was time for us to do some work, to prepare for our children's future, their formal education and things like that. So we had pretty much planned to record and do some minimal touring. So what I have done is just continue on our mutual battle plan.

Gone Again was Fred's title, it's what Fred wanted our record to be called. The last song we were working on together was called 'Gone Again'. It's a very straightforward American rock song, and originally he wanted it to be a woman coming down from a mountain to reassure her tribe that though things were not going well, the rain would return and children would be born and they would keep going. It has changed somewhat, because in Fred's passing, I wound up really writing it in memory of him, so it's more now that the woman comes down from the mountain and tells about the passing of a warrior. So it's a little rock song for Fred. By Fred and for Fred.

I'm definitely on another plane now, but I don't know how much of that can be attributed to mysticism, or even intelligence. A lot of it's to do with grief. So part of my elevation, if it is an elevation, is to do with that. I think of my new songs as gifts from Fred – his last gifts to me. When he died, my abilities magnified through him. At this point in my life, I'm trying to rediscover who I might be. I've been a wife for fifteen years, and my husband and I were very entwined: a lot of who I perceived mysself to be was an extension of him.

In an interview with Terry Gross on National Public Radio, Patti took the opportunity to discuss the inspiration that she had gained from her brother.

My brother was the same age as Fred, they were both 45, my brother was a very very supportive, high-spirited, youthful man. And he loved to see me work, he was in the last month of his life, trying to help me get back on my feet. Encouraging me to get back to work, and get back to performing and songwriting. He said that he would help me. And he did encourage me and fill me with a certain amount of energy. So when my brother passed away, all of the energy that he put into me, all of that encouragement, all of that love, I didn't want it to go in vain. And so I picked myself up and began to work really hard after my brother passed away.

The week after the release of *Gone Again*, Patti, backed by the band that would tour Europe with her, played two sold-out dates at the hip downtown punk club Irving Plaza. She opened with 'Piss Factory' and closed the two-hour show with 'Farewell Reel', the song about her recovery from her husband's death as she prepared to re-enter the world. Neil Straus, who reviewed the concert for the *New York Times*, noted the changes in Patti's subjects: 'Between these autobiographical sketches, an entire life unfurls. She sang lyrics of deterioration and recovery, scepticism and faith, bohemianism and motherhood.' Yet the concert was also a family event as her thirteen-year-old son Jackson was brought on to play 'Smoke on the Water' and her sister Kimberly came on to sing a song called 'I Don't Need'.

At the end of June, with an entourage that included Michael Stipe of REM, who would tag along for the fun of it, not taking part in the concerts but making a book of photographs of the tour; her children Jackson and Jesse; Tom Verlaine and the new band; Patti Smith took off to conquer Europe. From 30 June to 9 August she performed in Denmark, France, Italy, Spain, Belgium, Germany, Switzerland, the Netherlands, England, Scotland, the Czech Republic and Sweden.

The tour opened at the Olympia Theatre in Paris, host to the Beatles and the Rolling Stones in the sixties. According to Sam

Taylor, 'the sheer combustive brilliance of this show was entirely unexpected.'

The band, which had found its ground by the time they'd hit New York with Dylan, now hit its peak. Patti's improved, stronger and richer voice added a new dimension to the show and lent new energy to her dancing. Patti was brilliantly seguing from song to song (one of her best abilities), stirring the band up with a voodoo taste. Her face creased through fast changing expressions of pain, ecstasy and fear as she was concentrating so hard on the audience and the song. The set ended, as it did most nights, on a crowning encore of 'People Have the Power', with Patti yelling out the chorus, still promoting it as a new anthem of protest for peace everywhere.

By the time the Patti Smith tour hit Glasgow in early August it was, according to John Mulvey, who witnessed the Royal Concert Hall performance,

> Not a tour for revelling in tragedy. In other words, Patti Smith isn't exactly forgetting her troubles, but she is remembering how to have *fun*, too. This impeccably ruffled 50-year-old pulls her silver boots off and wafts her white sports socks in the air like an imperious stripper for 'Dancing Barefoot', a preternaturally well-preserved hippy mother decked out in crumpled outlaw hand-me-downs (much like her clothes on the *Horses* sleeve) while her, frankly, stellar band rock out. All of them, that is, except for laughing Tom Verlaine, slouched on a chair at the back, picking out fragile guitar lines with the vigour of a grouchy pensioner dozing on his porch.

Asked how it felt to be touring Europe again by every journalist who interviewed her at every stop, Patti replied:

> It's actually much nicer, although it was always interesting. I've always had the best people with me. Lenny Kaye is my oldest friend who's still amongst us. Tom Verlaine and I have known each other for 20 years. Strange as it might

sound, it's a great family unit and it's very good for my kids who still miss their father. Lenny and Jay were close to my husband and all the men in the band are great role models.

I feel pretty strong now. But there are times when I remember that the whole thing was Fred's idea – he would have loved it. At those times, it's heartbreaking.

In October 1997 Patti visited London to receive *Q* magazine's Inspiration Award. 'Looking more like the wicked witch of the east's funky younger sister,' Andrew Smith reported in the *Guardian*, 'she proceeded to regale a stunned, back-slapping crowd of musicians, journalists and industry officials with an acceptance speech that would have had Marlon Brando weeping with envy.' 'I just have one thing to say,' Patti said.

We must remember that artists are not here to serve the media. Nor is the media here to serve artists. If artists and media serve anybody, it's the people, and what have we been doing to serve them? I find all of this really pathetic.

And I'm not saying this in a mean way or to be funny or anything. We're moving towards a new century and *Q* magazine and all these other magazines and all of the cameras and people on the TV, this is a great thing we have. Media is potentially a great thing – let's do something better than this.

After telling a few more jokes, Patti accepted the award with a pastiche of a famous line from a Bogart movie, 'I don't need no fucking award, but thank you for giving it to me.'

At the height of the media campaign for *Gone Again*, in the summer of 1996, one of the most influential media commentators in America, James Wolcott, writing in the *New Yorker*, had said what had been circulating New Yorks's downtown underground all year: why was Patti getting away with building a completely mythological account of her married life in Detroit? '"Fred is dead," the album says, but "She Hath Risen,"' Wolcott wrote. 'At the risk of being offensive, I think she's overdoing her widowhood ... When she sings, "Our love comes from/above," I want to say, "Stop romanticising!"' Wolcott's question was further emphasized when no interviewer talking with Patti after its publication asked her to respond, and no reviews of her or her work mentioned it.

The answer is that one of Patti's talents had always been telling the Outrageous Lie. And furthermore, by 1996 she had metamorphosed from an entertainer into that position Richard Hell had prophesied in his 1974 essay on 'celebrity as an art form'. Such a character is a living piece of American history, a walking icon, like Andy Warhol, Muhammad Ali, Jackie Kennedy and, in her small world, Patti Smith.

Then between 1996 and 1998 Patti transformed once again from being a lifetime celebrity to something even stronger, that much beloved, rare figure, the wandering folk philosopher, represented in the flesh by Will Rogers or Woody Guthrie, in fiction by Huck Finn, in myth by Johnny Appleseed. That Patti was only too aware of this hierarchy there can be no doubt. In her first incarnation she repeatedly compared herself to Paul Revere, famous for riding a horse up the east coast in 1776 shouting, 'The British are coming!' The most fitting title she gave herself in the 1970s was the Field Marshall of Rock. The first label she was dubbed with in her comeback by the *New York Times* in 1995 was the godmother of punk. However, Patti saw herself in a bigger field than the tiny punk empire.

On 9 March 1998, Patti performed in a benefit concert for Tibet House at Carnegie Hall. She read parts of Allen Ginsberg's *Howl*, sang her song about the Tibetan troubles of 1959 and closed the show with 'Power to the People'. The song that Fred and Patti had written and recorded ten years earlier had finally taken its place next to 'We Shall Overcome' and 'Give Peace a Chance' as an anthem of the alternative culture. Inasmuch as there was still active in the United States any kind of underground resistance to Moloch the destroyer of the individual, then Patti was clearly its Godmother, its Queen. When she started her run in the early seventies, New York was the capital of the art world. Among the celebrity deaths she had attended or noted in her writing, Andy Warhol in 1987 and Allen Ginsberg and William Burroughs in 1997 had had the most impact. When Patti moved back from Detroit to New York in 1996, New York was no longer the capital of the art world, and one reason for this was that its previously thriving underground, without its leaders, had crumbled, its remnants scattered. It may come as a surprise to Patti, but now that she has returned to the city that has been her muse, it seems that the leadership of the New York underground is the position she is most needed in and best qualified for. It is a position she could hold for the rest of her life.

Epilogue

Patti Smith succeeded in the difficult task of creating a genuinely original musical persona, one that spoke to disaffected audiences everywhere. Then, after disappearing for over a decade, she returned in another guise and attracted an even broader audience. Who would have imagined in 1974 that the punk poet Patti Smith would be featured in *Time* magazine's 'Women at 50' cover story alongside Hillary Clinton? That she would be immortalized by the world's greatest photographers and that her face would grace the covers of dozens of magazines all over the world? That a top international clothing designer, Ann Demeulemeester, would name Patti as her muse, the inspiration for her highly successful fashion collections? Patti will undoubtedly be an important character in the two feature films currently in production about Robert Mapplethorpe's controversial life. She is also now one of those carrying the torch for the cause of Tibetan Buddhists, after the passing of Allen Ginsberg. The song she wrote with her husband Fred, 'People Have the Power', has become a universal anthem, sung at benefits by people around the world. Only Patti Lee knew these things would come to pass, as she lay awake, dreaming her dreams, alone in her room in her parents' house outside Philadelphia, somehow knowing it was just a matter of time.

Patti Smith metamorphosed from painter to poet to rocker in the seventies. In the nineties she's simply an artist. She expresses herself in music, art, poetry and prose, and devotes herself to her family as well as charitable, political and artistic causes. As always, she is masterful at using the press to further her agenda. As the writer James Wolcott pointed out in 1996, 'A decade before Camille Paglia, Patti Smith perfected the art of the interview as intellectual spiel.' From the beginning, journalists were in her thrall, and though some eventually fell out of love with her, in time the praise and acclaim outweighed the backlash. Her fans were always there.

After walking away from fame in 1979 and spending the eighties out of the spotlight, Patti had achieved something uncanny: as James Grauerholz said in *Please Kill Me,* 'She managed to be a rock 'n' roll death without having to die.' The Detroit years gave her time to contemplate and orchestrate her return.

Was Fred's death the event that set Patti free, and her brother Todd's the catalyst that spurred her return? It would be cynical to imply that Patti capitalized on the deaths of her husband and brother and friends, but it would also be disingenuous to ignore the level to which the motifs of death, grief, mourning and loss make up not only the content but the packaging and promotion of the albums *Gone Again* and to a lesser extent *Peace & Noise* (1997). Like Yoko Ono, who used a photograph of John Lennon's broken and bloodied glasses on the cover of the album released soon after his murder, Patti can be seen as an artist who uses the pieces of her life in her art, no matter how painful, but some wonder when the period of professional mourning will end.

By all accounts Patti seems quite happy these days, back in her beloved New York, living in a comfortable house in Greenwich Village with her two children and her lover, Oliver Ray. 'Presently, a really great day involves Oliver and I going to Matt Umanov's to check out guitars,' she recently told *Time Out* magazine. 'I just can't believe how great life is. Sometimes, when I'm felling a little dark, I'll come downstairs to see my children, Jesse and Jackson, laughing over some silly thing. And their laughter just resounds in the room. I look at them and shake my head, then I go back upstairs and ask myself, "How much better can life get?"'

Appendix
Patti Smith's First Interview:
15 August 1972

VICTOR BOCKRIS: Would you consider yourself to be the greatest poet in New York City?

PATTI SMITH: Um, the greatest poet in New York City? Um. Shit, I can't think of what to say. I don't think I'm a great poet at all. I don't even think I'm a good poet. I just think I write neat stuff.

VB: Why does it sell well?

PS: 'Cause I sell. 'Cause you know I gotta good personality and people really like me. When people buy my book you know they're really buying a piece of Patti Smith. That book is autobiographical. It sheds the light of my heroes on it. No good poet thinks they're good. Blaise Cendrars said he was a bad poet.

VB: How does it work in relation to people who don't know you? People in Omaha?

PS: Because I think I'm a good writer. I'm a good writer in the same way Mickey Spillane or Raymond Chandler or James M. Cain is a good writer. There's a lot of American rhythms. I mean I can seduce people. I got good punchlines, you know. I got all the stuff that Americans like. Some of it's dirty. There's a lot of good jokes. I mean I write to entertain. I write to make people laugh. I write to give a double take. I write to seduce a chick. I wrote 'Girl Trouble' about Anita Pallenberg. Anita Pallenberg would read it and think twice and maybe she'd invite me over to the south of France and have a little nookie or something. Everything I write has a motive behind it. I write to have somebody. I write the same way I perform. I mean you only perform because you want people to fall in love with you. You want them to react to you.

VB: John Wieners said to me yesterday that he figured he'd only just become a poet. He's thirty-eight and he figured this latest book of his [*Selected Poems*] was his first book. And it took him seventeen years to get there. What do you feel about that?

PS: The other day I reread my book and figured I had written my last book. I don't think that has anything to do with anything. Rimbaud writ his last book when he was twenty-two and sometimes I figure I did my best work as an artist from post-adolescent energy.

VB: Do you think you're a genius?

PS: I'm not very intelligent.

VB: But genius is something else. So you agree, right?

PS: Yeah yeah. It's like when I was a little kid I always knew that I had some special kind of thing inside me. I mean I wasn't very attractive. I wasn't very verbal. I wasn't very smart in school. I wasn't anything that showed physically to the world that I was something special but I had this tremendous hope all the time, you know, I had this tremendous spirit that kept me going no matter how fucked up I was. Just had this kind of light inside me that kept spurring me on.

VB: Why don't you take us back there to New Jersey in those days when you were a teenager beginning the great trail out? I mean, tell us when you first started to write and everything. How it happened.

PS: Well, I always writ. After I was seven when I read *Little Women* I wanted to be like Louisa May Alcott. The whole thing to me was in *Little Women*. Jo was the big move. It seems silly but Jo in *Little Women* with all those fairy tales and plays introduced me to the writer as performer. She would write those plays and perform them and get her sisters laughing even in the face of death so I wanted to be a chick like her, you know, who writ and performed what I writ and so I used to write these dumb little plays and then I wrote these banal little short stories but I wasn't good. I showed no promise and then when I went to high school I used to write these really dramatic poems just like any other kid writes. About everything I didn't know about. I was a virgin. I had never faced death. I had never faced war and pestilence and of course I read about sex, pestilence, disease, malaria, I read about everything but I never . . .

vb: What year is this?

ps: '62–'63. Then in '64 you know I started really getting involved in the lives of people. You know, it was like around '63–'64 I got seduced by people's lifestyles, like Modigliani, Soutin, Rimbaud.

vb: How did you get in touch with Rimbaud?

ps: Well, I was working in a factory and I was inspecting baby-buggy bumper beepers and it was my lunch break and there was this genius sausage sandwich that the guy in the little cart would bring and I really wanted one. They were like $1.45 but the thing is the guy only brought two a day and the two ladies who ruled the factory, named Stella Dragon and Dotty Hook, took these sausage sandwiches. They were really a wreck, they had no teeth and everything.

So there was nothing else I wanted. You get obsessed with certain tastes. My mouth was really dying for this hot sausage sandwich so I was real depressed. I went across the railroad tracks to this little bookstore. I was roaming around there and I was looking for something to read and I saw *Illuminations*, you know, the cheap paperback of *Illuminations*. I mean, every kid has had it. Rimbaud looks so genius. There's that grainy picture of Rimbaud and I thought he was so neat-looking and I instantly snatched it up and I didn't even know what it was about, I just thought Rimbaud was a neat name. I probably called him

Rimbald and I thought he was so cool. So I went back to the factory. And I was reading it. It was in French on one side and English on the other and this almost cost me my job 'cause Dotty Hook saw that I was reading something that had foreign language and she said, 'What are you reading that foreign stuff for?' and I said 'It's not foreign,' and she said, 'It's foreign – it's communist – anything foreign is communist.' So then she said it so loud that everybody thought I was reading *The Communist Manifesto* or something and they all ran up and, of course, complete chaos, and I just left the factory in a big huff and I went home. So of course I attached a lot of importance to that book before I had even read it and I just really fell in love with it. It was gracious son of Pan that I fell in love with it 'cause it was so sexy.

VB: At what point in this stage did you figure out and begin to understand what you were doing?

PS: Not until a few months ago.

VB: Why then?

PS: Well, see, what happened is I didn't really fall in love with writing as writing, I fell in love with writers' lifestyles; Rimbaud's lifestyle – I was in love with Rimbaud for being a mad angel and all that shit. And then I became friends with Janet and she was a writer, there was all these writers in New Jersey. There was just like this little scene. I was secretly writing. I was doing a lot of art. People knew me as an artist and so, like, I was secretly ashamed of my writing because all my best friends were great writers. So I didn't have no confidence in myself. I used to write stuff mostly about girls getting rid of their virginity and I used to write like Lorca. I writ this one thing about this brother raping his cold sister under the white moon. It was called 'The Almond Tree'. While his father raped the young stepmother and she died and he was . . . He looked at her cadaver and he said, 'You are cold in death even colder to me than you were in life.'

VB: What do you find are the major problems you have as a writer at this point?

PS: When I was a kid? Well, I had no understanding of language. I was so romantic and I thought all you had to do is expel the romance. I had no idea the romance of language was a whole thing in itself. I had no idea of what to do with language. I mean, all I had was I used to record my dreams. I had no conception of style of words.

VB: Tell me how *Seventh Heaven* got put together. It's a 48-page book. That's a lot of work.

PS: Right before I met Telegraph Books I started in the last two years reorganizing my style. I started feeling confidence in my writing. I just realized what language was. You know, I started seeing language as magic. Two things happened that really liberated me. The major thing was reading Mickey Spillane. Because I wanted to move out of . . . I was starting to get successful in writing these long almost rock and roll poems. And I like to perform them but I suddenly realized that though they were great performed, they weren't such hot shit written down. I'm not saying I didn't stand behind them, but here's a certain kind of poetry that's performance poetry. It's like the American Indians weren't writing conscious poetry, they were making chants. They were making ritual language and the language of ritual is the language of the moment. But as far as being frozen on a piece of paper is concerned, they weren't inspiring. You can do anything when you perform, you can say anything you want as long as you're a great performer, you know you can repeat a word over and over and over as long as you're a fantastic performer. You know you never understand what Mick Jagger is saying except 'Let it Boogie' or 'Jumping Jack Flash' but it's always so powerful 'cause he's such a fantastic performer.

VB: Well, how do you deal with that problem? That's a central problem in your work, Tony Glover says in his review of *Seventh Heaven.* He talks about the poetry of performance. I feel that's a central thing we're dealing with at the moment. How to get it down so you can have a book that people can read, but that you can also perform.

PS: That book to me represents me on the tightrope between writing and performing. I was writing stuff like 'Mary Jane' or the Joan of Arc stuff which is total performance poetry but, you know, I think they were worth of being printed because their content is important. The Joan of Arc poem is almost total rhythm masturbation but it puts Joan of Arc in a new light, it puts her forth as a virgin with a hot pussy who realizes that she's gonna get knocked off before she gets a chance to come. So there is a concept there that made the rhythm worth of being frozen. But like I said, I was reading Mickey Spillane. I couldn't get into prose 'cause I don't talk that well. I'm not good in grammar. I can't spell. I have lousy sentence structure. I don't know how to use commas so I just get very intimidated when I write something that isn't completely vertical. So I started reading Mickey Spillane, you know, and Mike Hammer, his hammer language: I ran, I ran fast down the alley. And back again. I mean he wrote like that. Three-word sentences and they're like a chill and they're real effective and I got real seduced by his speed and at the same time I started reading Céline. Well, I've never been able to go through a whole book by Céline 'cause it's just too intellectual but the idea that he could freeze one word and put a period. He dared put one word yellow and follow it by forty other words like forty movements, also like some kind of concerto or something. He's not as seducing to me as Mickey Spillane but I juggled the two.

And then the third thing, I was reading Michaux. He's so funny. He writ this thing called *The Adventure of Phene* and it's about this guy who's totally paranoid. He's so paranoid he goes to Rome and wants to see the Coliseum and the travel guide says, 'Stay away from the Coliseum, it's in bad enough shape already without a guy like you poking around it.' And Phene says, 'Oh, I'm so sorry. Well, could I at least have a postcard?' and he says, 'Don't be ridiculous.' And he says, 'Oh, I never really meant to have a postcard. I don't even know why I came to this country.' And he leaves.

So I mean I got three things. I got speed, humour, the holiness of the single word. So I just mixed them all up.

VB: Mostly European influences, Rimbaud, Cendrars, Céline, Michaux.

PS: Well, it used to be totally European. I had no interest in American writing at all.

VB: Why?

PS: It's because of biographies. I was mostly attracted to lifestyles and there just wasn't any great biographies of genius American lifestyles except the cowboys. And I'm a girl and I was interested in the feminineness of men.

VB: What you're trying to do in your writing is create a lifestyle. *Seventh Heaven* is a lifestyle.

PS: If I didn't think so much of myself I'd think I was a name dropper, but there's a difference. You can read my book and who do you get out of it? Edie Sedgwick, Marianne Faithfull, Joan of Arc, Frank Sinatra . . . all people I really like. But I'm not doing it to drop names, I'm doing it to say this is another piece of who I am. You know, I am an American. It's ironic I should be so involved with the French because I'm absolutely an American. I'm shrouded in the lives of my heroes.

VB: Would you find anybody in America now who you think influences you a lot?

PS: It's mostly dead people.

VB: Anybody alive?

PS: Dylan. You can't reject Dylan. But Dylan seduced me when he had a fantastic lifestyle. I'll always love Dylan all my life but Dylan was a big thing to me when he was BOB DYLAN. Now he's whatever he is but when he was there and had America in the grip of his fist, then I got so excited about him. As far as anybody living.

VB: I find the position of a writer is a fairly isolated one. It's a fairly lonely task. Do you find that?

PS: No, 'cause I don't have the balls to say I'm a writer. I don't think I'm good enough. See, I love my works. I think I've written some really good things. I think 'Judith' is just as good as anything ever written, but I couldn't sit down and do it all the time. Oh, Sam Shepard. I admire him.

VB: Do you find you learn from him?

PS: Sure, I learn from Sam because Sam is one of the most magic people I've ever met. Sam is really the most true American man I've ever met in as far as he's also hero-oriented. He has a completely western romance mind. He loves gangsters, he loves cowboys, he's totally physical. He loves bigness. You know Americans love bigness. In his plays there's always a huge Cadillac or a huge breast or a huge monster. His whole life moves on rhythms. He's a drummer. I mean, everything about Sam is so beautiful and has to do with rhythm. That's why Sam and I successfully collaborated because he didn't know that he was . . . intuitively he worked with the rhythm. I do it conceptually. I work with being a thematic writer. He just does it because he's got rhythm in his blood. I do it intellectually. He does it from the heart. And so we were able to establish a really deep communion that way.

VB: You're not working with him at the moment, are you?

PS: No.

VB: You don't associate with many writers?

PS: Well, my best friends are writers. I never collaborate.

VB: I wasn't thinking so much of collaboration. People who I feel more comfortable with tend to be writers nowadays because they tend to recognize me and I tend to recognize them.

PS: No, I don't think I have the modern writer's lifestyle.

VB: You don't take yourself seriously?

PS: Ultimately, I don't take anything serious yet I can take everything seriously. I'm too much of a cynic to take anything serious. If I'm in a good, pure, relaxed state I can look at certain of my works and like them. But most of the time I look at my stuff and say, Ah, this is a load of shit. Mick Jagger listens to his albums and says they're shit. Bob Dylan listens to his albums and says they're shit. It hurts me to read an interview where Bob Dylan says he hates *Nashville Skyline*. But I know how I feel. The best work to me is the work in progress. Which is why I produce . . . I almost hate to see my work go out. I'm more guilty of not being published than any publisher because I'm always in progress. I didn't like to finish my drawings. Yeats was like that. How many versions of 'Leda and the Swan' did he do? It's so difficult 'cause it means it's dead. De Kooning did twenty-eight dead women under *Woman 1* because you know he couldn't stand to say that she was done. It's like you know when a woman has a baby, she created it, it's just begun. But when an artist does a piece of work, as soon as he does the last brushstroke or the last period, it's finished.

VB: How did you feel when *Seventh Heaven* came out?

PS: I carried it around with me for weeks.

VB: Did it catalyse anything in your head about writing?

PS: I stopped writing for a while. I was like a kid at first, I didn't understand it. I saw it. It was in front of me. I liked to carry it on buses and hope people would recognize it was me on the cover. I stopped seeing the poetry as soon as it was printed. I'll stand behind that book, I think it's a damn good book, but the only two poems I like the best are the two last ones which are the most recent ones. I think 'Judith' is the best thing I ever writ.

VB: Would you say anything about the difference between being a man and a woman in relation to writing?

PS: I don't feel it that much.

VB: You write about it a lot.

PS: Being a writer?

VB: No, you're a woman. You used the image a few minutes ago of giving birth to a child. It rang a bell in my mind . . .

VB: I don't consider myself a female poet. It's only lately that I've been able to consider myself as a female at all. But I don't consider myself a female artist. I don't think I hold any sex. I think I have both masculine and feminine rhythms in my work. In the same sense I don't think Mick Jagger is just a masculine performer.

VB: You're bisexual.

PS: Completely heterosexual.

VB: You talk as if you were bisexual.

PS: Most of my poems are written to women because women are most inspiring. Who are most artists? Men. Who do they get inspired by? Women. The masculinity in me gets inspired by female. I get, you know, I fall in love with men and they take me over. I ain't no women's lib chick. So I can't write about a man because I'm under his thumb but a woman I can be male with. I can use her as my muse. I tried to make it with a chick once and I thought it was a drag. She was too soft. I like hardness. I like to feel a male chest. I like bone. I like muscle. I don't like all that soft breast.

VB: You find women inspiring from a distance. Anita Pallenberg, Joan of Arc, Marianne Faithfull, Edie Sedgwick, you knew . . .

PS: No, I don't know any of the girls I wrote about. I wrote about Judy, one of my best friends, but I could only write about her when she was away from me for a year. Then all of a sudden she became a muse. I don't like women close up because they're attainable. It's like I met Edie Sedgwick a few times and she had nothing to do with me. Who was I? But I thought she was swell, she was one of my first heroines. Vali's a perfect example. Vali's one of the only chicks I've ever attained and she didn't go in my nook. Vali has been a heroine of mine since I was fourteen years old. She was my original heroine. And when I met her she tattooed my knee. We kissed and all that. She suddenly vanished as one of my great muses. I didn't put her in the book and she's the one chick who deserved it because we touched.

VB: Tell me about the writing of a poem for you.

PS: Let me get the book out. I'll take 'Judith'. Most of my poems I write two ways. I write them from first writing a letter to someone who will never receive the letter or I write recording a dream. 'Skunk Dog' was a complete dream.

Judy was a girl I was in love with in the brain. I'm in love with her because we have similar brain energy. We can travel through time. We have this fantastic way of communicating. But she doesn't let me touch her. She's one girl that maybe I would have like to have done something to. At one point I was really obsessed with her and she wouldn't let me and at one point she went away to Nepal and right before she left she grabbed me and kissed me and I was so shocked I pushed her away and she said, 'You blew it' just 'cause I was too chickenshit. As long as she acted real tough . . . but as soon as she reached out for me I got scared. I'm a phony.

So anyway Judy was away and I loved her so much that I couldn't stand it. I started dreaming of her. So I was trying to write her a letter, but when you really love someone it's almost impossible to write them. It's people you love the most who you can't communicate with verbally. I had such a strong mental contact with this girl that I couldn't talk to her. So I was at the typewriter. It's made writing a much more physical thing. I write with the same fervour as Jackson Pollock used to paint. And all the things that we had, like, we loved the movie *Judex*, I started writing down in a line, just words but, you know, words that were perfect, words like 'kodak', 'radiant', 'jellybitch', and I just tried writing these words.

vb: You built the rest of the poem around the central words?

ps: Yeah, I had these words. I was trying to write her a letter but I had no idea where she was, so obviously it was a piece of narcissism. I was just trying to write this thing. Sort of jacking off. I was trying to project with words and language a photograph of Judy. So, anyway, I had all these words and they laid around for a couple of days and I looked at them and they were almost a perfect square and that's just how it is. I stretched them, put a few full stops in.

vb: How long did it take you to write that poem?

ps: About two and a half days. I think it's perfect. Another reason I like this poem is it explains our relationship through words like 'jewel', 'angelfood', 'avocado', it illustrates our personal aesthetic, then it illustrates our problem because it says she would not let me touch her. The other thing is it has my love for punch line. My favourite thing in it is 'ah spansule'. That's another thing. I love words. I heard some guy say 'spansule' as I was writing this. I said, 'That's a neat word, what does it mean?' He said, 'Spansule, gelatine, a hollow pill.' I love definitions. I writ that down and I like it so much and I wanted to put it in this poem but what was my motive for putting it in this poem? So I said, 'Ah spansule a hollow pill what's in it for me.' That's joke enough, but I kept carrying it, for love of Judy Judy Judy punch punch punch which . . . I think that's funny.

vb: Well, why do you find most other writers in America boring?

ps: I think I'm a timeless writer.

vb: You're a writer in the middle of a literary scene and you're totally ignoring the literary scene around you. How long can you keep going on your own?

ps: I can keep going because I'm constantly stimulated by earth's glitter. I'm constantly stimulated. I'm not at any loss for material.

vb: Are you satisfied with holding on to the same style?

PS: No, I write totally differently.

VB: What are you writing now?

PS: Back to Rimbaud again. 'Judith' is really a left-handed part of *Illuminations* and I'm writing more like that now. I'm allowing myself to get more obscure. I've always been against that. I like people to say what they mean. But what I'm moving into now is sort of the style of the *Illuminations* but more describing situations that have not happened. Like that thing I told you called 'Pap-rade'. I like to talk casually about things like I say 'regard I've popped out my eye, there it lies on the ground like some sick kodak. I pick it up and throw it in the face of an unsuspecting grandma, a pedestrian'. I like writing like a news reporter about more obscure events. In other words my writing is much more didactic. Documentaries of fantasies. That gives me a chance to get really obscure in terms of actions but it gives the reader a chance because it's written so rigidly they don't know something really bizarre is happening.

VB: Do you know what you're doing or is it hit and miss?

PS: I know what I'm doing. I was never an egomaniac . . .

VB: You're not?

PS: . . . until lately because I know what I'm doing.

VB: When did that moment come?

PS: It came when I started writing things like 'Judith'. I know that's a good poem. I know it'll be a good poem in ten years from now. To me when I am both inspired and have light emit-ting from me and feel real natural and intuitive but also at the same time clearly walk into my brain and look around.

VB: Before we get on to talking about things in the present let's clear up a few things in the past. Tell me about Cendrars and his influence on you and how that came about.

PS: I was working at Scribner's. I discovered Blaise Cendrars because of packaging. I should have discovered him years ago but people are so jealous and want Apollinaire to be the big spirit of the twenties and Blaise has really been sucked in the mud, you know. So I was working at Scribner's and Doubleday published *Moravagine*. It was beautifully packaged, had a drawing on it very similar to how I draw which immediately seduced me. I saw the drawing on the cover, it looked just like one of my drawings, I looked on the back and it said something about insanity and a collective unconsciousness . . .

VB: Do you write when you're travelling?

PS: Right now I've been in this room in this city for so long I don't see it any more and I'm not being stimulated. Lately I've just been doing a lot of cleaning inside my brain. My eyes are not seeing anything around me. So I've been dreaming a lot, recording dreams and trying to look within, but I'm not worried about it. I'm just waiting for the moment when I'll get to take a train or plane someplace and I know I'll spurt out because I've just got to see new things. I think Rimbaud said he needs new scenery and a new noise and I need that.

VB: Does the fact that you don't find any younger writers you learn from depress you?

PS: Their lifestyles don't attract me. I think I'm ballsier, a better performer. I think they can learn from me.

VB: So you feel the people you can learn from are the rock and roll scene?

PS: Yeah, in the sixties it was Jim Morrison, Bob Dylan, now it's still the Rolling Stones. There was Smokey Robinson. I can still get excited about Humphrey Bogart. I like people who are bigger than me. I'm not interested in meeting poets or a bunch of writers who I don't think are bigger than life. I'm a hero worshipper, I'm not a fame fucker, but I am a hero worshipper. I've always been in love with heroes, that's what seduced me into art. You know Modigliani, Jackson Pollock, de Kooning, people that were hot shit, you know. I want to know heroes, not eighth-class writers.

VB: Let's get into the poetry of performance. I've just finished an essay called 'The Poet is a Performer'. So that seems to me to be where it's at. What does it mean to you?

PS: Poets have been, I think, part of it because of Victorian England or something or how they crucified Oscar Wilde or something, but poets have become simps. There's this new thing: the poet is a simp, the sensitive young man always away in the attic, but it wasn't always like that. It used to be that the poet was a performer and I think the energy of Frank O'Hara started to re-inspire that. In the sixties there was all that happening stuff. Then Frank O'Hara died and it sort of petered out and then Dylan and Allen Ginsberg revitalized it, but then it got all fucked up again because instead of people learning from Dylan and Allen Ginsberg and realizing that a poet was a performer, they thought that a poet was a social protester. So it got fucked up. I ain't into social protesting.

VB: You obviously have a real belief in the possibility of poetry becoming a big public art again, which I really dig. But exactly how do you think that can happen?

PS: I've found it has more to do with the physical presence. Physical presentation in performing is more important than what you're saying, quality comes through of course, but if your quality of intellect is high and your love of the audience is evident and you have a strong physical presence you can get away with anything. I mean Billy Graham is a great performer even though he is a hunk of shit. Adolph Hitler was a fantastic performer. He was a black magician. And I learned from that. You can seduce people into mass consciousness.

VB: Don't you think you're directly competing with the Rolling Stones and how can you possibly win?

PS: It's not that I want to win. It's just that I think the Rolling

Stones aren't always around, you know. I think Mick Jagger is one of the greatest living performers. The other thing that gave me hope for the future of poetry is the Rolling Stones concert at Madison Square Garden because Jagger was real tired and fucked up. It was Tuesday, he had done two concerts, he was just really on the brink of collapse but the kind of collapse that transcends into magic. He was so tired that he needed the energy of the audience. And he was not a rock and roll singer Tuesday night, he was closer to a poet than he ever has been. Because he was tired he could hardly sing. I love the music of the Rolling Stones, but what was foremost was not the music but the performance, the naked performance. And it was like his naked performance, his rhythm, his movement, his talk. He was so tired he was saying things like 'very warm here warm warm warm it's very hot here hot hot New York New York New York bang bang bang'. I mean none of that stuff is genius but it was his presence and his power to hold the audience in his palm. There was electricity. If the Rolling Stones had walked off that night and left Mick Jagger alone he was as great as any great poet that night. He could've spoken some of his best lyrics and had the audience just as magnetized. Maybe just with Charlie's drum, Charlie's drums and Mick (I'm not renouncing the others, I love Keith Richards to death). Just the drum beat rhythm and Mick's words or refrains that are always magic could have been very powerful and could have I believe held the audience. And that excited me so much I almost blew apart because I saw almost a complete future of poetry. I really saw it, I really felt it. I got so excited I could hardly stand being in my skin and, like, I believe in that. That's given me faith to keep going.

VB: In as much as there is the possibility of poets becoming public figures, what is the public function of the poet?

PS: All I try to do is entertain. Another thing I do is give people breathing room. In other words . . . I don't mean any of the stuff I say. When I say that bad stuff about God or Christ, I don't mean that stuff. I don't know what I mean, it's just it gives somebody a new view, a new way to look at something. I like to look at things from ten or fifteen different angles, you know. So it gives people a chance to be blasphemous through me. The other thing is that through performance I reach such states in which my brain feels so open, so full of light, it feels huge. It feels as big as the Empire State Building and if I can develop a communication with an audience, a bunch of people, when my brain is that big and very receptive, imagine the energy and the intelligence and all the things I can steal from them.

VB: Would you give up writing tomorrow if you could continue performing in some other way?

PS: No, I can't give it up, I have no choice.

VB: Is that really true?

PS: I wanted to be an artist, I worked to be an artist for maybe six years and so as soon as I became a good artist all of a sudden I couldn't draw because in 1969 it began that I put my piece of paper and my canvas in front of me and I could see the finished product before I even touched the paper and it was frightening to me.

I like to work. I like that anguish you go through when you're writing something. I like to battle with language. When I started being able to see the finished product before I got a chance to work it out, it had no interest for me. I'm not interested in the finished product; I'm interested in creating the moment. I mean, the finished product is for the people who buy the stuff, you know. And I'm not interested in doing stuff so other people can get their rocks off only. I gave up art just like that in one day after putting seven years into it. And I was fucking good and then I writ and now what happens is I became so good at writing those vertical poems, those performing poems, they're no longer a challenge.

VB: So what did you do?

PS: I stopped.

VB: Are you in a transition phase?

PS: Yeah. Transition phases are very hard for me. They usually come in the summer and last about three months and they're usually the worst three months of my life. This one wasn't 'cause I happened to be in love. They usually come when I'm most fucked up. My brain is hungrier than it ever has been in my whole life but my pussy is being fed so I can ... So I'm not as fucked up as I could be. Last year when this happened I just wanted to kill myself. I thought I wasn't learning, I wasn't developing.

VB: Are you self-critical?

PS: Extremely self-critical. So much as I love my work, I hate it.

VB: If I was to offer you a reading tour with three other poets, who would you choose as the three other poets?

PS: Jim Carroll, Bernadette Mayer, Muhammad Ali.

VB: Why?

PS: Because they're all good performers. Ali's a good performer. He's got great rhythms. He's a good writer in a certain frame of reference. He's entertaining. Bernadette Mayer because I like what she does conceptually. She's a real speed-driven poet. Sometimes I don't like her because she's overly political and too influenced by St Mark's, but she's also a good performer. Jim Carroll because I think he's one of the best poets in America. At least he was when he was writing; I don't know if he still writes. Jim Carroll is one of America's true poets. I mean, he is a true poet. It kills me he's twenty-three, he wrote all his best poems the same year of his life as Rimbaud did. He had the same intellectual quality and bravado as Rimbaud. He's a junkie. He's bisexual. He's been fucked by every male and female genius in America. He's been fucked over by all those people. He lives all over.

He lives a disgusting life. Sometimes you have to pull him out of a gutter. He's been in prison. He's a total fuck-up. But what great poet wasn't?

I think the St Mark's poets are so namby-pamby they're frauds. They write about 'Today at 9:15 I shot speed with Brigid, sitting in the such and such'. They're real cute about putting it in a poem but if Jim Carroll comes into the church and throws up that's not a poem to them, that's not cool. If you could play with it in your poetry that's okay but if you're really with it, that's something else. They don't want to face it.

I think he's got all the characteristics of a great poet. He was St Mark's chance to have something real among them. And they blackballed him because he fucked up. I mean, he didn't come to his poetry reading. He was in jail. Good for him. 'Oh, well, we can't ask him to do poetry readings any more.' That's ridiculous.

VB: Are you at all interested in writing a long poem?

PS: I'd get bored. Blaise does that successfully 'cause it's like riding a railroad train. When you're riding a neat railroad train the whole ride is great, from the moment you get in till the moment it ends. And Blaise is able to sustain himself and seduce you page after page, but most people don't have power. I get bored.

VB: Do you read Pound or Olson?

PS: I like some of Pound. I'd rather read Eliot. I like pieces of Pound. I like Jules Laforgue better than either of them. I like Pound when he uses ditties same as Eliot, but I don't understand much of what they're saying. My intelligence is really dubious. I memorized 'Prufrock' when I was a teenager. I thought it was beautiful. It had a lot to do with instilling in me a love of flowing rhythms but I don't know what that poem's about.

VB: Do you find you learn a lot from Warhol?

PS: I used to think he was real cool in the sixties 'cause I like his lifestyle, I like the people he surrounded himself with and there was a lot of energy in the Factory. It paralleled with Bob Dylan but I think his whole family has gotten a lot tackier. But every time I want to say something about Andy Warhol I don't trust him. Socially, you know, I've met him a lot of times and he's always very nice. I don't know how to take him . . . Let me just say one nice thing about Andy Warhol: he gave Stevie Wonder a camera which was really cool, which is also what a good hustler he is. He has the ability to zoom in on the heart of things. Such an action reveals the two moods of Andy.

VB: Are you interested in interviewing people?

PS: I'd like to talk with Mick Jagger, mostly because I'd like to talk about performing. I'd like to talk to Dylan if he was in a certain mood, but that's why I stopped doing rock writing. I started interviewing people like Rod Stewart who I admire but because of my ego and my faith in my own work I don't like meeting people on unequal terms, so I figured I'd stop doing that and would wait until they discovered me and we can meet on equal grounds. I couldn't wait to meet Rod Stewart and then when I met him I didn't want to ask him anything, I wanted to tell him stuff. I didn't want to ask Rod Stewart about his work, I wanted to show him mine, that's because right now I'm into performing. I'm into extending myself rather than putting other people into me. I've spent half to three quarters of my life sucking from other people and now I'd like to give some.

VB: Do you think you're really a phony?

PS: When I say that I mean it totally endearingly, I say it with love, you know. I just think I get a kick out of myself. I act tough. I act like a bitch, a motherfucker, it's like when I'm doing this interview I act real tough and then my boyfriend comes in and I apologize to him and say, 'I'll be finished quick, baby.' I'm like a chameleon, I'm not a phony, I'm like a chameleon. I can fall into the rhythm of almost any situation as it calls for me. If I'm supposed to be a motherfucker I can be a motherfucker, if I'm supposed to be a sissy or a pansy I'll be that too. I'll be a sexpot, I'll be a waif. It doesn't mean I'm phony, it just means I'm flexible. I can marry the moment.

Discography

Albums

Horses **Patti Smith (Arista) 1975**
Producer: John Cale
'Gloria / in excelsis deo' (P. Smith), 'Gloria' (Van Morrison), 'Redondo Beach' (P. Smith/R. Sohl/L. Kaye), 'Birdland' (P. Smith/R. Sohl/L. Kaye/I. Kral), 'Free Money' (P. Smith/L. Kaye), 'Kimberly' (P. Smith/A. Lanier/I. Kral), 'Break It Up' (P. Smith/T. Verlaine), 'Land: Horses' (P. Smith), 'Land of a Thousand Dances' (C. Kenner), 'La Mer(de)' (P. Smith), 'Elegie' (P. Smith/A. Lanier)

Radio Ethiopia **Patti Smith Group (Arista) 1976**
Producer: Jack Douglas
'Ask the Angels' (P. Smith/I. Kral), 'Ain't It Strange' (P. Smith/I. Kral), 'Poppies' (P. Smith/R. Sohl), 'Pissing in the River' (P. Smith/I. Kral), 'Pumping (My Heart)' (P. Smith/I. Kral/J. D. Daugherty), 'Distant Fingers' (P. Smith/A. Lanier), 'Radio Ethiopia' (P. Smith/L. Kaye), 'Abyssinia' (P. Smith/L. Kaye/R. Sohl)

Easter **Patti Smith Group (Arista) 1978**
Producer: Jimmy Iovine
'Till Victory' (P. Smith/L. Kaye), 'Space Monkey' (P. Smith/I. Kral/T. Verlaine), 'Because the Night' (P. Smith/B. Springsteen), 'Ghost Dance' (P. Smith/L. Kaye), 'Babelogue' (P.

Smith), 'Rock n Roll Nigger' (P. Smith/L. Kaye), 'Privilege (Set Me Free)' (M. London/M. Leander with 23rd Psalm), 'We Three' (P. Smith), '25th Floor' (P. Smith/I. Kral), 'High on Rebellion' (P. Smith), 'Easter' (P. Smith/J. D. Daugherty)

Wave Patti Smith Group (Arista) 1979
Producer: Todd Rundgren
'Frederick' (P. Smith), 'Dancing Barefoot' (P. Smith/I. Kral), 'Citizen Ship' (P. Smith/I. Kral), 'Hymn' (P. Smith/L. Kaye), 'Revenge' (P. Smith/I. Kral), 'So You Want to Be a Rock n Roll Star' (McGuinn/Hillman), 'Seven Ways of Going' (P. Smith Group), 'Broken Flag' (P. Smith/L. Kaye), 'Wave' (P. Smith)

Dream of Life Patti Smith (Arista) 1988
Producers: Fred Smith and Jimmy Iovine
'People Have the Power' (F. Smith/P. Smith), 'Going Under' (F. Smith/P. Smith), 'Up There Down There' (F. Smith/P. Smith), 'Paths That Cross' (F. Smith/P. Smith), 'Dream of Life' (F. Smith/P. Smith), 'Where Duty Calls' (F. Smith/P. Smith), 'Looking for You (I Was)' (F. Smith/P. Smith), 'The Jackson Song' (F. Smith/P. Smith)

Gone Again Patti Smith (Arista) 1996
Producers: Lenny Kaye and Malcolm Burn
'Gone Again' (F. Smith/P. Smith), 'Beneath the Southern Cross' (P. Smith/L. Kaye), 'About a Boy' (P. Smith), 'My Madrigal' (P. Smith/L. Resto), 'Summer Cannibals' (F. Smith/P. Smith), 'Dead to the World' (P. Smith), 'Wing' (P. Smith), 'Ravens' (P. Smith), 'Wicked Messenger' (B. Dylan), 'Fireflies' (P. Smith/O. Ray), 'Farewell Reel' (P. Smith)

Peace and Noise Patti Smith (Arista) 1997
Producer: Roy Cicala
'Waiting Underground' (P. Smith/O. Ray), 'Whirl Again' (P. Smith/L. Kaye/O. Ray), '1959' (P.Smith/Shanahan), 'Spell'

Discography

(Footnote to *Howl*, A. Ginsberg/O. Ray), 'Don't Say Nothing' (P. Smith/J. D. Daugherty), 'Dead City' (P. Smith/O. Ray), 'Blue Poles' (P. Smith/O. Ray), 'Death Singin'' (P. Smith), 'Momento Mori' (P. Smith/L. Kaye/O. Ray), 'Last Call' (P. Smith/O. Ray).

The Patti Smith Masters (Arista) 1996

Boxed set of the first five albums. Unreleased tracks are included at the end of each album:

Horses 'My Generation' (Live in Cleveland, Ohio, 1976) (P. Townshend), *Radio Ethiopia* 'Chiklets' (P. Smith Group), *Easter* 'Godspeed' (P. Smith/I. Kral), *Wave* 5–4–3–2–1/Wave' (Jones-Hung-Mann/P. Smith), 'Fire of Unknown Origin' (P. Smith/L. Kaye), *Dream of Life* 'As the Night Goes By' (F. Smith/ P. Smith), 'Wild Leaves' (F. Smith/P. Smith)

US singles

'Hey Joe (Version)' (P. Smith) 'Hey Joe' (J. Hendrix) / 'Piss Factory' (P. Smith) (Mer records) 1974

'Gloria' (V. Morrison) 'In Excelsis Deo' (P. Smith) / 'My Generation' (Live Cleveland, Ohio 26.1.76) (P. Townshend) (Arista) 1976

'Hey Joe (Version)' / 'Piss Factory' (Sire) 1977

'Because the Night' (P. Smith/B. Springsteen) / 'Godspeed' (P. Smith/I. Kral) (Arista) 1978

'Frederick' (P. Smith) / 'Frederick' (live) (P. Smith) (Arista) 1979

'People Have the Power' (F. Smith/P. Smith) / 'Wild Leaves' (F. Smith/P. Smith) (Arista) 1988

'People Have the Power'/'Wild Leaves'/'Where Duty Calls' (F. Smith/P. Smith) (Arista) 1988

'Looking for You (I Was)' (F. Smith/P. Smith) / 'Up There Down There' (F. Smith/P. Smith) (Arista) 1988

UK singles

'Gloria' / 'My Generation' (live) (Arista 12" 45rpm) 1976

'Because the Night'/'Godspeed' (Arista) 1978

Set Free EP 'Privilege (Set Me Free)' (M. London/M. Leander)
23rd Psalm / 'Ask the Angels' (P. Smith/I. Kral) / '25th Floor'
(live version) (P. Smith/I. Kral)

'Babelfield' (P. Smith) (Arista) 1978

'Frederick' / 'Fire of Unknown Origin' (Arista) 1979

'Dancing Barefoot' / '5–4–3–2–1–Wave' (Arista) 1979

'People Have the Power' / 'Wild Leaves' (Arista) 1988

CD #1 'Summer Cannibals' / 'Come Back Little Sheba' (L. Kaye/
P. Smith) / 'Gone Again' / 'People Have the Power' (LP
version) (Arista) 1996

CD #2 'Summer Cannibals' / 'People Have the Power' /
'Beneath the Southern Cross' / 'Come On in My Kitchen' (R.
Johnson) (Arista) 1996

Miscellaneous

Rick Derringer, *All American Boy*, (Blue Sky Records 32481) 1973
(Patti wrote the lyrics for the track 'Hold')

Ray Manzarek, *The Whole Thing Started with Rock & Roll Now It's
Out of Control* (Mercury SRM-1-1014) 1974 (Patti appears on
'I Wake Up Screaming')

Blue Oyster Cult, *Agents of Fortune* (Columbia, CK 34164) 1976
(Patti contributed lyrics to and sang on 'The Revenge of Vera
Gemini')

Bob Neuwirth, *Look Up* (Watermelon Records) 1996 (Patti co-
wrote and sang on 'Just Like You')

Ivan Kral, *Nostalgia* (BMG/Ariola) 1996 (Patti appears with John
Cale on 'Perfect Moon'. A poem written by Patti appears on
the inside of the CD)

Discography

Les Nouvelles Polyphonies, *Corses in Paradisu* (Mercury/Phillips) 1996 (Patti introduces the track 'Dies Irae' with a poem)

Compilations featuring Patti Smith

New Wave (Vertigo/Phonogram) 1977 (features 'Piss Factory')
The Sire Machine Turns You Up (Sire) 1978 (features 'Hey Joe')
Times Square (Motion Picture Soundtrack) 1979 (features 'Pissing in a River')
That Summer! (Motion Picture Soundtrack) 1979 (features 'Because the Night')
Rock at the Edge (Arista) 1986 (features 'Gloria' and 'My Generation' [live])
Until the End of the World (Warner Bros Soundtrack) 1991 (features 'It Takes Time')
Just Say Yesterday Vol. 6 (Sire) 1992 (features 'Piss Factory')
No Alternative (Arista) 1993 (features 'Memorial Song' live) from NYC SummerStage, 1993)
Natural Born Killers (Nothing/Interscope Soundtrack) 1994 (features a remix of 'Rock n Roll Nigger' by producer Flood)
Aint Nuthin' but a She Thing (London) 1995 (features Patti's version of Nina Simone's 'Don't Smoke in Bed')
Dead Man Walking (Soundtrack) 1995 (features 'Walkin' Blind')

Bootlegs

Teenage Perversity and Ships in the Night, **30 January 1976**
Live recording of a show at the Roxy Theater in Los Angeles, California
Tracks: 'Real Good Time Together', 'Set Me Free', 'Ain't It Strange', 'Kimberly', 'Redondo Beach', 'Pale Blue Eyes', 'Louie Louie', 'Pumping (My Heart)', 'Birdland', 'Gloria', 'My Generation'

Hard Nipples, 1976
Live tracks: 'Real Good Time Together', 'G. Verdi', 'I Keep a Close Watch', 'Ain't It Strange', 'Free Money', 'Pale Blue Eyes', 'Louie Louie', 'Birdland', 'Gloria', 'My Generation'

I Never Talked to Bob Dylan, 3 October 1976
Live recording of a show in Stockholm
Tracks: 'Real Good Time Together', 'Redondo Beach', 'Free Money', 'Pale Blue Eyes', 'Ain't It Strange', 'Time Is on My Side', 'Radio Ethiopia', 'Gloria', 'Land'

Live in London, 16 May 1976
Live recording of a show at the Roundhouse, Chalk Farm.
Tracks: 'Real Good Time Together', 'Kimberly', 'Ain't It Strange', 'Set Me Free', 'Pumping (My Heart)', 'Free Money', 'Pissing in the River', 'Gloria', 'Time Is on My Side'

Live in Paris, 1978
Live tracks: 'Ask the Angels', '25th Floor', 'Rock n Roll Nigger', 'Till Victory', 'Set Me Free', 'Because the Night', 'Gloria', 'Free Money', 'I Was Working Real Hard', 'Keith Richards Blues', 'I Was Working Real Hard (Reprise)'

Superbunny, 1975
Live tracks: 'Real Good Time Together', 'Privilege (Set Me Free)', 'Ain't It Strange', 'Kimberly', 'Free Money', 'Redondo Beach', 'Pale Blue Eyes', 'Louie Louie', 'Hunter Gets Captured', 'Birdland'

Live May 1975 WBAI Radio, New York City
'We're Gonna Have a Real Good Time Together', 'The Hunter Gets Captured by the Game', 'Birdland', 'Redondo Beach', 'Son of Space Monkey', 'Snowball', 'Distant Fingers', 'Break It Up', 'Gloria', 'Scheherazade', 'Aisle of Love', 'Piss Factory', 'Land'

Discography

Live in Detroit, December 1976

Live tracks: 'Real Good Time Together', 'Kimberly', 'Redondo Beach', 'Poppies', 'Ask the Angels', 'Pissing in the River', 'Pumping (My Heart)', 'Ain't It Strange', 'Band of Gold', 'Radio Ethiopia', 'Rock n Roll Nigger', 'Gloria', 'My Generation'

Bibliography

Seventh Heaven (1972) Telegraph Books, Boston, MA. Paperback, 47 pp.

A Useless Death (1972) Gotham Book Mart, New York. Chapbook, 3 pp.

Kodak (1972) Middle Earth Press, Philadelphia. Paperback, 17 pp.

Witt (1973) Gotham Book Mart. Hardback and paperback, 45 pp.

(1977) Michel Esteban Editeur, Paris. 116 pp.

(1979) eco-verlag, Zürich.

Ha! Ha! Houdini! (1977) Gotham Book Mart. Chapbook, 8 pp.

Patti Smith-Gallerie Veith Turske (1977) Gallerie Veith Turske, Cologne. Paperback, 44 pp.

Babel (1974–78) G. P. Putnam's Sons, New York. Hardback and paperback, 202 pp.

Woolgathering (1992) Hanuman Books, New York. Paperback, 80 pp.

Early Work, 1970–1979 (1994) W. W. Norton & Company, Inc., New York. Hardback and paperback, 177 pp.

The Coral Sea (1996) W. W. Norton & Company. Hardback, 71 pp.

Source Notes

Appendices

The primary source for *Patti Smith* is the information she has provided about herself in the many interviews she has given throughout her career. The author did the first interview with the subject in 1972, on the occasion of the publication of her first book, *Seventh Heaven*. This interview provides a paradigm for all the Patti Smith interviews that were to come, illustrating how she has always been able to take the most mundane question and weave her answer into a piece of spoken poetry. Along with Bob Dylan and Keith Richards, Patti Smith remains among the best interview subjects in rock. Interviews and articles drawn on for this book were done by: Dan Acquilante, A. D. Amorisa, Carl Arrington, Robb Baker, Kate Ballen, Adele Bertei, Michael Bowen, Michael Bracewell, Chris Brazier, Julie Burchill, William Burroughs, Jim Carroll, Chris Charlesworth, Robert Christgau, Diana Clapton, Scott Cohen, Caroline Coon, Jonathan Cott, Sue Cummings, Michael Davis, Stephen Davis, Stephen Demorest, Ben Edmonds, Danny Fields, Stephen Frehr, Craig Gholson, Fiachra Gibbons, Tony Glover, Joe Gosciak, Gary Graff, Amy Gross, Penny Green, Mary Harron, Cynthia Heimel, Douglas Heller, Kristin Hersh, Clinton Heylin, Robert Hilburn, Tony Hiss, Cliff Jahr, Richard Johnson, Allen Jones, Jon Kaye, Nick Kent, Pattie Klenke, Stephen Lake, Gerrie Lim, Richard Lingeman, Shelley Lustig, Gillian McCain, Bob McCarthy, Evelyn McDonnel, Daisann McLaine, David McLelland, Legs McNeil, Greil Marcus,

Brett Milano, Thurston Moore, Suzan Moore, Paul Morley, Charles Shaar Murray, Lucy O'Brien, Jon Pareles, Tony Parsons, Ian Penman, Ramsey Pennybacker, Joy Presi, Paul Rambali, Dave Ramsden, Simon Reynolds, Dusty Roach, Lisa Robinson, John Rockwell, Shaar Murray, Andy Schwartz, Steve Shapiro, Susan Shapiro, Sam Shepard, Steve Simels, Ingrid Sischy, Wilson Smith, Matt Snow, Neil Straus, Jane Suck, Adam Sweeting, Nick Tosches, Jim Sullivan, Mim Udovitch, Lee Underwood, Jann Uhelski, John Walker, Andy Warhol, Paul Williams, James Wolcott and Charles M. Young.

Their pieces were published in: Andy Warhol's *Interview* magazine, the *Boston Globe*, *Big O* (Singapore), *Crawdaddy*, *Creem*, *Circus*, *Elle*, the *Guardian* (London), *High Times*, *Hit Parader*, *Life*, the *Music Gig*, the *New York Times*, the *New York Times Magazine*, the *New York Daily News*, the *New York Post*, the *Music Paper*, *New Times*, *Mademoiselle*, *Music News of the World*, the *Los Angeles Times*, the *New York Observer*, *Option*, *Pulse*, *Punk*, *Penthouse*, *Rolling Stone*, *Stereo Review*, the *Philadelphia Inquirer*, the *Philadelphia Weekly*, *Rock Scene*, *Trouser Press*, the *New Yorker*, the *New York Press*, *New York Rocker*, the *New York Times Book Review*, *Spin*, the *Oxford Literary Review*, the *Village Voice*, the *Philadelphia City Paper*, *Stereo Review*, *Zigzag*, *White Stuff*, *P.H.T.P.*, the *New Musical Express*, *Sounds*, the *Melody Maker* and *Mojo*, and broadcast on WNEW Radio.

The author conducted interviews for this book with: Gerard Malanga, Terry Ork, Miles, John Cale, William Burroughs, Allen Ginsberg, Clinton Heylin, Bebe Buell, Glenn O'Brien, Robert Mapplethorpe, James Grauerholz, Damita Richter, Legs McNeil, Christian Hoffman, Roberta Bayley, Lance Loud, Wayne Kramer and Andrew Wylie.

Secondary in importance to the interviews, but indispensable to any writer, are the numerous books about Patti Smith or that include information about her. They are:

Angry Women in Rock, vol. 1, New York, Re/Search Publications, Juno Books, 1996

Lester Bangs, *Psychotic Reactions and Carburetor Dung*, New York, Vintage, 1986

Source Notes

John Bauldie, ed., *Wanted Man: In Search of Bob Dylan*, New York, Citadel Press, 1991

The Book of Punk Legends, London, Q magazine, 1996

Julie Burchill and Tony Parsons, *The Boy Looked at Johnny*, Winchester, Massachusetts, Faber & Faber, 1978

Jim Carroll, *Forced Entries: The Downtown Diaries*, New York, Penguin, 1987

Robert Christgau, *Rock Albums of the Seventies*, New York, Da Capo, 1981

Scott Cohen, *Yakety Yak*, New York, Simon & Schuster, 1994

Gillian Garr, *She's a Rebel*, Seal Press, 1992

Lynn Goldsmith, *Photo Diary*, New York, Rizzoli, 1995

Trician Henry, *Break All the Rules: Punk Rock and the Making of a Style*, Ann Arbor, Michigan, UMI Research Press, 1989

Nick Johnstone, *Patti Smith: A Biography*, London, Omnibus Press, 1996

Clinton Heylin, *From the Velvets to the Voidoids*, New York, Penguin, 1993

Clinton Heylin, *The Great White Wonder*, New York, Viking, 1994

Clinton Heylin, ed., *The Penguin Book of Rock 'n' Roll Writing*, New York, Viking, 1992

E. Evelyn McDonnell, *Rock She Wrote*, New York, Delta/Dell, 1995

Merritt Maloy, ed., *The Great Rock 'n' Roll Quote Book*, New York, St Martin's Press, 1995

Patricia Morrisroe, *Mapplethorpe: A Biography*, New York, Random House, 1995

John Muir, *Patti Smith – High on Rebellion*, Babylon Books

Charles Shaar Murray, *Shots from the Hip*, New York, Penguin, 1991

Lucy O'Brien, *She Bop*, Penguin, 1995

Barbara O'Dair, ed., *Trouble Girls: The Rolling Stone Book of Women in Rock*, New York, Random House, 1997

Ellen Oumano, *Sam Shepard*, New York, St Martin's Press, 1986

Aida Pavletich, *Sirens of Song*, New York, Da Capo, 1980

Punk, the Original, New York, Trans High Publishing, 1996

Simon Reynolds and Joy Presi, *The Sex Revolts*, Cambridge, Massachusetts, Harvard University Press, 1995

Dusty Roach, *Patti Smith: Rock 'n' Roll Madonna*, South Bend, Indiana, and books, 1979

Aram Saroyan, *Friends in the World: The Education of a Writer*, Minneapolis, Coffeehouse Press, 1992

Jon Savage, *England's Dreaming*, New York, St Martin's Press, 1991

Irwin Stambler, *The Encyclopedia of Rock and Soul*, New York, St Martin's Press, 1989

Verbal Abuse no. 2, ed. Chi Chi Valenti, 1993

The Andy Warhol Diaries (ed. Pat Hackett), New York, Simon & Schuster, 1989

Richard Witts, *Nico: The Life and Lies of an Icon*, London, Virgin Books, 1993

Robbie Woliver, *Bringing It All Back Home*, New York, Pantheon, 1986

Acknowledgements

I want to primarily thank Roberta Bayley for the enormous amount of help she gave me in completing this book, and my editor Leo Hollis at Fourth Estate and Ingrid von Essen.

I also want to thank for their support: Andrew Wylie, Bridget Love and Zoe Pagnamẽnta at the Wylie Agency, Christopher Whent, Glenn O'Brien, Bobbie Bristol, Lisa Krug, Miles, Stellan Holm, John Lindsay, John Cale, Paul Katz, Gerard Malanga, Sharon Hird, Bunty Crawford, Anna Bockris, Steve Mass, Helen Mitsios, Chantal Rosset, Stewart and Jenny Meyer, Joe Gross, James Grauerholz, John Giorno, Ira Silverberg, William Burroughs, Allen Ginsberg, Chris Charlesworth, Andrew King, Dominic Anfuso, Ana DeBevoise, Bridget Behrens, Ed Friedman, Legs McNeil, Gillian McCain, Clinton Heylin, Chris McGuire, Gerrie Lim, Diana Rickard, Jim Condon.

Extract from William Burroughs interview with Patti Smith, © 1986, William Burroughs. Reprinted by permission William Burroughs estate / Andrew Wylie Agency.

Extract from Charles M. Young's *Rolling Stone* cover story 'Visions of Patti', © 1978 Straight Arrow Publications. Reprinted by permission of Straight Arrow Publication.

Extract from Gerrie Lim's interview with Patti Smith, © 1995 Gerrie Lim. Reprinted by permission of Gerrie Lim.

Index

Index

Index

Index

Index

Index